Malady and Genius

SUNY series, Insinuations: Philosophy, Psychoanalysis, Literature

---

Charles Shepherdson, editor

Malady and Genius

SELF-SACRIFICE IN PUERTO RICAN LITERATURE

Benigno Trigo

SUNY
PRESS

Cover art: *La escalera rota II*, by Rafael Trelles. 36" x 48". 2001.
Private collection of Benigno Trigo and Kelly Oliver.
Reproduced with permission from the artist.

Published by
State University of New York Press, Albany

Printed in the United States of America

For information, contact
State University of New York Press, Albany, NY
www.sunypress.edu

Production and book design, Laurie D. Searl
Marketing, Kate R. Seburyamo

Library of Congress Cataloging-in-Publication Data

Names: Trigo, Benigno, author.
Title: Malady and genius : self-sacrifice in Puerto Rican literature / Benigno Trigo.
Description: Albany : State University of New York Press, [2016] | Series: SUNY series, insinuations: philosophy, psychoanalysis, literature | Includes bibliographical references and index.
Identifiers: LCCN 2015036594 | ISBN 9781438461571 (hardcover : alk. paper) | ISBN 9781438461588 (pbk. : alk. paper) | ISBN 9781438461595 (e-book)
Subjects: LCSH: Puerto Rican literature—History and criticism. | Self-sacrifice in literature. | Literature and society—Puerto Rico.
Classification: LCC PQ7422 .T75 2016 | DDC 860.9/97295—dc23
LC record available at http://lccn.loc.gov/2015036594

Throughout time, women narrators have written for many reasons. Emily Bronte wrote to confirm the revolutionary nature of passion; Virginia Woolf wrote to exorcise her terror of madness and death; Joan Didion writes to discover what and how she thinks; Clarice Lispector discovered in her writing a reason to love and be loved. In my case, writing is simultaneously a constructive and a destructive urge, a possibility for growth and change.

—Rosario Ferré, "The Writer's Kitchen"

Contents

Illustrations

Acknowledgments

This book is profoundly indebted to my mother, Rosario Ferré (1938–2016), and it would not have been possible without Kelly Oliver's constant support and love.

It is published because Charles Shepherdson believed in the project, and it owes much to our conversations about literary analysis, psychoanalysis, and postcolonial studies. Since the beginning, Rubén Ríos Ávila was an enthusiastic supporter of the book. He has been a generous reader throughout the writing process, as well as a kind interlocutor over many years. Arnaldo Cruz-Malavé and Juan Carlos Quintero Herencia read early versions of the introduction, and I am thankful for their advice. Arnaldo also read chapter 2 and made helpful comments. His constant support has been a great source of encouragement for me. Both Vanessa Vilches and Mara Negrón (1961–2012) were open and receptive to my ideas, and they invited me to present versions of my work at the University of Puerto Rico. Their confidence gave me the strength to persevere and finish the manuscript. Juan Duchesne went beyond the call when he had an early version of one of the chapters translated so that it could be published in a Spanish-only journal. Thank you, Juan. Without the support of these friends and family, I would not have written this book. It is also indebted to many other friends, family members, students, colleagues, and inspiring models. I wish I could acknowledge each one of them.

My sincere gratitude also goes to Myrna Báez, Zilia Sánchez, and Rafael Trelles, for allowing me to use images of their works.

This book represents my insurmountable debt to the place where I was born.

Introduction

Scenes of Self-Undoing

MALADY AND GENIUS OF THE PUERTO RICAN SOUL

In a famous poem titled "A Julia de Burgos" from the collection *Poema en veinte surcos* (1938), the Puerto Rican poet Julia de Burgos (1914–1953) addresses herself as if she were in front of a mirror. The poem describes a self split into two grammatical persons that is composed of sets of irreconcilable opposites. At one point, Burgos describes her image as a submissive housewife, opposed to her image as master: "You in yourself have no say; everyone governs you. . . . Not in me, in me only my heart governs" (Burgos 1997, 3–5). The poem ends with Burgos, a torch in her hand, about to set fire to herself. "When the multitudes run rioting . . . against you and against everything unjust and inhuman, I will be in their midst with the torch in my hand" (ibid., 5). The threatening gesture at the end of the poem is intensely contradictory. It is on the one hand an attack against the self, even if it is an image constructed and defined by others. But the attack is also a defense against the social and cultural context that turns Burgos against herself. The gesture at the end of the poem is paradoxical, both suicidal and life-affirming. It is a scene of self-sacrifice or self-undoing that is repeated in the cultural production of Puerto Rico during the twentieth century: one hundred years lived as a nonincorporated territory of the United States.

The scene of self-sacrifice or self-undoing is as old as a painting that some have called "a synthesis . . . of our traditional, popular culture" (González 1983, 85).[1] Francisco Oller's *El Velorio* (1893) is a monumental painting that gives the form of a *baquiné* (an ancient funerary ritual in the countryside of Puerto Rico) to this scene of self-sacrifice or self-undoing, which the painter condemns as "an orgy of brutish appetites under the guise of a gross superstition" (Benítez 1983, 193). The president of the Puerto Rican Union Party, Antonio R. Barceló (1868–1938), repeated the scene in his famous reaction to the infamous Tydings Bill of 1936 that offered independence to Puerto Rico under punishing terms: he cried, "Give me independence, even if we die from hunger." The nationalist Lolita Lebrón (1919–2010) reenacted the scene during the attack on the U.S. Congress in 1954, and gave voice to it in her equally famous cry: "I didn't come here to kill anybody; I came to die for Puerto Rico."[2]

In this book, I focus on examples of this scene that appear in representative texts from the twentieth century written during the period of cultural debates that followed the period of nationalist unrest in Puerto Rico. Most of the texts are literary and they were written between the 1960s and the 1990s, and most are authored by Puerto Ricans born and living on the island—with some exceptions, such as Mayra Montero (1952–), born in Cuba, David Caleb Acevedo (1980–), born in Puerto Rico but raised in Hartford Connecticut, and Irene Vilar (1969–), born in Puerto Rico but living in the United States. All of the texts were also written during the gradual disassembly of the welfare state in the United States, and they all represent the impact of this important economic change on the social fabric of Puerto Rico. In all, I examine eleven literary examples of the scene of self-undoing, which include the suicide at the center of the now-classic short story "El Josco," by Abelardo Díaz Alfaro (1916–1999); the self-violence contained in two stories and one novel by René Marqués (1919–1979); the self-immolation at the center of a play by Luis Rafael Sánchez (1936–) inspired by Sophocles's *Antigone*; the imploding content and form of the influential literary journal *Zona. Carga y Descarga* (1972–75); the suicide of the main character in a novel by Montero; and the self-violent police novels of Edgardo Rodríguez Juliá (1946–). I end the book with an essay on the notion of internalized colonial shame and its effects on two testimonies from the early twenty-first century.[3] Vilar, the granddaughter of the famous nationalist Lolita Lebrón, authors one of them: *Impossible Motherhood: Testimony of an Abortion Addict*. In her testimony, Vilar suggests that there is continuity between the suicidal act of her grandmother and her own fifteen abortions, and she interprets them as acts "shrouded in shame, colonialism, self-mutilation, and family history," but also as forms of deliverance from a damned life (Vilar 2009, 4, 200).

The repeating nature of this contradictory scene of self-sacrifice or self-undoing raises a number of questions. Is it a reaction-formation after five hundred years of colonial relations in Puerto Rico, as some have claimed

(Gherovici 2003, 128–30)? Is it a "bugle call" to Puerto Ricans to manfully defend against a threatening abjection, or is it a restoration of that abjection to its rightful place as others have suggested (Perivolaris 2000, 188; Cruz-Malavé 1995, 159)? Does it bear witness to the paradoxical effect on the Puerto Rican imagination of what has been called the American Century? Beyond these questions, what are the conditions of possibility of the scene, what is the meaning of its contradiction, and how do we make sense of its various parts? In short, what does this repeating scene of self-sacrifice mean, and how do we respond to it, participants that we are in a long history of colonialism? In what follows, I offer answers to some of these questions while claiming that the repeating dramatic scene reveals four fundamental components, which together make up what I call the malady and the genius of the Puerto Rican "soul."[4]

First, the scene reveals the existence of a resilient psyche in general, and of a form of resilience that is particular to the history of colonialism in Puerto Rico. Indeed, the repetition of the scene bears witness to a resilience first recorded in the Caribbean psyche more than sixty years ago by Frantz Fanon. And the scene not only marks the survival of this psychological agency (even under extreme historical conditions) but it also continues to give form to an archaic impulse that drives this agency, and to a drive that is both out of bounds and necessary to the foundation of the subject. Kristeva calls this impulse and drive abjection.

Second, the repeating scene of self-sacrifice reveals the influence of history on the tragic nature of the Puerto Rican imagination. The scene repeats and suffers variations in tandem with what historians César Ayala and Rafael Bernabe have described as three different periods in the history of the American Century (to wit, the nationalist period from the twenties to the fifties, the period of cultural debates from the sixties to the eighties, and the period of postnationalism and postmodernism in the last decades of the twentieth century). But most importantly, the scene of self-sacrifice represents a Caribbean version of a slave-morality that Slavoj Žižek has described in another context, but which can be applied to the change in the Caribbean region from a "hard" form of colonialism to the "lite-colonial," as Juan Flores and Kristian Van Haesendonck have argued.

Third, the scene of self-sacrifice shows the difficulty of language, and the need for a form of analysis that does not ignore, disavow, or bury this difficulty, but instead tends to its aesthetic singularity and uniqueness. The repetition of the scene generates a tragic imagination, not only in the sense that it is an imagination tragically inflected and shaped by the long and changing traumatic history of colonialism, but most importantly in the sense that it is an imagination that can be traced back to the genre of tragedy, an imagination that reveals a tragic circuit of production and reception. As Charles Shepherdson suggests, language itself is part of this dramatic tradition. Language is a tragic form of representation, and in these scenes, language is deployed by interlocutors who are familiar with, and sensitive to this tragic irony and ambiguity. But language is also a paradoxical form of representation that contains hope and promise. As such, the scene of self-sacrifice reveals a complex aesthetic and literary difficulty that cannot be transposed easily and unilaterally to legal, political, psychological, economic, sociological, historical, or cultural forms of study, and that requires specifically literary forms of analysis.

Finally, the repeating scene of self-sacrifice reveals the agency of the body and its promise for the future of the Puerto Rican subject. The body in this repeating scene is far from being a passive site of contention or struggle. Instead, the scene reveals the nature of the body as a set of impulses, drives, or affects; as the material that subtends and gives support to the imagination; and as material that is necessary, that needs to be attended to, and that needs to be transformed. The scene reveals the body both as physically intervened, as suffering from what Kelly Oliver has called "social melancholy," but also as a site of imaginary passion that holds the potential for what Oliver has called "love" or "genius," and that sustains the abjection that is necessary for survival.

Psychoanalysis and Postcolonialism

Thirty years of scholarship about the effect on Puerto Rican cultural production by the modernizing impulse from the nineteen thirties to the seventies have included critical works that successfully combine postcolonial theory with psychoanalysis.[5] This book is a part of this critical tradition, even as it also questions some of its presuppositions. Indeed, this significant body of criticism is a testament to the power of Fanon's claim that the staying force of colonialism cannot be understood without studying the effect of colonial history on the psyche of the colonized. In other words, this scholarship has found it helpful to return to the technical vocabulary of psychoanalysis in order to explain the degree to which a colonial form of power or logic is still at work in what appears to be a postcolonial or a neocolonial moment. This is not to say that this scholarship has taken psychoanalytic theory at face value. In fact, these scholars repeat Fanon's criticism of the tendency of psychoanalytic theory to disregard such limiting constraints as colonial history and race. However, this scholarship also insists on an analysis that combines the history of colonial struggle (a history of the conflict between actors or social groups and their economic, social, cultural, and political interests) with an account of the imaginary forces at play. According to these critics, such forces subtend not only the struggle but also the very constitution of these actors and social groups. And their analyses go some distance in explaining the repetition of a colonial logic that will not stop.

This scholarship has also gone beyond Fanon in its emphasis on a dimension of the repeating colonial logic that Fanon was resistant to consider. Drawing mainly from queer theory and in particular from the work of Judith Butler, and from her influential interpretations of Rivierian, Lacanian, and Kristevan psychoanalytic theory in *Gender Trouble* (1990), this scholarship has redeployed concepts such as the "heteronormative matrix," the "phallic economy," and "abjection" respectively in order to explain the generative place of homophobia in the political unconscious of Puerto Rico and its repeating colonial logic. While it would be beyond the scope of this introduction to explain how this scholarship appropriates and reinscribes Butler's use of these psychoanalytic concepts, I would like to stress that generally speaking they all repeat a central tenet of Butler's analysis, namely, her understanding of the nature of power. And on the whole they place Butler's understanding of the nature of power at the center of their different analyses of the effect of colonial relations on cultural production.

Butler's Detour

In her book, Butler finds a free-floating "refusal" of love at the center of the logic of representative structuralist and poststructuralist theories (as well as of their feminist counterdiscourses). She also describes this refusal as an unstable interdiction, a speech act that is a "dissimulation" as well as a "self-subjection," an "injunction" that is simultaneously a prohibition and a disavowal (Butler 1990, 41, 49, 57). Further, she even finds this unstable interdiction at the center of the process that motivates paradigmatic shifts like the move from structuralism to poststructuralism. This injunction or performative speech-act is (for Butler) a "differentiating differance" (ibid., 40) that remains repressed in the unconscious of these systems of thought. It is a power (or a repressive mechanism) that can take the form of homosocial desire in patrilineal societies, as well as what she calls "distinct articulations of gender asymmetry in different cultural contexts" (ibid., 35). Put more simply, subjects in cultural contexts such as colonialism and engaged in asymmetrical relations like the colonized and the colonizer participate in a power struggle when they refuse each other's love. They stand in judgment of one another as each repeatedly disavows the other's refusal. Power is what happens when love is refused and when that refusal is in turn disavowed, according to Butler.

The postcolonial and psychoanalytic critical tradition I describe above repeatedly deploys Butler's definition of power as a free-floating refusal of love. It finds this repeated injunction or paradoxical prohibition at the center of reinscriptions of the master trope of the "Great Puerto Rican Family," as well as at the center of an obverse "point of resistance" (Butler 1990, 55). It finds this refusal at the center not only of the work of the writers from the Thirties Generation such as Antonio Pedreira and Luis Palés Matos, but also at the center of the queer literature of the male generation of writers that refused and disavowed them during the fifties and seventies, writers like Marqués, Sánchez, and Manuel Ramos Otero. Adding Eve Kosofsky Sedgwick's concept of "shaming practices" to Butler's notion of power as a refusal of love, this critical tradition studies Puerto Rican literature as a series of refusals of (same-sex) love that also includes points of resistance that in turn undo the patrilineal system that the shaming practices are meant to uphold. Further, this critical tradition deploys Butler's interpretation of Kristevan "abjection" as another name for this shaming or refusal of love, whose promise lies in the difference between its moments of repetition, a promise generated by its built-in point of resistance.

Back on Track

In this book, I challenge this interpretation of power as a free-floating refusal of love. Instead, I hope to prove that the power that enables acts of resistance to colonial shaming practices is neither a disavowal nor a free-floating refusal to love, but a necessary idealization of an absolute love object that Julia Kristeva also calls abjection (Kristeva 1982, *passim*). I argue that this idealization is based instead on the expression and elaboration of the symbolic lessons of the abject, or on the passionate form of support of an archaic not-yet-object, which I describe in some detail in chapter 2. And that the most significant lesson of this abjection is a hyperbolic forgiveness, which I describe in chapter 6 as "an attitude of radical responsibility that is both social and individual; an attitude that presupposes meaning from the get-go, before we hear the first word or read the first line that will be nothing but nonsense to us; an attitude that we take even before the first sound or mark is made by those who do not have a voice, by those without a sanctioned language, by those without a means to express themselves in writing, and/or whose expression is certain to revolt us."

Such a supportive attitude, which I call proleptic or hyperbolic forgiveness and Oliver in another context calls "love" (again, see chapter 2), is an antidote to the effects of colonialism on cultural production. It is an antidote to what Kristeva calls the malady of ideality and its symptoms. Kristeva claims that the right political context can turn our ideals into suicidal or anorectic behavior, or into a malady of Ideality.[6] She writes, "Accompanying the passionate adolescent in his procession is the triad disappointment-depression-suicide, or a more regressive, somatic form such as the anorectic syndrome or even, if the political context is ripe, the destructive tendency of the self-with-the-other which I call the kamikaze syndrome" (Kristeva 2009, 14–15). In this book, I argue that the colonized can (and should) elaborate the abjection of the colonizer, where abjection is understood as a form of hyperbolic forgiveness, a form of love, an ambiguous (supportive and disruptive) link that preexists the individual subjects and connects them both to their antagonists and to their environment.

As long as the colonized can express or put abjection into language, as long as the suspension of judgment that generates abjection is encouraged and remains in place, then repeated acts of interrogation of colonial affects like the colonial scenes of self-sacrifice or self-undoing that I study in this book, will remain meaningful. If these works of art remain meaningful, then they also remain as hopeful reactions to the colonial condition that Puerto Ricans continue to experience even today. And if they are hopeful, then they also guarantee the condition of possibility for continuing to overcome our colonial condition.

Malady and Genius of the Puerto Rican Soul

But, what do I mean by calling this scene the malady and genius of the Puerto Rican soul? At the beginning of her book *New Maladies of the Soul* (1993), Kristeva asks whether we have souls. By "souls" Kristeva does not mean the transcendental chimera to which secularism and fundamentalism have reduced what she believes to be a necessary component of our personhood or subjectivity. Instead, Kristeva means by "soul" the sign of a long discursive tradition that confirms that the person depends on a bond between something corporeal and something extracorporeal (or representational) that preexists and sustains the person. Organized religion, both in its orthodox and in its heterodox forms, is but one in a series of attempts at addressing and tending to this bond or "soul" according to Kristeva. Psychoanalysis and other secular attempts at finding the building blocks of the person are another example. In this book, I follow Kristeva in this long discursive tradition at a time when globalized and extreme forms of secularism and fundamentalism threaten to stop us from continuing to articulate this bond, at a time when speaking of the "soul" is considered either nonsense or a form of secular heresy. Such an interruption threatens to have catastrophic results in our individual but also our collective selves.

From this perspective, the scene of self-sacrifice or self-undoing is a return to the bond that makes subjectivity or personhood possible: abjection, the "degree-zero" of hatred, a negativity that is nevertheless also "the motor of psychical life" according to Kristeva (2010, 185, 183), a negative labor according to Oliver (2001, *passim*). This tragic scene is an elaboration in language of the familiar "pollution" that Sophocles called *Até* in his play *Antigone*: a paradoxical border that exists before the law, a place both fascinating and cruel according to Kristeva (2011, 1564). It is an elaboration of the bodily fright, the turning away, the jolt of the newborn when confronted with the abject. If the abject is a negative force that pulls the newborn toward a place where meaning collapses, then abjection is its reduplication, a reflex of the body of the newborn that tries to expel the abject. In other words, abjection is an example of a revolt against the most archaic of objects, the not-yet object; it is a form of turning inside-out of the body that is similar to throwing up or to sobbing. But abjection is also a social lesson learned in intimate relation with that not-yet-object. It is the redoubling of the negativity of the abject in language. It is what Kristeva calls an intimate revolt: "[A]bjection is the jolt that leads me into the abject but also separates me from it" (2010, 185). And the repeating scene of self-sacrifice is a redoubling and an elaboration of the bodily reflex and of the lesson learned in that historical abjection called colonialism. The scene of self-sacrifice in the American Century is an example of that jolt or reflex transformed into a form of the phrase "Not that!" by the Puerto Rican subject.

The scene of self-sacrifice in Puerto Rican cultural production also reveals the degree-zero of what Kristeva calls abjection. In fact, it reveals a regression of the subject to this archaic process due to cracks in the modern image of the self. The regression also suggests that the social support that helps the subject continue its struggle with the abject is waning in Puerto Rico. If the force of the contradictory process of abjection is easing, this suggests that the social context does not look kindly upon the practice of this process, that it does not support the expression of abjection, and that therefore the accompanying process of sublimation is becoming dangerously stale, fixed, and impoverished. An example of this poverty is the repetition of the scene of self-sacrifice, the return to a list of repeating words and ideas (even in the Puerto Rican diaspora, even in this book), or to what Sánchez called the dangers of the one-note-Johnny. The obsessive repetition of words such as "colony, colonial, colonialism, imperialism, [that] refer to the ideas of subjection, dependence, violence and poverty" suggests that a stifling environment of intolerance, domination, and colonialism has successfully reduced the language of the collective psyche to a minimum set of empty signifiers (Sánchez 1979, 119). In the words of Kristeva, this context produces self-hatred, and it "has transformed the uncertainty of abjection into a reversible dyad, sadomasochistic communicating vessels [that] does not assure any lasting independence" (2010, 191). Like a wooden wheel stuck in the mud of the abject, without the necessary social lever to give it traction, the Puerto Rican soul grinds, slips, and wears down, while remaining in place.

But the repetition of the scene of self-sacrifice or self-undoing in so many forms, in acts of political protest, letters, popular songs, painting, sculpture, drama, poetry, essays, short stories, novels, journals, *testimonios,* also suggests that abjection has found means, creative outlets, to express and transform itself, perhaps thanks to a social, cultural, political, and economic context where the work of art (i.e., the work of analysis and working-through) is still possible, perhaps thanks to alternative communities where the expression of abjection is still welcome and encouraged. In other words, the different forms taken by this scene of self-sacrifice suggest that the Puerto Rican subject remains alive inside its ready-made crypt. In fact, these scenes reveal that the Puerto Rican subject is under duress, but it still manages to spring out and claim its place in the world.

Kristeva states that at a time when technology, sexual liberation, and modernity threaten the space of the psyche with destruction, psychoanalytic interpretation offers a modern form of forgiveness that she calls pardon, something that happens through a gift, through a position that allows listening, a position without judgment and without calculus. She states that this position does not fight or submit to the abject; instead, it confronts the abject without ceasing what she calls its deconstructive elucidation of its contradictory bodily affect, of what Kristeva calls its love-hatred. She suggests that the success of psychoanalysis comes from the fact that it does not evacuate the contradictory feelings contained in the link to the other that she calls abjection, but rather depends on dismantling together with the analysand what she calls the cogs of negativity, the cogs that threaten to make the human psyche stop working, but also elaborate the labor of negativity that also makes the psyche work. This book is an attempt at similarly dismantling and elaborating the colonial psyche represented in a repeating scene of Puerto Rican self-sacrifice confident that we can keep putting the community back together again.

The Chapters of the Book

Malady and Genius is very much a mix of works of literature and theory originally written in Spanish, French, and English; and most of the works originally not written in English are readily available in translation. I've written all of the chapters with an English-speaking/reading audience in mind, but I've also tried to preserve some of the flavor of my Spanish mother tongue. Being as it is a work about U.S. colonialism and the Puerto Rican psyche, the issues raised by the literary and the theoretical works will be familiar to an American audience. My hope is that the literary works (originally written in Spanish) from the unincoporated territory of Puerto Rico also will pique the interest of English-speaking readers, and make them want to become more familiar with this corpus of American works.

In the first chapter of the book, I focus on the play *La pasión según Antígona Pérez* (1968) by Sánchez. I interpret the play as an example of the self-violent form of writing that Sánchez proposed to his generation as a response to colonialism, but also as an example that transcended the scene of self-undoing in its center. It is a play that confirms that the colonial psyche survives even if it does so at the limit of sense. It is a play that dramatizes the colonial logic according to which acts of excessive force and mercy are met with a similarly excessive reaction and resistance. It is a play whose deployment of ambiguity in language as a response to colonialism calls for a form of analysis that is specifically literary in nature. And it is a play where the act of questioning is intimately tied to bodily drives that must be sublimated if we are to survive the effects of a long-lasting colonial condition. Embodied writing is the hopeful material of this play about self-sacrifice in the context of colonialism, and its poetic and ironic language represents a call for literary interpretation as a necessary form of cultural intervention.

In the second chapter, I argue that the self-sacrifice in the works of Marqués is a way to approximate, moderate, and sublimate what Kristeva calls the abject and its processes: an archaic dread and joy that is necessary for the survival and development of the subject. I also argue that the dismembering and dismembered narratives of this famous and prolific Puerto Rican author are forms of the rituals of purification and defilement that are responsible for the survival and development of our social bonds. Marqués lived through the emergence, the consolidation, and the ossification and final decay of the Commonwealth of Puerto Rico. And his narratives are forms of the discourse of identity of the commonwealth State. But rather than reject them as superannuated sexist, homophobic, racist, and xenophobic narratives, I argue that they represent the dynamic and porous nature of this and similar discourses, and their sometimes unwitting production and sublimation of the material that is necessary for the process of subject formation. In the chapter, I take a close look at three works by Marqués from three different periods of his life in order to point out what I call the gift of the abject in the subject, in the object, and in the language of Marqués's works. The chapter is a rereading of the work of an author that has been interpreted (and sometimes dismissed) as an example of an obsolete way of thinking, a criticism that has not changed in forty years and that is sorely in need of revision.

In the third chapter, I focus on the spectacle of the struggle of the colonized slave and his master, and describe this struggle as a symptom of the malady of colonialism. I argue that the spectacle contains perverse desires such as masochism, sadism, and necrophilia. And I also find a symbolic matricide at the origins of this malady. I describe three different moments in the development of this symbolic matricide in Puerto Rico. The first moment generates a defensive sadism, the second generates a defensive masochism, and finally the third produces an explosive necrophilia (an unmediated immediate identification with the abject). In order to describe these three moments, I focus on three distinct works. First, I return to "El puertorriqueño dócil" by Marqués to find there a description of the masochism that characterizes Puerto Rican colonial culture, and his proposal that Puerto Ricans appropriate the sadistic position instead. At the origin of this proposal there is a symbolic matricide, or an abjection of the maternal body, which Marqués represents as weak, repellent, and base. Second, I move to Rosario Ferré's (1939–) *Zona. Carga y Descarga.* Ferré considers instead embracing the masochistic or subordinate position, and to search in that position for the resources to overcome the sadomasochistic binary, Ferré will empower the subordinate position of the child and its games while repeating the abjection of the maternal body in her journal. Unlike Marqués, Ferré will assign a negative kind of value to the abject maternal body. In the process, Ferré empowers a zone of maternal bodily affects that is represented by the literary journal. And she develops a feminist mode of body-politics in her writing. Third, and finally, I study Montero's novel *El capitán de los dormidos* (2002),[7] where I find the symbolic colonial matricide still firmly in place but now in the mind of the younger generation of Puerto Ricans represented by its protagonist, Andrés Yasin. The symbolic matricide takes a more virulent and necrophilic form in this novel, restricting even further the chance that Puerto Rican subjects can escape its self-destructive logic. In Montero's novel, Puerto Ricans become figurative sleepwalkers moved by an unconscious death-driven fantasy, but perversion becomes the psychological structure that, paradoxically, also helps to defend the psyche in a context of extreme colonial violence.

In chapter 4, I study the journal *Zona. Carga y Descarga* as an assemblage of minor literature, or as a form of literature that is reduced to a mere object in a violent colonial cultural context, and also as a form of minor literature that resists this reduction and instead tries to reanimate the material to which it is reduced. I interpret the self-violence that characterizes the journal as both an effect of its penal context (broadly understood) and as a simultaneous inversion of that effect and defense against the colonial context. More specifically, *Zona* inverts the perversions of a violent context with a symbolic operation of reanimation that I call a merversion: a turn to the material and maternal object, or to what Kristeva calls the abject. In the essay, I describe this symbolic operation with metaphors from the field of astrophysics, particularly with the metaphor of fossil light, and I also use this metaphor to describe the effect of *Zona* on our understanding of the so-called boom of Latin American literature during the late sixties. To do so, I focus on the influence of the work of Severo Sarduy (1937–1993) and Zilia Sánchez (1928–) on the journal. I specifically focus on their resignification of the tortured body in general and of the maternal body in particular as their greatest contribution to the effectiveness of the journal. I make connections between Sánchez's tactile approach to art making and Sarduy's homoerotic writing to make visible an otherwise invisible zone of motility and uncanny support that subtends the journal, and that challenges our most basic assumptions about the work of art. This zone is also coextensive with *Zona* and it represents a form of self-violence that is paradoxically generative and productive in a context that I describe as similar to that of Kafka's penal colony. In short, in this chapter I try to turn the relative invisibility of the journal and its minor writers into a sign of the forces that the journal contended with, and into a sign of the motor that drove its lasting effect.

Chapter 5 is a study of the short story "El Josco" (1948) by Díaz Alfaro, and of two police novels from the nineteen nineties by Rodríguez Juliá. It is also an attempt at describing them as forms of sublimation of the abject, or what I call a sadomasochistic Noir Eros. In the colonial context, the death-drive generates fantasies that haunt the Puerto Rican subject, such as the fantasy of the Victim Father and the fantasy of the Big Mother. This colonial version of the death-drive similarly produces affects that are related to those fantasies like colonial shame, which in turn lead to acts of self-violence or self-undoing, aimed partly at working through the death-drive and its sadomasochism. The works that emerge from this colonial context repeat these sadomasochistic fantasies. But these works also assume ownership of the sadomasochism at the center of the fantasies, and in doing so—in giving literary shape to the sadomasochistic impulse—they also create the condition of possibility for the continuing transformation of the fantasy. This possibility, in turn, is sufficient proof that a forgiving agency of the Puerto Rican psyche remains alive despite all evidence to the contrary (Kristeva called this agency the father of individual prehistory [2015]). And this agency is contained in the loss of inhibition and in the uncanny writing of Puerto Rican colonial authors such as Díaz Alfaro and Rodríguez Juliá. However, the forgiving agency at the center of this writing is also at a limit. So these works also represent a violent world of corrosive permissiveness, a world where the colonial subject denies responsibility for violent actions that it unconsciously repeats, and a world in a sadomasochistic embrace with the Big Mother. In short, these works represent a world steeped in the affect of colonial shame, which I go on to describe in the next chapter of my book.

Chapter 6 is a study of what I describe as two "queer Latino *testimonios*," a concept that I take from the work of Arnaldo Cruz-Malavé. I find in two recent Puerto Rican memoirs (one by Vilar and the other by Caleb Acevedo) ambivalent representations of abortion and homosexuality respectively that try to reverse the effects of colonialism on the Puerto Rican psyche, and that try to undermine a form of colonial shame that

Oliver has called social melancholy. These two works are characterized by three ingredients (shame, repetition, and forgiveness) that I describe in some detail after first giving an account of the debates about colonial shame in the field of Puerto Rican Studies. In this account, I offer four different descriptions of colonial shame, by Frances Negrón-Muntaner, Lawrence La Fountain-Stokes, Rubén Ríos Ávila, and Cruz-Malavé to establish my own approach to the affect of shame in the colonial context of Puerto Rico. Drawing from the work of Oliver on social melancholy and from the work of Kristeva on forgiveness I develop the notion of hyperbolic forgiveness as a preexisting relation between subjects, and between each subject and its most disturbing secrets. I argue that both of these writers rely on this hyperbolic forgiveness to work through the culture's rejection of their sexual preferences, and its abjection of their sexual beings. And I put the maternal body and its accidental temporality at the center of this forgiveness.

Malady and Genius: Self-Sacrifice in Puerto Rican Literature is not only a description of the surviving mechanisms within the Puerto Rican psyche that returns meaning to a repeating scene of self-violence. It is also an argument against an interpretation of the scene of self-violence in Puerto Rican literature that reduces the scene to an unconscious repetition of a constitutive lack, or that reduces the scene to a social and cultural subversive act. Instead, I understand the repeating scene of self-violence as the sure sign that the Puerto Rican imagination is alive and well, but also as a signal that, more than ever before, we have to be prepared to hear and to reciprocate its urgent interpellation.

1

Psyche, History, Language, and Body in *Antigona Pérez* by Luis Rafael Sánchez

"Be quick, Creón, be quick. Give me, give me death."

—Luis Rafael Sánchez

La pasión según Antígona Pérez by Sánchez is a representative example of the repeating scene of self-undoing in Puerto Rican cultural production during the American Century. This scene is made of four components, all of which are found in the tragedy by Sánchez. The four components are: (1) The colonized yet flexible and surviving Puerto Rican psyche, which is represented in ambivalent expectation, in preparation for, and in anticipation of, the next scene of self-undoing; (2) The distancing effect that temporarily interrupts the effect of absolute power on the psyche, which allows the representation of the historical nature of absolute power; (3) The sublimation of a bodily impulse into words, which turns the scene into a disturbing and negative morpheme of a collective metaphorical language; (4) A body that responds despite a social context where no response is forthcoming, which suggests a body with a forgiving nature.

Sánchez has been described as "the island's most important writer" (Perivolaris 2000, 15). He is perhaps the most renowned Puerto Rican author of the last third of the twentieth century. He is mainly a playwright, but is also a fiction writer and essayist.[1] Notably, he is the author of a collection of short stories, *En cuerpo de camisa* (1966),[2] which marked the beginning of a literary movement in Puerto Rico that culminated in what Juan Gelpí calls "the three fundamental texts of Puerto Rican narrative during the seventies: *Papeles de Pandora* by Ferré, *La guaracha del Macho Camacho* by Sánchez and *La novelabingo* by Manuel Ramos Otero" (Gelpí 1993, 134). The play *La pasión según Antígona Pérez; crónica americana en dos actos* (1968) repeats many of the features of *En cuerpo de camisa* and *La guaracha del Macho Camacho*, which make them representative of Sánchez's generation. In the play, Sánchez makes references to a colonial society in crisis, and practices an irreverent style of writing that mixes popular with literary discourse (Ayala and Bernabe 2007, 258–259).

Much criticism about *La pasión* associates the play with the Theater of Protest or political theater in Latin America, or with Experimental Theater or Third World Theater.[3] This criticism emphasizes the similarity of the concerns of Sánchez and those of the playwrights from the Theater of Protest. For example, R. L. Shaw describes the claims of political theater in Latin America as a protest "against threats from abroad to the independence of Latin American countries and against arbitrary presidential power," and Eliseo Colón Zayas characterizes the plays by Sánchez as a protest against "an imperialist system of oppression" and similarly highlights its "concern about the economic and cultural dependency of the country" (Shaw 1968, 31; Colón Zayas 1985, 26). Similarly, Waldman concludes that "Sánchez belongs to a generation of Latin American playwrights concerned with social change" (Waldman 1988, 334).

But many other critics also highlight the difference between Sánchez's play and this Theater of Protest. They call attention to the fact that Sánchez belongs to a generation of playwrights that react against the realism of an earlier form of Puerto Rican theater modeled after the Latin American theatrical tradition.[4] These critics suggest that Sánchez represents a turn away from the social realism of a nationalist theater, a turn begun in the forties by Emilio Belaval and followed by playwrights such as Francisco Arriví (Phillips 1972, 16). Sánchez follows the work of playwrights like Marqués and Myrna Casas, who were responsible for a resurgence of Puerto Rican theatre in the fifties and sixties, and infused their plays with fantastical elements from the Theatre of the Absurd (see Colón Zayas 1985, 18–28; Irizarry 1993, 16–33). Like the experimental playwrights of this generation, Sánchez writes plays that have a "tragicity" to them He writes in a tragic mode (Ben-Ur 1975, 16, 20; Shaw 1968, 31). "Clearly our best playwrights use farce and tragedy to both express themselves better and also to better express Puertorricanness," writes the critic María Teresa Babín (quoted in Waldman 1988, 332). But Sánchez's plays are also different from the so-called farcial tragedies of Marqués and Casas. His plays are also about the language that conveys the message. And Sánchez not only makes of language his object of study (as in the language of the media in *La pasión*), but his plays are also characteristically rhythmic and self-referential.

Sánchez's turn to language is part of the linguistic turn of the late sixties, but he also inflects this turn with local and political concerns. In a widely read essay, Sánchez describes the writer from Puerto Rico as saddled by an overwhelming guilt. The guilt that Sánchez describes is one that overcomes the writer who resists repeating a vocabulary and ideas that refer to a long-standing colonial reality that does not appear to change. Sánchez refers to the words *colony, colonial, colonialism, imperialism,* and to the ideas *subjection, dependence, violence, and poverty* as signs that have lost their power, that have become stilted clichés, slogans, even as he also refers to the guilt that the writer from Puerto Rico feels when turning away from them ("Cinco problemas," 119). What is to be done? he asks. He responds with a form of linguistic self-violence. He advocates "putting a drill" to the stilted language of nationalism, exposing it to a corrosive agent that will precipitate its decomposition. He suggests producing the identity of the Puerto Rican writer out of this act of self-violence. *La pasión* is an example of this self-violent form of writing. But as I hope to show, it is also a form of poetic practice that goes beyond the self-undoing that Sánchez advocates in his prose.

La pasión was first performed in Puerto Rico at the end of the sixties, when a "new cohort of historians, social scientists, and artists . . . sought to remake the inherited visions of the past, offer new analyses of the present, and renew literary and artistic expressions and discourse" (Ayala and Bernabe 2007, 247).[5] The new analyses of this cohort consisted of a different account of both colonialism and nationalism in Puerto Rico. Earlier Puerto Rican accounts of colonialism had emphasized the notion of an "American 'dumb imperialism,' which had stumbled into an expansionist adventure in 1898" (ibid., 248). Members of the new generation argued instead that there was an inherent connection between colonialism and advanced capitalism. Earlier accounts of Puerto Rican nationalism (both cultural and political) also repeated and celebrated a discourse of renunciation and self-sacrifice and elevated its main figures to near-sacramental status (e.g., the "Apostle" Pedro Albizu Campos, "The Leader" Luis Muñoz Marín). The new cohort instead looked on nationalist movements as promoting conservative religious and cultural values that often reflected a nostalgic, elitist, Hispanophile, sexist, and racist mentality. These critiques were partly indebted to the rise of new cultural currents and global conflicts such as the attention to social and economic dynamics, and the protests against the Vietnam War, but they also reflected the influence on this generation of Fanon's theorization of colonial mentality, and his account of the effect of a dying colonialism on the psyche (ibid.).

Psyche: Forgiving Cathartic Self-Violence

As critics have noted, Sánchez continues the work of Fanon insofar as he also describes in his works the survival of a Caribbean postcolonial subject (Perivolaris 2000, 187). In fact, the influence of Fanon is manifest from the beginning of *La pasión*. The play begins with a set of detailed instructions for the music, the lighting, and the set, followed by a general description of its parts. The description highlights not only the absolute theatricality and the poetic quality of the play, but also its disturbing nature and the equally disturbing psychological makeup of the tyrant, Creón (*La pasión*, 12). Moreover, the stage directions also associate the form of the play (its minimalist set, its low-pitched and arcane music, its extreme lighting, and the freedom of movement of Antígona) to the arbitrary and limitless nature of memory, which together with the full title of the play (*The Passion According to Antígona Pérez; An American Story in Two Acts*) further suggests a link between the disturbing form and content of the play and the similarly disturbed mind or psyche of Antigona. Indeed, from its very first line, the directions suggest not only that the play is Antígona's "American story" but that her words will invest, cover over, and adorn her suffering or passion, a paradoxical experience that is both embodied and imaginary (*La pasión*, 11). The disturbing and disturbed nature of Antígona's story is further emphasized by the lilt of her strange voice, which is poignantly described as the effect of poetry becoming dust inside the mouth (ibid., 13).

The plot of the play is loosely based on the plot of the ancient Greek tragedy by Sophocles, although, as the criticism has noted, it is a condensed version of it. The events of the play are arranged in a sequence of twelve oneiric scenes whose psychological link to Antígona is emphasized by the fact that she not only acts in them but she is also a witness to the scenes, and provides a running commentary on them. The sutured scenes combined with the open plan and two-platform stage set, further suggests that the play is a dream remembered by Antígona: a space divided into upper and lower platforms, into light and dark areas, where the events take place. Most of the scenes happen in the lower platform, which also represents the dark dungeon where Antígona is held prisoner. Creón visits Antígona three times, and the other characters in the play also visit her in an effort to change her mind, and to make her confess where she buried the bodies of the Tavárez brothers.[6] Only two scenes in the play are set on the higher platform, always in plain view of Antígona and the audience. The first scene (between Creón and his wife Pilar) takes place in the private chambers of the palace, and the second (between Creón, Monsignor Bernardo Escudero, and Pilar) happens in a reception hall. The scenes are arranged in such a way as to suggest a repeated assault on the mind of Antígona, as well as to underscore the increasing strength of her resolve. In fact, the plot seems to suggest that Antígona's unrelenting drive to her death is the paradoxical effect of the increasingly poignant and emotional attempts to convince her to save her life (more on this later). At the end of the play there is a plot-reversal, and Antígona's fate is sealed by the straight-talking Pilar who describes Antígona's self-sacrifice as the exact obverse of Creón's resolve (*La pasión,* 118).

Indeed, both the form and the content of the play combine to suggest that Antígona's apparent death wish is a perverse kind of ironic agency that inverts the roles played by the characters, until the dictator must bend to Antígona's self-undoing will: Creón says, "I will give you what you want, I will give you what you want right away. Antígona likes pain. Antígona will have all the pain she wants" (*La pasión,* 47). At first, her mother compares her stubborn idealism to the imaginary ravings of a madman and of a classic literary figure (ibid., 23), but then she traces her idealism back to Antígona's father, executed by Creón before the play begins (ibid., 26). Later, Creón compares Antígona's actions to those of her suicidal friends (ibid., 68). But then he reveals—to Antígona's surprise—that she not only repeats the Quixotic and insane actions of her father, as well as the suicidal actions of the Tavárez brothers, but that her steadfast opposition is in fact the result of a family resemblance: Creón says, "Antígona, you are just like me" (ibid., 8).

Antígona learns that she is in fact related to Creón on her father's side. It turns out that Antígona's father is Creón's half-brother. The fact suggests that her stubborn idealism to the point of self-sacrifice is also her tragic patrimony, already inscribed in the name her father gave her. Indeed, her father named her Antígona, an extraordinary and literary name in ridiculous contrast with her ordinary surname (Pérez). Her name is a sign of pride, of hubris, and of a family trait: the tendency to give themselves self-important poetical names and titles (*La pasión,* 78). The booming names, Antígona,

Santisteban, Generalísimo, Creón, in fact hide and cover over the profound fears of the characters who carry them. Most of all, the theatrical names screen the doubt that haunts and undermines their apparent resolve (ibid., 93). The prescient Pilar will later add that Creón's iron will in fact requires the disavowal of a growing doubt (ibid., 53). Antígona's self-sacrifice is then the clearest sign that she is her father's daughter, the true heir of the patriarchal line. And her dramatic commitment to a political cause is similarly the surest sign of the doubt behind her resolve.

From this perspective, the play represents the Manichaean and paradoxical colonial logic that Fanon so famously diagnosed in his works, but also explained and, in a way, forgave as well. Fanon asks how to explain the abnormal defensiveness of the Caribbean black man in the twentieth century, his attitude of being already on guard before conflict ever arises, when he has never had any relations with the white man, when there is complete identification with the white man, when there has been no real trauma, when the modern Caribbean black man has not seen his father beaten or lynched by a white man. Fanon writes that that there is an early and imaginary trauma, or a trauma of the imagination that explains this so-called abnormal defensiveness. At first, Fanon suggests that the trauma of the Caribbean man is no different from that of the European subject diagnosed by Freud in *Beyond the Pleasure Principle* (1920). Like Freud, Fanon suggests that there is an archaic and paradoxical tendency in man to repeat unpleasurable situations in order to master a deadly bodily impulse, or what Freud will call the death drive. The game of *Fort/Da* is an example of how we learn as children to turn a passive situation into an active part "by repeating it, unpleasurable though it was" according to Freud (Freud 1981, 16). In other words, the very compulsion to repeat unpleasure in childhood games and dreams is an attempt to work through an overpowering principle that is beyond pleasure according to Freud (ibid.). For Freud, this impulse finds expression in the primary experience of the death drive.

Elaborating on this psychoanalytic model, Fanon explains that the development of a collective consciousness requires a similar imaginary practice (e.g., a game, a dream, or a story). This practice releases or channels the often sadistic aggression against the otherwise internal and normal threats of the death drive to consciousness. That is to say, it masters the bodily impulses. Aesthetic, literary, or imaginary expression performs what Fanon calls a necessary cathartic function by generating defensive images for both the consciousness and for the threats sustained by that consciousness. The aggression, Fanon continues, is often represented by an agency that is the very opposite of the threat. In this way, the European subject imagines a white, active, and good mind as threatened, haunted, and fascinated by a black, passive, and evil body, in order to return agency to a subject who feels mastered by its death drive. Paradoxically, this mastering fantasy is also phobic and causes unpleasure.

But Fanon takes the psychoanalytic model even farther by transposing it to the colonial context. In colonial societies, he argues, these imaginary expressions for the threat to the self are represented in a similar Manichaean way but with another complication. In the colonial context, the operation of these phobic fabrications is significantly altered by the fact that in them the agency becomes identical with the threat. In other words, the colonized subject identifies himself simultaneously with the agent of the aggression and with the object of its sadism. The young colonized subjects who consume these fictions then invest the heroes of their imaginary dramas with a self-violent agency, with a sadistic aggression that they act out and aim squarely at their abject selves (Fanon 1967, 147).

The doubleness of this imaginary practice is what is distinct about the colonial version of the psychoanalytic drama, and this doubleness explains the hypersensitivity of the colonial subject in general and of the Caribbean black man in particular, according to Fanon. The fact that they imagine themselves as simultaneously occupying the position of the good agent and the evil object puts colonial subjects in a uniquely awkward position. They don't act out their aggression against an imaginary other, they act it out against their imaginary self. That is to say, the only act of defense or mastery that is possible for the colonial subject is an act that undermines the imaginary, or the seat of that very defense and mastery. And their position is made even more awkward by the fact that the colonial subject is already on guard before conflict ever arises. In other words, unlike the European subject who learns to protect himself by repeating in the imagination a trauma that he experiences in reality, the colonial subject arrives at a scene that has been already imagined for him. He proleptically hurts himself, before there is a need for protection. Fanon might have said that the Caribbean colonial subject is always already late to the European game of *Fort/Da*.

Fanon argues that the nationalist literature during the early phases of decolonialization, or during what he will call a dying colonialism, repeats this unique form of imaginary trauma. But nationalist literature also performs a necessary if also very problematic cathartic function (Fanon 1067, 148). From his perspective, the scathing denunciations, the outpourings of misery, and the heated words of the poetry and tragedy of nationalist literature during the period of decolonialization repeat the earlier fictions of the colonial period. But the fact that they take the paradoxes of the imagination to a feverish point, the fact that they reach the extreme of self-violence, also makes an important difference. Insofar as they are fictions of their own making, nationalist tragedies of self-undoing are different from the colonial fictions after which they are modeled.[7] And this difference makes it possible for the colonized to avoid acting out the trauma, the problematic aggression, or the hypersensitivity, that they put into words instead. In this way, nationalist poetry and tragedy helps to clear the air, even if it also steals the thunder from a necessary struggle according to Fanon (Fanon 2004, 173).

Influenced by Fanon's account of the paradox of the colonial psyche, Sánchez writes a cathartic tragedy that reveals the complex and resilient nature of a compromised psychological agency. If, as it has been claimed, the play is an example of the Hegelian and Marxist account of catharsis, where the tragic hero affirms his true humanity by means of an apparent self-sacrifice, it is also an ironic example of this cathartic affirmation (Colón Zayas 1985, 91). Indeed, like the nationalist tragedies described by Fanon, the play gives form and voice to the traumatized psyche of a hypersensitive subject during the period of a dying colonialism (*La pasión*, 24). Through lighting, music, sets, and inflection the play dramatizes the effects of an archaic trauma for an audience familiar with its symptoms. Through its plot and events the play gives a narrative arch to the Manichean process (a colonial patrimony) that inevitably leads to a self-violence, which is just as therapeutic as Antígona's breaking point in the play (ibid., 107). The imaginary and cathartic self-violence of the play temporarily clears the air, relaxes the hypersensitive muscles of the characters, and even tempers the hysterical violence of the social order. This relaxation is evident in the final reports by the press (ibid., 122).

Like many of the scenes of self-undoing studied in this book, *La pasión* reveals a flexible colonial psyche that survives at the border of the possible. This is not the triumphant survival that Perivolaris finds in the theatre of Sánchez, a survival that celebrates the potential of crisis as the necessary condition for subversive transformations (Perivolaris 2000, 188). Instead, the play represents a psyche (the psyche of Antígona) that survives in a mode of sustained crisis. The hope of this survival cannot be separated from the limit and borderline state of the psyche. The promise of the survival is entangled with the disquiet of the psyche. At the end of the play, an embodied psyche in a state of ambivalent expectation emerges as the curtain lowers. It is represented by the beating of a heart that pounds ever so loudly to an uncanny rhythm. It is the heart and the soul of Antígona, the surviving colonial psyche, beating in preparation for, and in anticipation of, the next tragic scene (*La pasión*, 122).

History: The Effect of the Lite-Colonial on the Psyche

The stage directions of *La pasión* indicate that the last rhythmic lines of Antígona ("Be quick, Creón, be quick. Give me, give me death") are inflected with a joyful music. They are compared to a joyful hallelujah (*La pasión*, 121). The ecstatic delivery of the lines is a repetition of an earlier moment in the play when Antígona describes to the audience the torture she is about to experience (ibid., 47). Indeed, the music that accompanies Antígona's suffering or passion is a motif of the play. The joyful music is part of the sumptuous and imposing Christian spectacle that also surrounds and accompanies the characters of Monsignor Bernardo Escudero (a high official of the Catholic Church) and Generalísimo Creón Molina as they enter the stage (ibid., 59). What is the meaning of this musical motif? The joyful music that marks both the scene of Antígona's self-undoing and the entrance of the powerful figures of authority is a sign of a paradoxical form of agency and domination under what has been called the "lite-colonial," an elaboration of Nietzsche's slave morality into Christian Democracy. The musical motif suggests Sánchez's attempt to redefine the scene of self-sacrifice as an act that is proper to (but also symptomatic of) an equally extreme, excessive, and absolute display of power.

Religion is central to Sánchez's play. The references to the passion of Christ and to the role of a high official of the Catholic Church, the set directions that call for a background wall or mural pasted with slogans including "CHRISTIAN DEMOCRACY," and the ecstatic musical motif all confirm this. Some of the criticism about the play has commented on its religious dimension in an effort to politicize it (Ben-Ur 1975, 18–19). Barradas, for example, argues that Sánchez modernizes Christian self-sacrifice through Antigona's martyrdom. It is a reference to Liberation Theology according to him (Barradas 1981, 36–37). Others suggest that the play de-sacralizes the Christian passion and instead represents it as a material and worldly experience (Ben-Ur 1975, 19; Santos Silva 1981, 439) or as a radically individual experience with national repercussions (Bettaglio 2012, 48). And yet, none of these critics addresses a troubling aspect of the play, namely, its association of Christian passion with death, and with the pleasure that death promises to bring Creón and Antigona.

I mentioned before that the play suggests that Antígona's unrelenting drive to her death is the paradoxical effect of the attempts of the other characters to convince her to live. And none of the characters are more sincere and invested in the effort to save Antígona from death than Monsignor Escudero and Creón Molina. The Monsignor tries to convince Antígona to confess by insisting on the beauty of life (*La pasión*, 83). Creón blames the victim and claims his Christian opposition to the death penalty (ibid., 73–74). In fact, Creón also orders Antígona to live and to give herself over to her love (ibid., 97). Indeed, Creón and Escudero are both representatives of a Christian regime that idealizes life and is afraid of death. When Aurora describes to Antígona how she pleaded with Creón to let her visit her daughter, Antígona stops her and tells her it would have been better if Aurora had protested at the gates of the palace. When Aurora replies that the guards would have ignored her, Antígona answers that after two days of screaming, Creón himself would have begged Aurora to visit her daughter, just to make her stop (ibid., 30).

Perhaps because Antígona realizes that there is fear behind the regime's command to live, Antígona fanatically embraces death with a strange form of pride, as Pilar suggests when she visits Antígona in prison (*La pasión*, 116). Antígona suggests that she can do what Creón cannot do himself. She turns Creón's own words against him and asks him directly for the death that he cannot order. When Creón first visits Antígona, he commands her to look at him when he speaks (ibid., 38). But when Creón visits Antígona a second time, it is Antígona who challenges him to look at her as she asks him for blood, for revenge, and for death (ibid., 96).

Creón's merciful Christian Democracy and Antígona's fanatical self-sacrifice are two sides of a symbiotic and passionate embrace that Slavoj Žižek has described, in another context, as an archaic form of slave morality. Žižek writes that "Christianity is the true religion of the superego," suggesting that the excessive, disproportionate, unexplainable, and unjustifiable pardon, mercy, and love of Christianity generates an agency of absolute and arbitrary power (Žižek 2004, 503). He further suggests that Christianity produces a Nietszchean slave morality in the sense that, like Creón in Sánchez's play, the Christian master will not admit he is a master. But Christianity also leads to the unmasking of this very morality, insofar as it leads to a similar absolute radical politics, according to Žižek. Christianity generates an attachment or an embrace of this arbitrary and absolute power based on a similarly excessive, indelible, and unforgiveable guilt and crime, according to him (ibid., 518). Žižek uses Sophocles's *Antigone* as an example of absolute radical political opposition, suggesting (against Nietzsche) that slave morality in fact predates Christianity. For Žižek, Antigone's self-violence is the mirror image of Creón's arbitrary and absolute power, an absolutely radical act that by its very excess calls into question the slave morality or the antiauthoritarian tolerance of Creón's regime.[8]

Žižek's account of slave morality and his extension of it to the simultaneous charitable and profiteering developed nations of global capitalism has resonated with critics of Puerto Rican cultural production of the last twenty years such as Flores and Van Haesendonck. These critics suggest that the transition to transnational global capitalism in the final decades of the twentieth century is an example of slave morality that has similarly affected colonial relations in the Caribbean and more particularly in Puerto Rico, turning them into what they call examples of the "lite-colonial." Van Haesendonck echoes Žižek's argument suggesting that the Caribbean is in fact a model for an invisible form of expanding global repression and domination. He suggests that subjects in the global empire are becoming increasingly enmeshed, perhaps defensively entangled, in ambivalent relationships with the absolute power of the "lite-colonial," negotiating with it and trying to circumvent it, like the trickster of old. He calls this negotiation a kind of madness, and finds that it defines the present condition of the Caribbean intellectual. This condition is a defensive madness that is productive and creative at the same time. The madness makes it possible to survive as an intellectual in the Caribbean, but this is not the same as living free, according to Van Haesendonck.

Flores similarly defines the "lite-colonial" as a discursive diversion, thick with symbols, that has shifted attention away from the material conditions of colonialism, that is, from the body and from the violence done to the body. But the "lite-colonial" has also produced its own counterdiscourse in narratives of the Puerto Rican diaspora, according to Flores. These narratives practice what Flores calls an inversion of the diversions of the "lite-colonial." On the one hand, like Van Haesendonck, Flores argues that these narratives are a carnivalesque displacement of colonial reality. On the other, he goes farther than Van Haesendonk in emphasizing their necessary return to the point of entanglement with colonial power.

The first performance of *La pasión* coincided with a period of economic crisis and intense cultural debates in part due to the participation of Puerto Ricans in the Vietnam War that resulted in an island-wide state of crisis. In fact, the play made oblique references to a conflict at the University of Puerto Rico that reflected this wider state of political unrest. One year before its first performance, the first of six violent confrontations between 1967 and 1971 took place between students and riot police. The confrontation led to the arrest of sixteen pro-independence students, who received a harsh sentence two years later during the tenure of the first pro-statehood governor of the island, Luis A. Ferré (1904–2003). The judgment led to three more confrontations, leaving ten people wounded and one student dead. Facing the escalating violence, Ferré spoke to student groups making reference to the democratic form of government enjoyed in Puerto Rico after the occupation of the United States in 1898, and opposing this form of government to harsh Spanish rule (R. Ferré 1972, 130). The speech was one of many calls by the governor to a form of government that would teach the youth how to enjoy life (!), rather than resort to violence (ibid., 131). His calls led to one of the slogans made famous by the Ferré administration: "Reason doesn't scream, reason persuades" (ibid., 143). Fatefully, Ferré's calls to reason also led to what one historian describes as "the most violent university uprising and confrontation in the history of Puerto Rico" (Baralt 1998, 120–21). The 1971 bombing of the ROTC building in the university left sixty-two wounded and three dead including an ROTC cadet, a policeman, and the chief of the riot police sent into university grounds to impose and preserve order. In short, the Christian Democracy that arrived with the United States in 1898 is an example of slave morality unwittingly triggering and embracing fanatical protest in a passionate conflagration.

Flores and Van Haesendonck suggest that the invisible and yet absolute deployment of power under this contemporary form of slave morality produces a madness, a making-fun, but also a disavowal, a refusal to see, and a willful blindness that temporarily diverts but also eventually returns the colonial subject to its attachment with colonial power. The joyful music that accompanies Antígona's act of self-undoing is a sign of this return and overpowering attachment. Its joy reveals a paradisial plenitude, the ecstasy of a final and kamikaze reunion with the shadow, or with the other in the mirror that will only be postponed. In other words, the "lite-colonial" results in a scene that represents the fanatical repetition of the excess of that absolute power: a disturbing reaction-formation to the effect of such absolute power on the colonial psyche. But, following Žižek, these critics also suggest that the repetition of this scene has the potential of unmasking the raw power of the "lite-colonial" by means of the distancing required to represent the effect. These critics suggest that from this distance a measure of meaning can be returned to an otherwise meaningless act of suicidal self-undoing.[9]

Language: The Tragic Meaning of the Words of the Master

Beyond revealing the pliable nature of the psyche and the effects on the psyche of the history of colonialism, *La pasión* also displays the central (and also ambiguous) place that the language of tragedy occupies in Puerto Rico's repeating scene of self-undoing. In the play, Antígona chooses tragic irony over the transparent and objective language of the media. She prefers poetic ambiguity to the transcendental language of the Church or to the decisive language of the Law or the State. She also gives up her authority, or the need to have the last word. Instead, Antígona recognizes that one is never fully in control of one's language, of its meaning, or of its effect. In doing so, the play dramatizes a tragic view of language as a powerful device in the hands of men who are too clever for their own good. In this way, Antígona's tragic language becomes the means to their self-undoing, but also the promise of their salvation.

Antígona tells Creón he does not realize what he is asking for when he commands her to confess, and to give herself over to life with her lover, Fernando (*La pasión*, 97). Antígona poetically suggests that words and language cover over and protect a more meaningful love. And so, to renege on her words, to repent and disavow her pledge to the Tavárez brothers, is to leave this love unprotected and without cover. But Antígona also suggests that the very opposite is true: that to give yourself absolutely to this love, without the protective cover of words and language, is to give yourself over to an uncontrolled and destructive passion whose effect might be a profound challenge to the law of Creón. So, to undermine one's words, to disavow them as Creón demands that she does, will pose a challenge to him that is more disturbing than he realizes. In other words, Creón does not know that what he is asking of Antígona will be his undoing.

In fact, Creón's inability to understand the meaning of his own words is perhaps the most poignant example in the play of a linguistic crisis that is widespread in the imaginary Republic of Molina. This crisis is brought about by the constant struggle between divergent, even opposite versions of the truth. The crisis reaches the point where several characters can't make themselves understood even to Antígona (*La pasión*, 21, 112). Others, such as Pilar, try to return clarity and transparency to a ruler who confuses even himself with democratic language (ibid., 57). Paradoxically, the crisis leads Creón to insist that Antígona have the last word, that she give him a final decision. Creón mistakenly believes that Antígona's last word will not only seal her fate, but also put an end to the uncertainty, the doubt, and the political crisis that the conflict has produced in Molina (ibid., 119).

Creón's insistence on quickly closing Antígona's account of the truth is but a form of what Antígona calls the century's great *persecución,* the noun form of the verb that means to hunt down in Spanish, a hunt that the play suggests will lead to a similar violent form of resistance. According to Antígona, the century is characterized by linguistic and moral relativity (*La pasión*, 104). As a reaction to this language play, the State defends itself by looking for absolutes (ibid.). The American Century is not only characterized by doubt, but also by the need to erase doubt with categorical statements of allegiance. However, if the hunt for absolute truth leads to propaganda, the same propaganda also undermines truth and returns doubt (ibid.). From this perspective, the violent disavowal of doubt, and the pursuit of absolute truth (or of certainty), paradoxically also generate the rallying cries of the opposition to the State, they generate the slogans that Antígona is forced to repeat (ibid.).

Antígona gives in to the slogans, but she also does it while expressing regret at the loss of something else, the loss of a form of signification that lies beyond the literal or dictionary definition of words, a form of signification beyond the strict laws of the State or the Church, a kind of nonsense perhaps, or the very negativity that undermines perfect clarity and absolute sense. When her sister tells Antígona that she does not understand her, Antígona replies, "I would like nothing better than to not understand you, to not understand so many things" (*La pasión*, 112). Antígona's words are ambiguous. They suggest that despite her inability to hear Irene's concern for her, she does understand the deeper meaning of the words of her friend. Antígona refers to the ambition that the words of Irene betray, an ambition that escapes even Irene (ibid.). But Antígona also says that she would prefer not to understand Irene's words, as if this disavowal would allow her to feel the love that subtends even the ambition of her friend.

So, when Creón asks Antígona to decide between two radically different options (between salvation and damnation (*La pasión*, 119)), Antígona chooses to "not understand" the choice. Instead, she insists that salvation is not opposed to death, and that death will be her salvation (ibid.). Her choice is to confuse the terms, to scramble the opposing choices into one paradox.

In fact, Antígona often speaks in riddles in the play—poetically, as Pilar contemptuously describes her speech—inverting meaning and scrambling the words of the other characters like an ancient Greek Oracle.[10] Not even Creón is immune to Antígona's strange, archaic, oracular, and paradoxical language. Like Oedipus in *Oedipus Rex*, Creón interprets Antígona's oracle. He tells her that blood is indeed her fate, and he means not only the literal blood that Antígona will spill (her own), but also the blood that runs through her metaphorical veins: her bloodline. Family is destiny Creón says, and with the same words he unwittingly predicts his own downfall (ibid., 90).

The strange language of Antígona repeats what Shepherdson describes as the "tragic way of thinking" that is also the dramatic lesson of Sophocles's *Antigone*. In Shepherdson's reading of the play, Creón is a tragic hero. Like Antigone, Creón is a descendant of the disobedient Laius (the father of Oedipus) and the sins of his father will be visited upon him. The story of the play is then the story of a divine vengeance exacted on the house of Labdacus. It is the story of what Sophocles calls *Até,* something that for Shepherdson does not fit either with the idea of a crime or of an unjust law (Shepherdson 2009, 57). It is instead the story of a pollution that extends beyond Laius, Oedipus, or Creón, a family curse, passed on across generations.

This fate is clear to the audience of the tragedy, according to Shepherdson, but not to Creón, the legitimate ruler of Thebes. In fact, Creón's tragic flaw is that the hubris of the tragic hero doesn't allow him to understand his role in the play or his fate. Like the words of the ruler of Molina, the words of the ruler of Thebes are his downfall. Creón is a clever man, he is particularly clever with words, but he is oblivious to their tragic meaning. He promises to the Chorus that his actions will speak for him, that actions speak louder than words. And yet Creón's tragic actions are in fact the effect of his obliviousness to words, to the irony of the words of tragedy, to the meaning of the discourse and of the story that antecedes and frames him. Creón is oblivious to the point of arrogantly disavowing the ambiguity of language, of words, and this arrogance is the reason for his fall. "Actions speak louder than words," Creón says, and the audience of tragedy smiles knowing better.

Shepherdson argues that Creón embodies the tragic view of man or the view of man according to tragedy. Man as *deinon* or as "self-undoing" (Shepherdson 2009, 71). In tragedy, man is too clever for his own good. He is inventive and disastrous at the same time. His clever words have the opposite meaning that they ostensibly carry. And, Shepherdson further argues, we repeat Creón's tragic flaw when we take a tragedy such as *Antigone* out of its literary and dramatic context and use it to argue for a certain philosophical, legal, political, or cultural point, bending its ironic words to our will, clever and tragic as we are wont to be of late. Instead, Shepherdson suggests, we should heed the lesson of tragedy, as Creón does by the end of the play, when he hears of the death of Eurydice (ibid.). For Shepherdson, tragedy, tragic irony, and language, are all embodied in the strange dyad that couples the words of Creón with a strange and "feminine" tone. Tragic irony or language is for Shepherdson the carrier of an eerie music, an uncanny poetry, a negativity, and an undoing that is closer to us than we might want to admit. Like Creón, like Antígona Pérez, we must tend to this strangeness in ourselves in the effort to transform this negativity into a song, as Shepherdson suggests.

Antígona's need to listen for the strangeness in our own language, her attentiveness to the signs of its undoing, is also the dramatic and tragic lesson of the scene repeated by the Puerto Rican imagination. Like the play, and like the character of Antígona, this scene is also paradoxical, even contradictory to the point of self-sacrifice or self-undoing. But also like the play, the scene is a warning to heed the ambiguity of our words, and to follow the tradition of knowledge most familiar with their double-meaning negativity, if we are to prevent ourselves from repeating the mistakes of Creón. In other words, the scene of self-undoing, like the play, is a call to the study and interpretation of language in its many forms (art, literature, linguistics, and aesthetics) at a time when "action speaks louder than words," when the study of language broadly defined has become ethically questionable and suspect.

Body: From Affect to Sublimation

The tragedy of *La pasión* is also the story of the transition of a twenty-five-year-old young woman from an adolescent into an adult. From a rebel who screams No! into a subject who repeatedly questions authority. It is a tragic story because the development of Antígona meets with an unsupportive social environment, and with an interlocutor who purposefully ignores her questions. The effect is that the character is put in an uncomfortable and paradoxical position. In the end, Antígona asks the only question that is allowed her: she "asks" for her own death. The statement is not literally a question, and yet it is a request that like a question provokes a response. It is both a provocation and a self-destructive act. But it is also a defense in two senses. On the one hand, these are the last words that stand between Antígona and her death. They are a temporary buffer postponing the inevitable. On the other, the words also affirm the capacity to respond, a response whose nature remains unknown until it is given. Antígona's final request is a question of last resort, a final revolt, but also a hyperbolic act of forgiveness: she says that "what is important is that there always be someone who is predisposed to give. It's our last hope" (*La pasión*, 117).

Antígona's request is the last in a series of statements that interrogate not only the authority of a tyrant, but also the place of women in the imaginary country of Molina. The origin of the questions is the abject status of the female body. At a certain moment in the play, groups of men and women respond to Creón's second visit to Antígona in prison. They react to Creón's inflexibility with contradictory exhortations. The men ask Antígona to give up her struggle against the ruler, while the women ask her to continue to resist. The scene is important because it suggests that sexual and gender difference is a key to understanding the play. Indeed, the chorus suggests a widespread persecution of women that Antígona experiences not only at the hands of Creón, who tells her that he was counting on her "feminine weakness" (*La pasión*, 92), but also at the hands of her own mother, who tells Antígona that she is only a woman and she should stick to her domestic chores (ibid., 28). Together, these statements suggest that Antígona's crime, beyond stealing the corpses of her friends, is her sexual difference. The suggestion is contained in the epithet repeatedly used by the press to describe Antígona as wicked or *fascinerosa*. The word is an archaic Spanish word meaning one who commits crimes frequently, habitually, and it suggests not only an identification of Antígona's actions with a crime, but also of her very essence with absolute evil.[11] Faced with this widespread social abjection of women, Antígona describes her century as the century of the great persecution, and she repeatedly asks, "What is the meaning of this hunt?" and whether the century is "forcing us out of our very selves?" (ibid., 104).

Antígona's questions hark back to Fanon's description of the colonial paradox. But they also complicate Fanon's analysis of the injection of a racialized bodily schema into the psyche of the colonial subject with an added abjection now also based on sexual difference. It is significant from the perspective of this sexual complement to colonial pathology that Antígona's questions at the end of the play develop out of negative responses that begin with the character of her mother: Aurora. During her visit to

Antígona, Aurora tries to convince her daughter to confess to her crime by painting an image of future marital "bliss" with Fernando, Antígona's beau: a home in the country surrounded by children. The stage directions emphasize that a certain rhythm accompanies the words of Aurora and that Antígona repeats this rhythm even as she refuses the life that her mother imagines for her (*La pasión*, 28). It is as if the lilt that subtends the sexist words of Aurora also provided Antígona with the necessary support to say No! to her mother. It is as if something in Aurora's voice gives Antígona the permission to go against her mother. Something that remains and resists even after Aurora has been forced out of her self, and has become the model for Molina's femininity. It is as if the bodily impulse of Aurora, contained in the rhythm of her words, were a form of archaic musical signification that inverts or negates the meaning of her words, and leads Antígona to ask her mother questions and to revolt against social injustice. Antígona suggests that the protest in her own voice is a sign of suffering, a form of passion (ibid.).

The complex passion of Aurora contained in the lilt of her voice is the bodily impulse that subtends Antígona's revolt, and it is also the force that gives form to the language of the adolescent Antígona (and gives the title to the play). Her language has not had the time to become smooth with time, it is compared to the neighing of a horse or an animal language that carries wounds and suspicions (*La pasión*, 80). This language begins with her No!, and is followed by the questions she puts to her mother. These questions in turn are followed by Antígona's vehemence, by her extreme form of love and hatred, simultaneously expressed by her screams of anger and cries of joy in the play. And Antígona's vocalizations return emotion to the sick, heartless, and cold language of the media. They return volume to the voices of Molina, where there is a tendency to lower the voice in fear. They revolt against Creón's demand for a language of reason (ibid., 40). They contain a disturbing tone, a shrill bitterness that filters through Antigona's laughter (ibid., 64). They turn into the poignant questions that Antígona asks Creón (ibid., 129). And the questions make Creón feel desperate. They make him feel trapped. Indeed, Antígona's vehemence provokes a crisis in Creón, it makes him lose his patience, his mind, his control, his sovereignty even over himself. And Antígona's vehemence or passion also spreads to a larger audience. In the poetic language of the play, Antígona's vocalizations, her vehemence, and her questions act as a catalytic agent that decomposes or "ferments" (in the words of the play) a collective language. A legend is woven out of this process, a legend that is also an act of insubordination (ibid., 65). The play is a corrosive legend told in a corroding tongue that transforms passion or bodily impulses into powerful words.

Oliver gives a detailed account of this transformation of bodily impulses into words. And she insists that this transformation must take a social form if there is to be an antidote to what she calls the colonialization of psychic space. In Oliver's account of the play by Sophocles, the criminal trespass of Antigone is her unforgiveable sexuality, and Oliver suggests that this abjection of the female body, and the shame that it injects into the body of women, is the archaic model for later forms of domination and subjection, including colonialism (Oliver 2004, 220–21 n.1). Oliver argues that the domination inherent in colonialism is similar to the treatment of *Antigone* by Sophocles. Following Fanon, she argues that colonialism is a series of longstanding social practices of shaming, humiliation, and devaluation that hollow out the psyche of the colonized subject, that injects the hollowed-out core with a phobic and cruel superego, and that finally secretes an artifact that is made pathologically self-violent (ibid., 51, 67). The malady of the secreted artifact is that it can no longer transform its bodily impulses into words. The body of the colonized subject is the crypt inside which she remains interred.

By contrast, a subject that transforms its bodily impulses into words (or that is able to question authority) is a subject that can step outside this social crypt, according to Oliver. To question authority in this sense amounts to allowing the expression of the unconscious bodily impulse (or affects) even in the face of a form of domination that abjects the body in general and the racialized female body in particular. Such questioning is an antidote to the colonialization of psychic space in two specific ways, according to Oliver. First, it profoundly undermines the illusion of sovereignty that subtends all authority, and that is actually an effect of the malady of colonialism. Questioning instead has its source and origin in the body, in the unconscious bodily affects, rather than in the so-called mind. Second, questioning interrupts the injection of the phobic and cruel superego and the ensuing collapse of the ego of the colonized by transforming or inverting the negativity of the unconscious bodily impulse into the positive force of sublimation. But this positive outcome, she stresses, is the result of a movement that comes from sustained negativity: the sustained struggle against giving a primacy to either the body or to language. Finally, such paradoxical questioning depends on the trust that an accepting and supportive social attitude preexists, precedes, antedates, the subject, the belief in the preexistence of the necessary conditions of possibility for the transfer of these affects or the sublimation of bodily drives. Characteristically, such social trust is modeled on our relations to the maternal body, and Oliver calls this trust forgiveness. In an earlier piece, Oliver also associates this trust with the environment, and she calls the negative labor of this trust the "Look of Love."

The play *La pasión* is an example of the vexed and negative form that this necessary questioning can take. From this perspective, the play is a series of negations and questions that add up to an imaginary disavowal of reality, a disavowal of the evacuation of the colonial self, an interruption of a process of self-evacuation, and an antidote to the colonialization of psychic space. Antígona's No's and her questions repeat, invert, and elaborate her mother's melancholy and sad regretfullness, as well as the confession and disavowal that Creón asks of Antígona. She turns Creón's command to retract, to confess, to admit wrongdoing first into a resounding No!, then into a scream, and finally into questions. Her poetically inflected negations, screams, cries, and questions are followed by a catharsis. They prepare the way to a cathartic future of social upheaval, but they also postpone the immediate breakdown of the self. In fact, her final demand for death paradoxically turns the negativity of her abjected body into the language of a command. Her demand undermines Creón's sovereignty, and it negates the pulverizing effect of inevitable death by asking for it, by turning death into the response of an otherwise unresponsive tyrant, and by transforming the patrimony of his violent actions into a hyperbolic forgiveness.

The paradoxical nature of *La pasión* culminating in Antígona's scene of self-undoing is at the heart of the Puerto Rican scene of self-undoing during the American Century. Like Sánchez's play, the negative scene stops the injection of an abjected body into the psyche of the Puerto Rican subject. It represents or gives symbolic form to the only kind of agency left for the abjected subject: a dramatic self-undoing. With this vexed representation, the Puerto Rican subject continues to hold the seat that generates agency: the seat of the imagination. The surviving Puerto Rican imagination finds a form of support for itself in the strange rhythms of the abject body, turning around the social abjection of the colonized, its racialization, erotization, and sexualization. The genius of imagination undermines the notion of sovereignty and absolute power that the malady of colonialism generates (and of a sovereignty that is always already beyond the grasp of the colonial imagination), and instead it insists on the unconscious and bodily origin of action and agency. And it replaces an ideal of social forgiveness with a more sober ability to respond, the minimum requirement for the subject to continue to say No!, to ask questions, and to sublimate. In the melancholy words of Antígona, this ability to respond is our last hope.

Almost fifteen years after *La pasión* was first performed in Puerto Rico, Rosario Ferré, another member of Sánchez's generation, published *Fábulas de la garza desangrada* (1982),[12] a heterogeneous book of poems, short stories, letters, that contained four poems dedicated to the figure of "Antígona Labdácida" (R. Ferré 1982, 36). The poems can be interpreted as a response and a reaction to the repetition by Sánchez of the figure of the self-sacrificing woman in the face of overwhelming force. Like other poems in the book, similarly dedicated to anthological and familiar female figures that commit suicide or die at the hands of their loved ones (Shakespeare's Ophelia, Cervantes's Dorothea, Daphne, Ariadne, St. Catherine, etc.) the poems that Ferré dedicates to Antígona listen to an uncanny voice and represent a voice that returns from the grave. The poems begin where the play by Sánchez ends. They recover Antígona from the crypt where Sánchez leaves her, and make her speak again with an ever-increasing anger. The third poem of the series, for example, reaches an apocalyptic climax of destruction, and inverts the self-sacrifice of Antígona with a revolting image: "may the golden feces of the princes / turn implacably in their fertile ground / and may their fields and their trees be razed by my memory" (ibid., 39). The poetic voice imagines her disturbing effect on the abject remains of the rulers of Thebes, who (like Antígona) also turn in their graves.

But the abjection, the regression, and the confrontation with negative human matter, is also followed by a gift, the fourth poem "Antígona Delonix Regia" (R. Ferré 1982, 40). This poem makes an oblique reference to the red flowers of the poinciana tree, abundant in tropical Puerto Rico. Its blood-red flowers become a metaphor for Antígona's spilled blood. In other words, Antígona's blood still flows, it boils over at night, but it is also transformed into the metaphor of the poinciana tree, a poem whose language is also a source of shade and rest for all past and future rebels. The metaphor of the poinciana tree, with its bleeding but protective branches, is a form of the ambiguous but necessary collective tradition of imagination and interpretation contained in the poems, in the play, and in the scene of self-undoing that they repeat. Most importantly, the metaphor is also a sign of the support that this tradition continues to give to the Puerto Rican subject.

2

The Gift of Abjection

THE LOOK OF LOVE IN RENÉ MARQUÉS

To each ego its object. To each superego its abject.

—Julia Kristeva

"Look me in the eyes!" He obeyed and was surprised not to see the dreadful anger he had expected.

—René Marqués

Marqués's last novel, *La mirada* (1976), begins with a flashback to a scene of punishment that is also a familiar, archaic, and changing ritual. The punishment both purifies and defiles (constitutes and undoes) the main character of this coming-of-age novel: a young and nameless adolescent.[1] The ritual is familiar in the sense that it internalizes a threat of dismemberment that is characteristic of much of Puerto Rican literature, as I argue in this book, a threat that is also a repeated scene of self-undoing, self-sacrifice, or self-castration in the narrative of Marqués. The ritual is archaic not only in the sense that it is in the past of the narrator, but also in the sense that it refers us back to an irreducible dread and joy that are at the origins of all subjectivity and of social organizations. Kristeva calls this dread and joy abjection. Finally, the scene also represents the changing nature of the rituals of prohibition and its effects both on Marqués and on Puerto Rico. Indeed, Marqués rewrites this scene so familiar to Puerto Rican readers when facing his own mortality (he died three years after the novel was published), and when the Puerto Rican Commonwealth and its discourses of national identity were facing their own end.

In the novel, the adolescent main character remembers a moment in the distant past when he was a boy and he was punished by his father for masturbating naked with a friend (Julito). He remembers his father hitting him with a riding crop. The blow separates the two friends but it also has the unforeseen effect of making the main character ejaculate from the shock. The flashback is quickly followed by another where the father gives his son the "look" that also gives the novel its title. "Look me in the eyes!" he commands his embarrassed son, who dares not meet his gaze for fear of what he might find there. But when the docile son finally raises his eyes and meets his father's gaze, he is surprised to see something he did not expect. The narrator tells us that the boy sees the absence of dreadful anger. In this chapter, I will argue that this absence that the boy sees in his father's eyes is something that is latent in the early work of Marqués and becomes manifest in his last novel. This so-called absence is the strange hold that Kristeva calls abjection and that Oliver calls love.[2]

The Commonwealth and Its Weak Prohibitions

Marqués writes his novel at the end of what historians have recently characterized as "the epoch of PPD hegemony" (Ayala and Bernabe 2007, 201). The Popular Democratic Party was founded in 1938, but its solution to decolonization through self-government was institutionalized in 1952 when President Harry S. Truman signed Public Law 82-477. With this act, President Truman enacted a new constitution for Puerto Rico, which indicated that the relationship between the island and the United States was a compact between two parties rather than an imperial imposition. This relationship, in turn, generated the Estado Libre Asociado, known in English as The Commonwealth of Puerto Rico. Together with this new legal entity, the landscape of Puerto Rican politics, economy, and culture also changed. For example, the nature of the economy went from agricultural to industrial production. This fundamental economic change was followed by mass migration from the countryside to urban areas, and eventually to the United States. Moreover, the Commonwealth called for a cultural form of nationalism that affirmed Spanish language and Spanish values, including a discourse of national identity that invoked, among others, the figures of the patrician patriarch, of the good peasant, of the self-sacrificing wife, and of the great Puerto Rican family, as historian Quintero Rivera famously argued (1976, passim).

And yet, the Commonwealth also represented what could be described as a weaker, a more porous and forgiving law. It was, after all, a negotiated solution between the extremes of dependence and independence, colonialism and sovereignty. Unlike the Nationalist Party that it helped to eradicate, the Commonwealth did not promote a sense of nationhood predicated on armed conflict and political opposition to the United States. Nationhood was predicated instead on the resistance to the cultural influence of that country. Similarly, the new constitution, drafted by Puerto Ricans, approved in a local plebiscite, and signed into law by President Truman, did not change the official status of Puerto Rico as an unincorporated territory of the United States. Instead, the constitution only granted autonomy to the island over its local affairs. Finally, the Commonwealth was partly developed in consultation with the New Deal liberals and as such was an extension of the welfare state that they helped to create. The new economic model of the Commonwealth (called Operation Bootstrap) also articulated a humanitarian and optimistic discourse of national identity (called Operation Serenity) that generated a Puerto Rican subject that was euphemistically described as serene, peaceful, tolerant, and democratic, according to Marqués.

The flexibility of the Commonwealth and its official discourse were sorely tested, however, during the recession that hit the United States between 1974 and 1975.[3] At that time, the hegemony of the once invincible PPD political party came to an end in the polls. Puerto Rico transitioned from a one- to a two-party system, giving the lie to the exaggerated democratic claims of the earlier regime. One year later, in 1976 (the same year that Marqués published his novel), two groundbreaking works were published that represented the growing ossification of the discourse of national identity but also the coming changes in the rituals and prohibitions of the Commonwealth. These works not only documented the ossification of the discourse and the changes in the law, but they also gave a literary form to both. From this perspective, *La guaracha del Macho Camacho* (1976), a novel by Sánchez, and *Papeles de Pandora* (1976), a collection of short stories by Ferré, represented the closing of the racial, sexual, class, and demographic boundaries of the discourses of national identity. But they were also a testimony to the flexibility of the rituals and discourses governing the

Commonwealth of Puerto Rico. Like Marqués facing his death, these writers adapted their narratives to the pressures of an impending transformation, and to a new reality. Together with Marqués, these writers opened the way to what Kristeva calls the sublimation of abjection.

Readings of Marqués

Marqués was probably the most celebrated, and later the most reviled literary figure of the Commonwealth from beginning to end.[4] And this should come as no surprise since Marqués's claim to fame in great part resided in what literary critic Rubén Ríos Ávila has called his "frontal assault" against the political, economic, and cultural programs of the Commonwealth (Ríos Ávila 2009, 181). Indeed, Marqués criticized the mass migration of Puerto Ricans to the United States in what is perhaps his most famous award-winning play, *La carreta* (1951). He also criticized the cultural program and the optimistic rhetoric of the Commonwealth in award-winning essays such as "Pesimismo literario y optimismo político: su existencia en el Puerto Rico actual" (1959) and "El puertorriqueño dócil" (1962). Influenced by critics of New Deal liberalism like Lionel Trilling and Alfred Kazin, Marqués opposed the humanitarian optimism of the Commonwealth with a tragic pessimism that described the abject figure of the docile Puerto Rican. Finally, Marqués also exposed the psychological effects of rapid industrialization, urbanization, and compulsory military service in his widespread edited collection *Cuentos puertorriqueños de hoy* (1959), and in his widely acclaimed collection of short stories *En una ciudad llamada San Juan* (1960).

Paradoxically, and significantly, by the time Marqués published his last novel, his works had become synonymous with the orthodox values (social, moral, and political) of the Commonwealth that he so vehemently opposed. Feminist and sociological critics identified his works with a nostalgic and bourgeois longing for the conservative, patriarchal, Catholic, lost world of the displaced Creole landowning class that was romanticized by the ideologues of the Commonwealth.[5] Twenty years later, poststructuralists, cultural critics, and queer theorists have continued to identify the work of Marqués with these orthodox and conservative values. And they have also added to the criticism of Marqués his so-called exclusion and/or repression of homosexuality (including his own) for the benefit of a homosocial and heteronormative matrix in Puerto Rico, a criticism inspired by the influential work of Judith Butler. To their credit, some of these critics moderate their criticism by noting that Marqués's exclusions, and particularly his so-called repression of homosexuality, also produce revealing "tics," as well as haunting returns of the repressed, that are worthy of continued study.[6]

Of these readings, one stands out for its bold attempt to change what was (at the time) a twenty-year-old interpretation of the work of Marqués (see Cruz-Malavé, "Toward an Art of Transvestism"). In an ambitious rereading of the legacy of Marqués's last novel, Arnaldo Cruz-Malavé argues that *La mirada* is the first text to make visible a perspective that he calls "transvestite abjection." From this perspective, homosexuality has been systematically repressed and condemned in Puerto Rico; it has been turned into an abject spectacle. But the abject homosexual writer has also turned the tables on the system that victimizes him, and has become a power of resistance and provocation. Cruz-Malavé also finds this perspective in the works of Sánchez and Ramos Otero, two writers traditionally believed to have broken away from the works of Marqués. But he credits Marqués for being the first writer to reveal, albeit in a negative way, the fact that the discourse of national identity "abjected" (read excluded or repressed) homosexuality from Puerto Rican literature. He also argues that Marqués was the first to take stock of this systematic exclusion by documenting and dramatizing its corrosive and degrading effect in *La mirada.* Cruz-Malavé then argues that the writers who wrote after Marqués developed his dramatization of Puerto Rican abjection first into a form of resistance against the discourse of national identity, and then into a form of subjection of this discourse. In short, he argues that Marqués's novel is the first to make a spectacle of the abjections of the discourse of national identity in Puerto Rico. In doing so, Marqués sets the conditions of possibility for a negative reversal of this discourse. Later writers, Cruz-Malavé concludes, appropriated and exaggerated the abjection first represented by Marqués, making it run amok in their queer works.

A Different Approach to Abjection

In this chapter, I use "abjection" to reread the work of Marqués, but my interpretation of this concept differs from that of Cruz-Malavé. Following Kristeva's aphorism that "to each ego its object, to each superego its abject," I reread the writing of Marqués as the abject to the Commonwealth's superego (Kristeva 1982, 2). On the one hand, I understand that the abject is a polluting power that is directly proportional to the prohibitions of the superego (ibid., 69). On the other, I understand that the Commonwealth is the weak superego that gives form to the writing of Marqués. Most importantly, like Kristeva, I insist on the difference between foreclosing exclusion and porous prohibition. Rather than claim that the dismembered and dismembering writings of Marqués are forms of the foreclosing exclusions of a discourse of national identity, I will argue instead that his narratives are forms of its porous prohibitions, or the remainder of a necessarily imperfect and always limited set of ritualized purifications and defilements practiced by the Commonwealth in its discourses. From my perspective, the figure of the feminized, docile, Puerto Rican subject, as well as the sacred nonobjects or eroticized part-objects that emerge from the so-called perverse narratives of Marqués (more below), are actually a testament to a speaking subject that survives through the weak disavowals of the discourses of national identity of the Commonwealth and beyond.

In other words, the psychotic and phobic narratives of Marqués are elaboration in language of the rituals of defilement or purification of the Commonwealth. They dramatize and elaborate in fiction the production of clean and proper subjects (that are also psychotic and phobic speaking subjects) by the Commonwealth discourse of national identity: subjects that always unsuccessfully try to displace, disavow, negate, and become almost impermeable to the matter that constitutes them; and subjects at the limit of language and its sublimation of the uncanny material that gives them life. But the narratives of Marqués also, and simultaneously, give form to subjects that inevitably represent and make visible something that should remain invisible: a pollution, or the abject to which their subjectivity is always already connected. In other words, the abject is not a repressed that returns. It is instead a sublimated remainder that holds.

Marqués's elaboration in narrative of the catastrophic formation of the Puerto Rican subject is a symptom of a context that has taken language to its limit. And it is a warning against the consequences of continuing to do so. From this perspective, Marqués represents clean and proper but also borderline speaking subjects who are separated from their polluting matter only at a great cost. Also from this perspective, he simultaneously represents the emergence of sacred, eroticized and idealized nonobjects, partial objects that haunt these subjects, and that are a testament to the continued dependence of these subjects on the abject. But the narratives of Marqués are also increasingly shaped by the power of an asymbolic authority or law that is also contained within the weak prohibitions, the ambivalent rituals of defilement and purification, and the porous borders of the Commonwealth: a law Kristeva calls abjection. From this perspective, they are narratives that become increasingly ambiguous, polyphonic, figurative, and oneiric—poetic, in short.

An Old Approach to Abjection

My rereading of Marqués's narratives is indebted to Kristeva's notion of abjection as she develops it in her groundbreaking work *Powers of Horror* (1980).[7] In that book, Kristeva offers a provocative account of the abjection at the origins of all subjectivity and of all social formations drawing from the psychoanalytic theory of Sigmund Freud, from the anthropological work of Mary Douglas, from the poetic works of George Bataille, and from the tragedies of Sophocles. Perhaps most significantly, in this work, Kristeva shifts emphasis away from the arguments of *Totem and Taboo* (1913)—particularly its focus on the ritual murder, or parricide, as the supposed origins of all social formations—and away from the primal role played by the sacrificial rituals represented by the Greek tragedy *Oedipus Rex*. Kristeva instead focuses on what she considers to be the earlier dread and joy of incest, and on the rituals of purification and defilement whose object is to moderate, give form to, and work through the archaic law. She argues that these rituals and prohibitions generate the difference between the clean and proper self and a sacred object, whether it is pure or defiled.

Kristeva bases her argument at least in part on the last works of Sophocles and Freud (*Oedipus at Colonus* and *Moses and Monotheism*, respectively). She finds in them what she calls a different approach to abjection as well as a way to sublimation. Her suggestion is that at the end of their lives, and faced with a change in the law brought about by the turn to democracy (in the case of Sophocles) and by the flight from the Third Reich (in the case of Freud), the playwright and the psychoanalyst achieve a similar moment of clarity. In that moment, they see the true nature of abjection and its fundamental contribution to the social order.

For Kristeva, abjection is both a remainder from the rituals of defilement and purification and an earlier law that she traces back to polytheistic and endogamic cultures with the aid of the anthropological work of Mary Douglas. Indeed, perhaps Kristeva's most important challenge to the psychoanalytic and poststructuralist theories that posit exclusion, castration, or lack as the origins of language, subjectivity, and social order, is her insight that endogamic polytheism gives us what I will call the gift of abjection.

In other words, the transition from endogamic to exogamic social orders, or from polytheistic to monotheistic religious orders, preserves, repeats, and elaborates rituals of defilement and purification that are porous, weak, fragile, or compromised from their first manifestation. Kristeva's claim is that these weak rituals or prohibitions (what she will call the paternal function or the father of individual prehistory) are the inheritance of polytheistic and endogamic cultures, and in turn they bequeath abjection to monotheistic and exogamic cultures. In other words, they allow what we dread and desire the most—a condition or an incestuous state of temporary fusion with another body, an archaic law—to pass through the rituals, but to pass through them changed, moderated, pacified, or sublimated. Kristeva calls this archaic law abjection and, in the short history of the individual, it takes place during the temporary fusion of the mother-child dyad, or during the libidinal stage of primary narcissism.

The effect of these porous and fragile rituals of defilement and purification are what Kristeva calls the clean and proper self on the one hand and the sacred preobject or the nonobject on the other. These are but forms of the original unstable material that is transformed by the rituals sometimes to the point that we become blind to the true nature of our origins. And Kristeva warns that we do this at our own peril. For to lose sight of the true nature of these forms, and to become blind to our own otherness, to the law of abjection at the center of the rituals that make us, is also to generate phobias and paranoid phantasies that will lead us to our premature demise. Indeed, for Kristeva, the phobias and paranoid phantasies of the contemporary world are based on our current separation from our otherness (understood as the archaic law of abjection) relative to other times. These war-producing contemporary phobias and paranoid phantasies are but the underside of our unconscious allegiance to the erotic sacred objects with which we have unwittingly surrounded and accessorized ourselves according to Kristeva.

Poetry and narrative for Kristeva are representations of these rituals of defilement and purification that approximate us to a greater or lesser degree to the law of abjection, to the dread and the joy at the center of our selves. This is not to say that all poetry and narrative possess and sublimate this experience or law to the same degree. Certainly for Kristeva, the baroque mystical poetry of Saint Theresa, or the high modernist novels of James Joyce are examples in language of rituals of defilement and purification that succeed more than others in the effort to open the way back to abjection. It is to say, however, that all poetry and narrative to some degree has the potential to allow this return insofar as art in general and literature in particular are rituals that are at a second remove from the prohibition they represent. In other words, by taking the form of literary language, the rituals of defilement and purification become fragile, weak, and porous enough to represent a royal road back to abjection.

For Kristeva, poetry in particular, whether it is more or less successful at guiding us back to the law of abjection, represents a fragile and thin protective skin, an overtly porous defensive boundary. And it is also a set of formal condensations. Poetry is made of the building blocks of language, it reduces sense and signification to music, to rhythm, sometimes even to negative and empty space, a form of nonsense for Kristeva. The revolution of poetic language is for her a sudden and almost immediate return to the site of abjection and its experience of dread and joy. By contrast, narrative for Kristeva is a form of the rituals of defilement and purification that separate and guide us back to abjection in a more protracted way, allowing for more space and time to work through what we dread and desire so much. If poetry works along the axis of condensation, narrative works along the axis of displacement. But poetry and narrative are not exclusive forms, and they constantly combine to form new articulations. For Kristeva, poetry and narrative are relative forms of condensation and displacement, the so-called primary structures that the structuralists discovered at the foundation of myth, and that the psychoanalysts placed at the center of the dream and of the unconscious. Kristeva retains but also inverts the nature of these so-called primary structures by making them the effect (rather than the cause) of abjection, and of what she calls its archaic parceling or separation, its hold (Oliver would call this hold "relationality" or "love"). This parceling is the degree-zero of abjection for Kristeva. It is what Sophocles, Freud, Douglas, and Bataille describe, study, and elaborate in their works: the experience at the center of abjection (the origin of its dread and joy). It is also what rituals of purification and defilement approximate and what they sublimate when they turn abjection into language. And this parceling is also the loose bond or the ambivalent hold at the center of the rituals, prohibitions, or language that bring us together in society.

In *Powers of Horror*, Kristeva explains why Sophocles and Freud change their approach to abjection, or why Sophocles goes from *Oedipus Rex* to *Oedipus at Colonus* and Freud goes from *Totem and Taboo* to *Moses and Monotheism*. Why they emphasize in their later works the rituals of purification and defilement rather than the ritual of sacrifice, the taboo of incest rather than the taboo of murder, and the social imperative of symbolic matricide rather than the expectation of symbolic parricide. According to her, two things lead to this change in their approach to abjection. First and foremost, events in their lives motivate this change. From this perspective, the rituals of defilement and prohibitions are always biographical for Kristeva. They are as intimately tied to the psyche of individuals as they are to their historical and social circumstance. Kristeva emphasizes that both Sophocles and Freud were on the verge of death when they wrote *Oedipus at Colonus* and *Moses and Monotheism*, respectively. And this proximity to death partly led to the change in their approach to abjection. In fact, Kristeva suggests that when faced with our own mortality, we try to think through the advent of language, culture, and the social order "in order better to establish [their] effectiveness" (Kristeva 1982, 72). In other words, approaching death makes us think of the promise that these porous rituals ultimately hold: the promise of putting mortality and death into circulation, the promise of allowing death (our inheritance, so to speak), to be shared, transmitted, and bequeathed to others. By working through the abjection at the origins of the rituals that give birth to our speaking selves (and also to our social orders), we approximate a form of survival based on sublimation. In the end, sublimation allows us to say with *Oedipus at Colonus*, "I am abject, that is mortal and speaking" (ibid., 88).

Second, the change in the approach to abjection is also shaped by history. Kristeva emphasizes the fact that the social order is never fixed. The rituals of legal, phallic, linguistic, and symbolic separations that give rise to the social order are never radical. In other words, like the embodied hold that they elaborate, these rituals of purification and defilement are always transitory and temporary. They are historical and determined by the twists and turns of local conditions and geopolitical events. To a greater or lesser degree their transitory nature sets the conditions of possibility for the change in the approach to abjection by Sophocles and Freud. Such is the case of the transition from tyranny to democracy in Athens in 508–507 BC, which Kristeva suggests prepared and allowed the writing and the insights of *Oedipus at Colonus*, written one hundred years later in 406–405 BC. And such is also the case of the rise of the Third Reich in 1933, which led Freud to escape to London in 1938, and to publish *Moses and Monotheism* one year later. The weak prohibitions and the porous nature of the rituals that these writers encounter in the wake of history are the conditions of possibility for their sublimation of abjection. And thanks to their sublimation we can see our abjection without gouging out our eyes as Oedipus does in *Oedipus Rex*.

The Docile Puerto Rican and His Discontents

The narratives of Marqués are rituals of purification and defilement that represent both a clean and proper Puerto Rican subject and its intimate and paradoxical relation with the laws, prohibitions, and discourses of the Commonwealth. Some of these narratives represent the uneasy transition of Puerto Rico from one social order to another, from one set of prohibitions to another, without foreclosing or disavowing the abjection that remains as a part of the Puerto Rican subject and its social order. No narrative is more representative of this process than Marqués's ambitious short story "Otro día nuestro," which gives the title to his first collection of short stories, published in 1955.

In her prologue to the first edition, literary critic Concha Meléndez considered "Otro día" not only the best story in the collection but also a valuable addition to the Latin American short story (Meléndez 1955, 9). In her insightful commentary, she suggested that "Otro día" showed with clarity and without sentimentality the effects on Puerto Rico of a transformation of global proportions. What she calls a "new order" is the rapid industrialization and secularization of the island, precipitated by the arrival of the United States in 1898. And the story represents for her an existential realization by its main character: the realization that he has outlived the traditions, beliefs, and sacred law of his earlier way of life. This realization in turn leads him to the conclusion that he must make an adjustment. The character is under house arrest and he comes to see in the course of the story that his age and its social order have been passed by. Unable to die according to the sacred rituals of the old order and its laws, the nameless prisoner gradually turns into a complex but patient figure, both resolved and resigned to live the rest of his life according to an archaic law that still inhabits (and will survive) the law of his jailer.

The nameless prisoner of the story was widely believed to be a cipher for Pedro Albizu Campos (1891–1965), president of the Puerto Rican Nationalist party since 1930. His life of service to the nationalist ideal, long imprisonment, and tragic death summarized a deadly chapter in the history of colonialism in Puerto Rico: the tragedy of persecution and nationalist uprising that took place from the nineteen-thirties to the nineteen-fifties. Two years before the publication of the collection of short stories *Otro día*, in 1953, the then-governor of Puerto Rico (and founding figure of the Commonwealth) Luis Muñoz Marín (1898–1980), had pardoned Albizu

Campos after thirteen years in prison. Albizu Campos had been charged with sedition against the United States government on the island and had been imprisoned twice, once for the murder of Colonel Frances E. Riggs by a nationalist in 1936, and a second time for the nationalist insurrection, and for the simultaneous attempt on the life of President Truman by two nationalists in 1950. One year before the publication of the collection, in 1954, Albizu Campos was placed under house arrest after the attack on Congress by four Puerto Rican nationalists. At the time the collection was published, in 1955, Albizu Campos was on his way to serving another eleven years in prison. He was pardoned a second time by Governor Muñoz Marín in 1965, and he died shortly after his release. Albizu Campos served a total of almost twenty-five years of prison time. The short stories in *Otro día* allow us to sublimate this chapter of Puerto Rican history. The story "Otro día" in particular gives meaning to the life of Albizu Campos rather than purify him into a sacred scapegoat or defile him into a madman.

It is the story of a nameless man held under house arrest in the capital city of Old San Juan for reasons that are never spelled out. We follow him from the moment he first opens his eyes in the morning, to a moment later in the day when he sits transfixed and "waiting for death to pass through" (*Cuentos,* 134). Not much happens in the story, and most of it takes place in the mind of the main character. We see him going through his ablutions and briefly exchanging morning greetings with a young neighbor who is sweet to him. Mostly, we hear his thoughts, his memory of his wife and his longing for his son. We also hear other voices, Biblical phrases that give him the aura of a mystical and sacrificial figure: "Teacher, you have the countenance of Christ," or "My kingdom is not of this world," among many others (ibid., 118, 128). The story progresses gradually, giving us the sense that the character is doubly imprisoned, first by the external walls of his small second-story apartment in an old colonial house, but also by the voices in his head, which cause him great anguish and lead him to an inevitable conclusion: "I do not belong to this age that I am living!" he almost screams out loud (ibid., 128).

The character realizes he is a prisoner of another time, and indeed time stands still for him for most of the story. The epiphany leads him to action. He decides to step outside his home knowing full well, and even wishing, that he will be shot dead by his jailers. He gets dressed and walks out in full view of his captors, still hearing the sacred voices inside his head: "Blessed are those who are persecuted because of righteousness, for theirs is the kingdom of heaven" (*Cuentos,* 129–30). He braces for the order to stop and for the bullet that will end his life, comically hoping that the guards are good shots. But instead, he is stopped by the voice of a young lieutenant calling him "Teacher." When he turns around to meet the gaze of his jailer he shudders when he sees in them an early form of the look of *La mirada*: something he does not expect, a request described as an "anguished plea" (ibid., 131). The look of the young lieutenant leads the prisoner to his second epiphany. He realizes that the government will not execute him because his jailers belong to a different order, "too civilized to believe in the death penalty," he says to himself (ibid., 129). And also because the athletic young lieutenant sees him as an old man, instead of as a martyr. At this point, one could say that the sacred evacuates from the prisoner, even as he says to himself, "Father, take this last cup away from me" (ibid., 132).[8] Realizing he is but an old and tired man, the prisoner retraces his steps back to his apartment to finish his prison sentence. At the end of the story, he sits patiently but also with determination in his eyes, waiting "for death to pass through" (ibid., 134).

In the story, the prisoner struggles to remain a part of an old transcendental order of sacrificial rituals. The story is prefaced with verses from the mystic Saint John of the Cross that refer to the purifying vision of the Christian soul: "Without light or guide / save that which burned in my heart" (*Cuentos*, 115). And it begins with the main character in bed, looking up, barely opening his eyes, half-dreaming half-awake, and hallucinating. When he looks up from his bed he looks back four hundred years to old "virgin forests" of young saplings instead of seeing the ceiling of local hardwood. He tries to remain in this almost mystical state against an intrusive reality. He fights against the present. He tries not to go see the modern truck noisily collecting garbage from the street. He tries to protect himself from the blinding light of a naval communications tower. He struggles to remain true to a law that punishes disobedience: "Thou shalt sow, but shalt not reap; thou shalt tread the olives, but thou shalt not anoint thee with oil," the old law commands (ibid., 127). He clings to the teachings of the mystics who welcome a fight with the devil in hand-to-hand combat: "He understands clearly where the devil is going to strike, flees from him and crushes his head," writes Saint Theresa (ibid., 118). And he remembers the cries of his followers similarly possessed by his purifying vision of self-sacrifice: "We are ready to die for you, teacher" (ibid., 125).

But his efforts to remain in that old order are futile. Indeed, without realizing it, he has already joined a new order of things. Twice he is faced with this fact. The first time happens after the changing of the guard, when the prisoner feels pity for the jailers who keep him under house arrest because they have to obey a secular law that he believes feeds their stomachs but not their souls. He confidently steps out into the balcony and greets them. But his action prompts the officer in charge to plead with him to put on a shirt and step back inside. The prisoner apologizes to the lieutenant, smiles, and follows his orders. The narrator tells us that he suddenly feels guilty and embarrassed at showing himself in public like that. He realizes for the second time that his reality has changed when he steps outside his apartment again and the lieutenant pleads with him to return to his cell. Yet again, the prisoner complies, this time empathizing with the other. He makes eye contact with the lieutenant and feels touched by his anguish. He sees himself through his eyes, and senses the lieutenant's pity for his old body. The narrator tells us that the eyes of the prisoner well up with tears, filled with a "painful gratitude" for his jailer (*Cuentos*, 132).

The prisoner shuttles between the opposite sides of the binary that divides his world into inside and outside, light and darkness, sacred and secular orders, nationalism and the liberalism of a welfare state. One side of his world belongs to an order that codifies sacrifice with a flag, a crucifix, and an old, Spanish sword. Its values are patriotism, self-sacrifice, and honor. Its struggle is the heroic fight against evil. It demands self-sacrifice. Its nature is mystical, transcendental, and eternal. Its look is a purifying gaze. Its language is the sacred language of Scripture: "The light of the body is the eye," it booms (*Cuentos*, 126). The other side of his world belongs to an order that does not ask him for the supreme sacrifice, and does not practice the death penalty.[9] Its mundane symbols are the garbage truck and the radio tower. They stand for the modern values of hygiene, progress, and civilization. Its demands are sentimental. Its nature is earthly. Its temporality is linear. Its look is the sympathetic gaze. Its language is euphemistic and tender: "He gives me alms by calling me 'teacher,'" the prisoner realizes and says under his breath (ibid., 132).

The prisoner is caught in the middle between these two extremes. Indeed, he seems to be made of the worst of both worlds. He is too polluted to be sacred, and too pure to be defiled. Too doubtful to believe, and too insecure to renounce belief. Too sensitive to be self-righteous, and too old to be a threat. In short, he is radically ambiguous. He is just like the world around him: robotic like the trash collectors, affectionate like his neighbor, friendly like his jailers, obedient like Juan, meek like the lamb on Puerto Rico's coat of arms, passive like the lieutenant (*Cuentos*, 118, 120, 122, 124, 125, 131). He is part of a world where "the miserable ideal of daily survival" is barely alive (ibid., 129). He is "silently sad, resigned, docile," just like the world he tries to revive with violence (ibid.). He is abject even to himself, feeling shame at his own naked and decrepit body. And yet, he is also loved by the mother of his child, and more importantly he is respected by the narrative voice who also sees through his mask of martyrdom: "I will die before you," his wife says to him (bid., 130).

Marqués represents the prisoner as a sympathetic if also tragic figure who can step outside of himself and see things from the perspective of the other. In fact, the abject ambiguity of the prisoner is what allows him to appreciate the difficult position of his "antagonist," who is sworn to uphold the law but can't punish a decrepit old man. And the prisoner's sense of his own abject condition allows him to see that the jailer in fact shows him consideration when he withholds his support, when the lieutenant stops himself from offering his arm to steady the old man in his slow return to his cell. But it is the last scene of the story that suggests Marqués's respectful attitude toward the abject docility of his prisoner. Tired and conscious that he is condemned to live the rest of his days in a cell, the old man fixes his eyes on the old sword that hangs from the wall of his room, and waits. The narrator says that he waits not just for the gift of death, but he waits "also for death to pass through" (*Cuentos*, 134). With this ambiguous phrase, the narrator suggests that death is neither the sacred ideal of the old empire, nor is it the pollution that must be purified of the new. It is more than the desired end of a transcendental order. It is more than the feared end of a secular life. Death, the ultimate abject, is what remains after the sublimation of our rituals, after the prohibitions that constitute the subject. And abjection is the remainder that ultimately becomes the speaking subject present, past, and future.

Sublimation and the Maternal Abject

Two works by Marqués that follow "Otro día," "Purificación en la Calle del Cristo" and *Los soles truncos*, are further examples of rituals of purification or forms of abjection that Kristeva calls a scription (i.e., purification rituals with a linguistic structure, Kristeva 1982, 73). And they look back at an "archaic parceling," at a simultaneous jettison and defense of a nonobject or preobject, that Kristeva calls the abject (ibid.). What I want to emphasize in this section is that Marqués gives a maternal form to abjection without dehumanizing it. Instead, Marqués suggests that the maternal abject is the remainder of a social ritual of purification and defilement. It is the remainder of a "scription without signs" that subtends even his own writing. If "Otro día" is a study for the abject subject that emerges from the narratives of Marqués, these later works are studies of the maternal abject, and of abjection proper. They dramatize our joy and dread, our fascination and repulsion, and our desire to possess and to evacuate the maternal abject. But they are also a testimony to the survival of the abject despite our conflicted feelings and desires. They represent the connection of the abject to our ambiguous selves, and the role of writing as the means to sublimate abjection. Like much of Marqués's writing, these works allow us to approximate the abject and to recognize it is a part of life, and as a parcel of the ambiguity of language. At one point, Hortensia, a character from *Los soles truncos*, says to her sister, Emilia: "There is much ugliness . . ." Emilia answers "Yes, much ugliness in the outside world." And Hortensia clarifies: "No, in ourselves, Emilia" (Marqués 1976b, 53–54).

Both "Purificación en la Calle del Cristo" and *Los soles truncos* first appeared in 1958. The short story was later included in the collection *En una ciudad llamada San Juan* (1960). Pilditch ranks the story as among the "the best examples of Marqués storytelling art," and he praises it for its masterful technique and poetic quality (Pilditch 1976, 50). The play is one of the most successful by Marqués, having been produced in Spanish and English, and presented in Puerto Rico, the United States, and internationally. Pilditch considers it the summit of Marqués's dramatic production. According to him, Marqués brings to the play all of the technical elements and experiments from his earlier dramas (ibid., 186). Rivera de Álvarez, also praises the play *Los soles* and places it at the same level as the best examples of contemporary theater (1983, 608). If Pilditch calls attention to the technical innovation and experimentation of these works, Rivera de Álvarez emphasizes their study of the collective personality of Puerto Ricans. Echoing the prevailing criticism, she sees in them a conservative Puerto Rican tradition that is threatened with disappearance but refuses to give in (ibid., 497).

Both of these works by Marqués were written four years after the notorious attack on Congress by Lolita Lebrón and three other Puerto Rican nationalists in 1954.[10] On the island, Lebrón became a figure of mythological proportions after her suicidal act followed by the statement, "I did not come to kill, I came to die for Puerto Rico." These works by Marqués can be interpreted to be in part a sublimation of this chapter of Puerto Rican history, and of this suicidal act by a patriotic woman, understood by many in his generation as a cathartic form of heroism, a kind of acting out against the trauma of colonialism. Marqués's generation had lived through several wars (World War II and the Korean War), and they were preoccupied with the effect of war on the psyche. The literary critic Francisco Manrique Cabrera became famous for calling the generation of writers who lived through the invasion of Puerto Rico by the United States the "Trauma Generation" in his *Historia de la literatura puertorriqueña* (1956). Two novels published the same year also represented the effects of colonization on Puerto Ricans as a kind of shell-shock: *Los derrotados* by César Andreu Iglesias and *La ceiba en el tiesto* by Enrique Laguerre. Their concern echoed in part that of the developing psychological sciences in Puerto Rico in the fifties and sixties, and the focus of these sciences on the vocational aptitudes of veterans of wars (Rivera Ramos 1991, 2).

Like the other members of his generation, Marqués was concerned with trauma and its psychological effects on the psyche of Puerto Ricans. And he was particularly interested in the effect of war in the context of colonialism, as evidenced by his first book of poems, *Peregrinación* (1944), and by his essay "El puertorriqueño dócil," which opened with a mediation on the effects of the Korean War on the Puerto Rican psyche, and was first delivered as a lecture during the sixth congress of the Puerto Rican Psychological Association in 1961. But in the two works that are the focus of this section, there is a notable shift away from the effects of war on Puerto Ricans, and toward a psychological disturbance that precedes the Korean War, World War II, and even the Spanish American War. In these works, Marqués focused on the role of an archaic maternal abject in the context of colonial trauma.[11]

The short story and the play are narratives about the apparent loss and eventual recovery of the maternal law of abjection, a law that is anterior to what in Lacanian psychoanalysis is known as the law of the Father (the law that mediates between the child and the mother). This law is represented by a maternal inheritance, a set of jewels that are hidden by one of three daughters in order to protect them from creditors. As the story unfolds, we learn that the three sisters have lived together for a long time in a decaying colonial mansion in the capital of San Juan and in relative isolation from the world. We also learn that they are the heirs to a significant fortune, but have gradually lost their inheritance due to a series of unrelenting crises. These crises are of various natures and proportions: personal (anemia and cancer), natural (the hurricane San Felipe), and historical (the U.S. invasion of Puerto Rico and the revolt of the Nationalists). At the origin and at the center of these losses is the character of the mother, Mamá Eugenia. Her death coincides with the transition of the island from being a colony of Spain to being a colony of the United States in 1898. The loss of the mother has a monumental effect on the destiny of the family and begins its gradual degeneration. Mamá Eugenia is a formidable figure whose wealth and blinding brilliance are reflected by the objects that decorate her body: a diamond tiara, a pearl ring, a golden fan, among others. She represents for her daughters a time of security that is economic, social, and political. Her jewels are presumed lost or pawned by Inés, one of the three daughters. But they reappear at the end of the narrative, when Inés brings them out in the final scene, and decorates herself and her two sisters with them, before she sets fire to the old house with the help of Emilia.

The maternal jewels at the center of this story are a figure for the abject and its hold. They are objects that are sacred and are brought back out from hiding during the purification ritual that ends the narratives, a ritual that gives a name to the short story and transforms Inés, the middle and ugly seventy-year-old sister, into a beautiful vision. The maternal objects are both defiled (in need of purification, hiding in secret) and pure (blindingly brilliant). They give the maternal figure an uncanny power of attraction and repulsion. They represent an incestuous law that brings the daughters together. The law attracts them to their mother first, and then to each other. But the same law also divides them into distinct beings with separate qualities, each with a desire to separate from Mamá Eugenia and become an independent being. The brilliance of the maternal jewels is figuratively transposed into the truncated suns that give the play its title, architectural features of the old colonial home that repeat the same shape but in different primary colors: red, blue, and yellow. The distinct colors of the truncated suns also signal the different virtues and vices of the sisters: strength and envy in Inés, pride and beauty in Hortensia, innocence and illusion in Emilia.

The dilapidated house on Cristo Street, the house of the truncated suns, is the house of Mamá Eugenia. It is the maternal house, a figure for the original preobject, a cipher for the monumental abject. As such, the house of the truncated suns is governed by the maternal law or by the law of abjection, a set of flexible prohibitions that connect opposite worlds, a set of rituals that allow the transference of ambiguous material from the outside to the inside, the circulation of fluid matter from one order into the other. The house is furnished by the mother. It is a depository for her objects, for her furniture, the Louis XVI chairs, the grand piano, but also a cleaning water bucket and its dirty rag. It is the safe house for the jewels of the mother. And its signature architectural features (the translucent stained glass windows that give the house its name) are signs for the women that live in it, extensions of, but also separations from the maternal abject. In fact, the house is the prism that projects the different colors of its translucent, truncated suns. The house is the object, or better yet, the abject. It both defends, holds, but also jettisons, choke-holds its three feminine inhabitants: Hortensia, Inés, and Estela. The house on Cristo Street, the house of the truncated suns, the house of Mamá Eugenia is so old, so archaic, so decayed, that its walls are porous. It allows passage between the inside and the outside. The porous walls of the house stand as a set of laws and rituals that allow the speaking subject to survive, that withstands the force of natural or historical events such as the invasion by the United States, or the hurricane San Felipe whose destructive force sent the Puerto Rican economy into a tailspin in the nineteen-thirties. The walls of the house, the objects that give it a structure, a form, also produce a mark, a great water stain in the shape of a continental map: two worlds joined and or separated by an isthmus. This geographical figure is also a metaphor for a link that joins the maternal abject with its progeny (with its three daughters), but also for a boundary that pushes them out and makes them search for other love objects.

The sisters search for an other love object. They are encouraged by Mamá Eugenia to fall in love, to create new ties, at the same time that they feel themselves drawn ambivalently to each other, and to the abject at the center of each other. From this perspective, the ambivalent movement to and from the abject is at the center of both of these narratives, and it is informed by taking stock of the shame that lies under the apparent guilt of the daughters. This underlying and primary shame is not a feeling that comes from the judgment of a punishing law.[12] Shame is instead the feeling that comes from realizing the hold, the abjection, the strange form of incestuous love and hate that is at the origin of each one of these characters. "I am the shame of a family where beauty is queen," says Inés to the ghost of Hortensia (*Los soles*, 21). And the narrative of these works is a gradual realization that what the sisters think is their guilt is really the profound passion that constitutes them. The sisters are a jealous bunch, they envy and resent each other for the virtues and gifts that distinguish them and make them different parts of the same original material: the gifts of a poet (Emilia), a beauty (Hortensia), and a master (Inés). In their different ways, they are all drawn to the same Spanish ensign, the same external love object that promises to separate them from their family, from their mother and from each other. But they all conspire simultaneously to undermine the escape. In different ways, directly, indirectly, obliquely, they remain true to each other. They remain passionately in love with each other, possessed by an incestuous bond that pulls at them, even as they simultaneously struggle to betray it and pry each other free. Each believes that she is guilty and that they remain in the house to expiate this guilt. But this so-called guilt also brings them together. They think that they are guilty of violating the patriarchal law, the commandment to not covet your neighbor's wife, the law of sexual property and difference. But as women coveting the fiancé of their sister, they also disturb the punishing law. In the end, they feel, even if they do not consciously realize, that the passion and emotion that drives them is not only the love of the other, or of the nameless Spanish ensign. More importantly, what drives them is the source of their shame: their love of the mother, and the love they have for each other. It is the ambiguous experience of that love, of that hold that is also a chokehold, of that motherly tenderness that is also a betrayal that keeps changing them, transforming them, and also keeps them bonded to (and separate from) the abject. That love, that maternal law, is a flexible and porous set of rituals that connects and separates worlds, centuries, and bodies. The stain on the wall of the house is a figure for this love.

The most important ritual in the narratives is the purification that gives the short story its title and that takes the form of an elaborate three-way marriage ceremony at the end of the play. Faced with a world increasingly hostile to their permutations and transformations, increasingly challenged by the difficulty of keeping alive the link back to the maternal abject, the two surviving sisters decide to burn down the house at the end of the narrative. But before they do, they dress the corpse of Hortensia, the most beautiful of the three, with the wedding gown that she never wore, and Inés brings out the family jewels. In ceremonial fashion, Inés tenderly divides the maternal inheritance. She places the small embroidered fan of mother of pearl hanging from a thick golden chain around the neck of her sister Emilia, and crowns her head with the diamond and sapphire tiara. She places the pearl ring on the finger of the dead Hortensia. And she takes the ring of Father Burkhardt for herself. "Of all of the jewels, the only one that I want for myself," she says (*Los soles*, 63). The marriage ceremony is uncanny. It is both familiar and defamiliarized. It is a clear reference to the familiar ritual of marriage under the patriarchal law that establishes agency, property, and sexual difference along the lines of a gendered binary that separates the male from the female. But this reference also dramatically changes the ritual, and refers back to an earlier, more archaic law, where the ritual of sacrifice is now substituted by the ritual of abjection. The three-way incestuous marriage between the sisters divides property evenly, makes the binary separation and hierarchy impossible, and introduces the bisexual subject of Inés, a phoenix that rises out of the ashes of the patriarchal law of sexual difference.

In the end, as the fire consumes them, in an act of generosity that recognizes the transformation taking place, Emilia takes the tiara off of her head and puts it on the head of Inés. The ritual that ends the short story and the play sublimates the sacred maternal object, the defiled and pure object, and produces the maternal abject incarnate in Inés, giving birth to a new bisexual subject. The self-undoing that ends these works has often seemed tragic, and yet I believe that it is also hopeful and transformative, and it is a figure for the ambiguous power of Marqués's writing, which Eleanor Martin calls its ambivalent "subtlety."[13] In a profoundly moving final moment of the play, Emilia exclaims "Inesita, the fire has made you beautiful. . . . We have won over time. We've won" (*Los soles*, 65). The sisters set the fire that consumes them. But the fire also sublimates them in a chemical reaction that purifies and constitutes an ambiguous triumph over the forces that they struggle against, a melancholy triumph to be sure, but a triumph nonetheless. The triumph is over the temporal forces that threaten their survival throughout the narrative: the aging and decaying body, the whirlwind of history, the implacable forward motion of time. The triumph is by the process of transformation and metamorphosis that the fire represents: the sublimation of the love and the passion between the sisters.

"Purification" and *Los soles* are works that go deeper into the meaning of the archaic law that fascinates and holds the subject prisoner in "Otro día." If the main character of the earlier story comes to inhabit an ambivalent position between an old Spanish order and the new order of the Commonwealth, the main character of the later narratives (Inés) represents the surviving tie to an embodied language more archaic still than the Scriptures holding the prisoner. Inés is a code name for the abject and for the remainder of the process that gives the abject its name. Inés is Spanish for the English Agnes. Both names are forms of the Latin *agnus*, or "lamb," which gives Saint Agnes her name and her animal sign. In Greek, *hagnos* means chaste or pure, and the story of Saint Agnes is the story of a young virgin who is martyred for trying to preserve her virginity for God. Agnes is not executed by the Romans but thrown into a brothel, defiled. She is eventually killed by the sword, but only after fire fails to consume her. The name Inés is then a sign that points to a ritual of purification and defilement. And it is a sign that points to the survival of the abject in a different form, sublimated into a new symbolic order, changed into a new name. In other words, Inés is a code for approximating abjection and the porous nature of our prohibitions. And as such, the poetic language that Inés speaks at the end of the play is an elaboration of her name. It is a form of scansion that codifies, moderates, and that also sublimates our dread and our joy of the abject: "The poetry of Hortensia's cancer, and the monstrous multiplication of the cells in the beloved breast of Hortensia, and the deep hurt that decays without screaming," recites Inés out loud (*Los soles*, 50). Inés becomes a poetry-speaking subject that suspends, holds, supports, and jettisons a familiar other. At the end of the short story, she gives out an "extraordinary . . . light of [her] own" ("Purification," 61). At the end of the play, she "looks at Hortensia and smiles" expressing her love for her sister with a look that is repeated and returned by Emilia (*Los soles*, 65). Together, this blinding light and meaningful look are early versions of the material and ambiguous language that also gives form and title to the last novel by Marqués.

Ethical Reflections in *La mirada*

The last novel by Marqués is a form of scription that is more poignant still than "Otro día," "Purificación," or *Los soles*. Like those earlier works, the novel is a literary form of the porous and archaic law that contains the abject. Also like them, it is a form of abjection at a second remove, signifying the nature of the prohibitions as a crucible for the abject. But more so than its predecessors, the novel is also a writing practice that tries to take both Marqués and his readers beyond survival, and into ethical or self-critical reflection. More than the earlier works, *La mirada* reflects on the insurmountable debt owed to an abjection that is now also tied to the environment: an inheritance that we continue to dismiss at our peril, according to Marqués. The self-critical recognition of this otherness both inside and outside our voice, both inside and outside of language and writing, is what allows the character of the story to change his attitude to life and to the future, from one of alienation and uncertainty to one of acceptance of his fate and of trust in the justice of the other.

More so than the earlier works, *La mirada* describes a world that has made a ritualized transition to a new order and law. The old order and social law, represented by the repeated figure of the father in the novel, is now either irreparably broken, absent, or simply left for dead. The broken paternal law is represented in the novel by the nameless father of the nameless main character, a veteran from World War II, who is "taught to kill" but is unable to meet his parental responsibilities. The absence of the paternal law is more emphatically represented by the main character's older brother (Carlos), who leaves his home in Puerto Rico to become a successful drug lord in the United States. He ends up murdered in Mexico, leaving his infant daughter an orphan. When we meet her, Carlos's daughter (María) has been adopted into the family of the main character and is living with him in the same house. Like a modern day Rhea (the wife and sister of the Titan God, Cronus), she both joins and resists her brother/uncle in the new upended social order represented by their generation. The new order is marked by an apparent absence of authority and a lack of prohibition. It is characterized by permissiveness of all sorts (sexual and otherwise). And it turns the adolescent siblings into haunted and borderline figures. By the end of the novel, "brother" and sister (uncle and niece) become sadomasochistic lovers haunted by phobic and paranoid violent sexual fantasies that appear to leave them alienated in the face of an empty future that they foresee from the beginning of the novel (*La mirada*, 27).

La mirada insists on the turbulence of the transition to the new social order, as well as on its archaic nature, with direct references to the Greek myth of Cronus. The reference to this myth also harks back to Marqués's infamous theory of the so-called matriarchal pattern articulated in many of his works, which has been severely criticized by his readers.[14] According to the myth, Cronus was the Titan who deposed his father (Ouranos) at the instigation of his mother (Gea). He castrated his father and then ate his children in an effort to preserve his own power. His effort, however, was only temporary, and he was eventually defeated by Zeus, who was hidden by Rhea, the wife and sister of Cronus.

In the novel, Marqués is concerned with the incestuous rule and permissive regime of the offspring of a similarly castrated father figure. The world of his modern Cronus is deeply influenced by the rise of a new titanic culture that surrounds Marqués. From this perspective, the novel is deeply critical of the influence of the United States on Puerto Rico, and specifically of its countercultural hippie culture during the nineteen-sixties. Marqués represents this culture and its new permissive order as abundant in mind-altering substances that uninhibit the sexual impulses and lead to all kinds of uncensored expression and perverse excess. And yet, the novel also makes direct references to the passion of Christ. From this perspective, the forty sections of the novel can also be interpreted to tell a secular version of the temptation of Christ in the Judaean desert. In other words, Marqués suggests that the new regime is but a temporary state. It is a passing purification ritual that prepares the son of man for yet another transition, this time for his inevitable death, except that Marqués substitutes the ascension of Christ with the abjection of man.

Like the works by the younger members of his generation, the last novel by Marqués reflects the end of a Commonwealth that had ruled essentially unchallenged for more than twenty years, as well as the end of its hegemonic discourse of cultural identity. Marqués published his novel at the end of his life, but also at the end of a period of Puerto Rican history that Ayala and Bernabe have called "the American Century." The end of this period came about partly because of the influence of the counterculture movement in the United States on Puerto Rico. The civil rights movement, the protests against the Vietnam War, and the rise of organized labor during the sixties and seventies supported a critical revision of the history of colonialism in Puerto Rico. As Ayala and Bernabe have convincingly summarized in their work, the history of colonialism underwent a radical rewriting during the seventies that opened a space for previously marginalized members of Puerto Rican society: women, workers, blacks, Nuyoricans, and homosexuals. The new history revealed and criticized the class privilege, racism, sexism, xenophobia, and homophobia of the identity discourses of the Commonwealth. It was partly responsible for a new paradigm for Puerto Ricans as entangled in an endless commute between the island and the mainland, the colony and the metropolis. Sánchez famously described this suspended form of identity in his influential essay *La guagua aérea* (1994). The change in turn led to a new wave of literature with a new language that codeswitched between English and Spanish, that inflected the popular expression of the emerging urban working classes, and that eschewed both the rhetoric of self-sacrifice of the defunct Nationalist party, and the rhetoric of autonomy and stable identity institutionalized by an ossifying Commonwealth. This literature was a memorial, a purifying ritual if you will, to the passing of the social order of the Commonwealth, foreshadowed by the stroke of its seventy-eight-year old founder, Governor Muñoz Marín, in 1976, and confirmed by his death four years later. This scription or literary ritual of purification and defilement was perhaps best represented by the essay *Las tribulaciones de Jonás* (Rodríguez Juliá 1981): a baroque memorial to the dearly departed patriarch. But it was also a ritual anticipated and repeated by the leading writers of the young generation spearheading the new literary wave: Ferré, Sánchez, and Ramos Otero (Gelpí 1984, 134). Like the emerging experimental works of these young writers, *La mirada* was also a witness to a developing new social order, to its emerging discourses, and to the hold of the abject.

The look that gives title to the last novel by Marqués is the abject look of the witness to this emerging order: both polluted and pure, desired and dreaded. It is the look of an archaic remainder after the transition from the old to the new social order. It is a look without sense, or better yet a look of nonsense that eerily collapses the senses of touch, sound, and sight into one urgent gesture: "He was correcting the part about Cronus devouring his children when he sensed the steady, persistent look. He raised his eyes and saw him seated there. . . . He hadn't seen or heard him come in, but there he was staring at him with his affectedly faded and ragged jeans" (*The Look*, 27). It is an archaic look from a ragged figure that perhaps can be traced back to the crazed look of the mythical Saturn in the famous painting by Francisco de Goya y Lucientes: "Saturn Devouring his Son" (1819–1823). But it is also a look that is repeated in the literature of Puerto Rico, and can also be traced back to the diseased perspective of its colonial abject. As such, it is a form of the contaminated look that opens the Puerto Rican novel by Manuel Zeno Gandía, *La charca* (1894). It is a version of the "palpitating" look of Silvina, the young and anemic peasant whose epileptic visions reflect the contaminating influence of her abandoned and degenerate colonial environment. And it is a version of an earlier abject look elaborated by Marqués in *Los soles* (as the joyful look of the sisters), in "Otro día" (as the docile look of the lieutenant), and in his first book of poems, *Peregrinación*, where it appears as the atrophied look from the moss-covered pupils of the dying motherland: "Atrophied well of suffering / crystalizing / the anguish of my motherland / in the relentless green / of its pupils / dead for all eternity!" (27).

The invasive strangeness of the look of *La mirada* is marked by the green set of eyes that travels from character to character in the novel, and that allows them, or urges them, to fulfill their desires no matter what they might be. As such it is a look characterized by a law of the embodied senses over logical sense. The look touches, presses, corners, and holds the main character in its gaze, as if it were a filament that extends from its uncanny green eyes: "And he sensed the urgency of the look. His? Another's? It didn't matter; only the urgency," writes the narrator (*The Look*, 21). The origin of its invasive and palpitating filaments is an uncertain, confused, disordered, and split body. The narrator does not know whether the look comes from the other or from the self. It is simply described as a form of urgency (from the Latin to press), an invisible force or impulse that pushes to act without direction. This permissive impulse displaces the main character, it brings him down from his place of origin, the mountainous region of Puerto Rico, and its traditional values. It pollutes him and contaminates him. But it also embraces him, even as it takes the main character off of his high horse, and brings him down a notch: "He saw him raise his arms slowly as if in flight or the form of a cross and look at him. In spite of the distance he was certain that he was looking at him. And he felt the irresistible impulse to descend" (*The Look*, 53). It changes the main character into a stranger to his own family and to himself. He becomes docile prey to his own sexual and violent impulses (ibid., 55), a fool without direction (*La mirada* 32), an extraterrestrial, a Martian even (*The Look*, 39). It makes him more hateful and more forgiving. It makes him more human.

The permissiveness of *La mirada*, its implied docility, also extends to the voice of the characters in the novel who, like the father of the main character, react without anger to the world that surrounds them, merely expressing disbelief: "[W]hen he told his father that he was not going to return to the university, he perceived in the latter's voice not the anger which he was expecting but rather an infinite disbelief. 'Are you crazy?' " (*The Look*, 31). The disbelief of this voice is translated into the writing of the novel making it almost unreadable. Its ironic tone subtends a language that is radically split, interrupted by self-critical questioning. It is a form of broken and collapsed language that is often split apart from reality, paranoid and hallucinating. It is a form of psychotic writing that hears voices including those that interrupt its flow with parenthetical remarks. It emphasizes breaks in space and time. The sections jump back and forth in time without warning. They take us from place to place, from country to country without transition. And there are no transitions either between sections that are written like some of the characters speak: "Without pausing, he asked "And Chile?"—"What Chile?" (*The Look*, 45). It is a language ruled by the law of an archaic parceling, producing a weak grammatical structure, perpetuating a state of constant change, transformation, and displacement: a form of nonsense.

But the look, its voice, and its writing are also signs of another component of the same law. As the novel descends into the Age of Aquarius, it also engages with its countercultural law. Marqués's characters go on existential trips, searching for meaning through altered states of consciousness reached by means of hallucinogenic substances, similar to trippy works such as the influential road movie *Easy Rider*, whose music is mentioned in the text (*The Look*, 85). This psychedelic law and its rituals are informed not so much by nonsensical separations as by meaningful environmental correspondences of cosmic proportions. As such, the novel does not signal a nostalgic desire for the old romantic discourse of the Puerto Rican peasant or *jíbaro*. Instead, it looks forward to the dawn of New Age Spiritualism: "Mom, let's not talk about that. War is always bad. Let's talk about peace here, in Alto del Monte, why do you think it's so strange that I want to share this peace with you and Mom and the kid? I've learned a lot here and I can keep on learning," says the main character to his mother before a fight breaks out between the parents (ibid., 33). From this perspective, the writing of the novel is also modeled after a law of relationality that insists on the link between the character's speech and his changing environment (the countryside, the university, Washington, D.C., the hippie commune, the prison, the discotheque, or the cosmos).

Many passages of the novel, particularly those that follow the ingestion of hallucinogenic substances, are characterized by a linguistic form of this law of New Age correspondence or relationality. Its paragraphs are marked by long improbable sentences with multiple subordinate clauses. The sentences create the sense of a repeating, breathless, musical, and suspended voice. This voice always defers the anticipated end, and is similar to the high modernist writing of the famous "Yes" paragraph that ends James Joyce's *Ulysses* (1922). Marqués also takes farther his characteristic experimentation with free indirect speech in this novel, blending the first and the third-person narratives in what is sometimes a seamless flow.[15] He adds to this the condensation (rather than the split) of time and space to create a sense of infinity or eternity in some passages, the confusion of identities in hallucinogenic dream narratives, and the mix of Spanish and English. On the one hand, Marqués models this breathless writing on the movements and rhythms of bodies in the thrall of sadomasochistic relations. On the other, he also models it on the necessary dependence between the heavenly bodies of the cosmos: "[T]he comet shone in all its rigorously limited astral freedom. And the Puerto Rican humanity viewed it with docile objectivity. . . . And the fact is that freedom is much the same thing: [to] revolve in the orbit of something or someone else," the narrator concludes (*The Look*, 90).

Throughout these shifts from nonsense to sense, from parceling to relationality, there is also a constant of self-referentiality and self-criticism throughout *La mirada*. This aspect of Marqués's writing is evidenced by several direct and indirect references to the author's works, ranging from parodic references to his first novel (*La víspera del hombre*) to ironic repetition of scenes from his infamous short story "En la popa hay un cuerpo reclinado." The self-critical nature of the novel is perhaps best represented by the final confrontation between the main character and his "sister"/niece after an incestuous love scene degenerates first into a graphic moment of sexual assault, and then into a farcical and sadistic allegory of colonial relations at a café concert. After confessing her love for her "brother"/uncle, María turns the tables on him and dresses him down, first defiling "that look of yours . . . that I was in love with" (it "is after all just 'pure shit,' " she says) and next criticizing his abusive behavior, indirectly also meaning the early writing of Marqués: "But you'll still just be some crazy kid in favor of independence who can only play at 'revolutionary theater' and beat up a woman in public" (*The Look*, 84). From this perspective, the novel is faithful to its epigraph by Karl Jaspers: "It is characteristic of Man . . . to direct his look toward the foundation of truth. Truth always exists in him and for him by means of a language, however obscure and rudimentary this may be." Marqués takes a hard look at his abject writing in *La mirada*, but he also remains ethically committed to self-reflection and self-criticism as a way to both approximate and also live with abjection. In other words, the novel is an example of an ethical form of writing founded on always imperfect, always porous, but also always necessary rituals of purification and defilement that reproduce and sublimate the abject.

The narratives of Marqués are not only an effect of the necessarily limited rituals of defilement and purification of the Commonwealth (e.g., the cultural discourse of national identity), but they are also the representation of the constitutive porosity and ultimate weakness of these and of all such rituals. As representations, his narratives of self-undoing are rituals of defilement themselves, but of the second order, purification rituals to the second degree. They do violence not only to their objects and subjects, but most importantly they do violence to the syntax of language itself. Marqués's narratives parcel language, like the high modernist writing of William Faulkner (an early literary model for Marqués), or like the experimental writing of José Donoso (a literary model for the writers who came after Marqués). Indeed, they are narratives that go so far as to both release and defend the abject in language: the nonobject at the origins of all speaking subjectivity. They are narratives that function like asymbolic signs of separation and relationality that are the least common denominators of language (such as hyphens or slashes), signs that insist on the fundamental connection between sense and nonsense. Like the discourse and the law of the Commonwealth, these narratives insist on the surviving and necessary hold between pollution and prohibition. In doing so, Marqués's narratives reveal that they are governed by abjection not in spite of, but because of the porous nature of the rituals of defilement and purification, because of the changing discourse and law before and beyond the Commonwealth.

3

Vicissitudes of Perversion

FROM "EL PUERTORRIQUEÑO DÓCIL" TO *EL CAPITÁN DE LOS DORMIDOS*

She was also caught in our love triangle, and she shuddered just like me.

—Bobby Capó

Embalmed, Lita is as dangerous as a bomb.

—Rosario Ferré

In his book *Vieques y la prensa: el idilio fragmentado* (2001), Félix Jiménez describes the explosive international spectacle that the island of Vieques became after the accidental death of David Sanes in 1999.[1] Sanes was a Puerto Rican security guard who was killed when a missile fired by the United States Navy missed its target by two miles and hit him instead. The bomb not only killed him, it also set off protests that became widespread and briefly turned Vieques into an international *cause célèbre* televised all over the world. Celebrities such as the Dalai Lama, Jesse Jackson, Robert Kennedy, Ricky Martin, Benicio del Toro, and Edward James Olmos joined the leaders of the main political parties on the island of Puerto Rico in protests that eventually resulted in the departure of the Navy from Vieques in 2003, continuing a vexed history of occupation, expropriation, and protest begun in 1898.

Mayra Montero's novel about Vieques, *El capitán de los dormidos*, published in 2002 at the height of the spectacle, suggests that the epical account of Puerto Rican history rehearsed during the crisis as a struggle of "good" nationalist forces against "evil" imperialism, is part and parcel of what Oliver has described as the "pathology of colonialism" (2004, 6). Montero suggests in her novel that the nostalgic rehearsal of a spectacular struggle between the colonized slave and the colonial master that followed the death of Sanes, far from being a liberating act, was instead a turn in the screw of this pathology. She suggests that this rehearsal of colonial pathology traps all sides in its spectacle rather than liberates them. It creates a self-sustaining circuit of perversity, a closed circuit of perverse desires.[2] It reproduces a colonized way of seeing and being that is represented by Andrés Yasin, the central character of the novel, who never grows up, whose growth is stunted, and who is shaped by a voyeuristic necrophilic desire. She further suggests that the spectacle of Vieques screens (both repeats and reveals) a foundational symbolic matricide on which this pathology of colonialism depends.[3]

From this perspective, the suspicious and spectacular neoNationalism surrounding the struggle for Vieques in 2003 (as well as its quick reversals) are not just a phenomenon driven by the ideologies of the globalized state, as postmodern critics of Puerto Rican culture such as Carlos Pabón would have us believe.[4] Montero suggests instead that the apparent struggle for political control between an imperial master and its colonized slave that Vieques became between 1999 and 2003 was also a struggle for control over an eroticized abject corpse. This necrophilic struggle was in turn the effect of a sentimental education in a context of expanding colonialism, and the effect of the perverse desires that the continuing colonial presence generates even today. In particular, Montero suggests that the spectacle reproduces an economy of disavowal in the colonial subject best represented by Andrés, a voyeur who denies what he so eagerly watches. At the end of the novel, caught in the spectacle of his family relations, Andrés watches as the corpse of his mother is raped. The scene, I will argue, is more than the rape of an individual called Estela. Her corpse is also a metaphorical stele, a monument to the social and political violence that surrounds and eventually sacrifices the symbolic maternal body in Puerto Rico. These same forces generate Andrés's necrophilia, an obsession with the abject that eroticizes a symbolic maternal corpse, and a mode of identification that preserves intact the necessary foundations for the pathology of colonialism.

Also from this perspective, Montero departs (both in the sense of a point of origin and of a point of separation) from a longstanding and still widespread Nationalist tradition in Puerto Rico, and from its production of a particular colonial identity and subjectivity. According to this tradition, the Puerto Rican subject is pathologically perverse in its proximity to the feminine in general and to the maternal in particular. Consider, for example, Antonio Pedreira's (1899–1939) account of the Puerto Rican subject always afraid to leave the figurative womb of his island. Or think about many of the narcissistic, weak-willed, and cowardly male figures in the work of José Luis González (1926–1996). A crippling perversity that results in a suicidal melancholy haunts Puerto Rican allegorical subjects in his stories, ranging from Andrés Morales in "Paisa" (1950) to Melodía in "En el fondo del caño hay un negrito" (1954).

Indeed, Montero's novel is but the latest installment in a series of works from Puerto Rico that screen (both reflect on and repeat) a colonial matricidal pathology. The contemporary perverse form of this pathology of colonialism is first found in works by Marqués. As we shall see below, his notion of a perverse colonized Puerto Rican subject is a departure from an earlier discourse about the so-called traumatized and diseased nature of the Puerto Rican subject. Writing in the fifties and sixties, Marqués emphasized the importance of taking over the position of the sadist master in his revolutionary account of the discourse of colonial perversions. If Marqués helped to initiate a discourse of constitutive perversion of the Puerto Rican subject, this discourse suffered an important shift during the seventies. Ferré and the generation of writers who published their work in the important literary journal she helped to publish (*Zona. Carga y Descarga*) suggested a related but different account of colonial perversion, one that paradoxically empowered the position of the abject maternal and the masochist slave that identified with her.

Writing twenty years after *Zona*, and during the Vieques crisis, Montero makes a further turn on the road of this discourse of colonial pathologies. She suggests that the perversions of colonialism are alive and well in the struggle for power and control over Vieques. In her novel, she suggests that the spectacle of Vieques screens (hides even as it reveals) a still-unresolved foundational symbolic matricide that is at the center of colonial relations, and that is perpetrated by all sides of what becomes a self-fulfilling and self-sustaining perverse cycle. Her account is clearly indebted to Ferré's melancholy turn to the maternal, but she also describes the paradoxical nature of this turn in the matricidal colonial economy. Taken as a whole, these vicissitudes of the perverse in the literature of Puerto Rico suggest that perversion is a defensive, and flexible, psychological structure whose specific forms change together with the developing, shifting, and expanding modes of an equally resilient structure of colonial relations.

Marqués and the Perverse Puerto Rican Subject

The Puerto Rican allegorical subject appears in its most representative docile and emasculated form (it was always a masculine subject for the generation writing during the fifties and sixties in Puerto Rico) in some of the short stories and essays by Marqués. His sadomasochistic, incestuous, and necrophilic nature is perhaps most evident in the infamous figure of the self-emasculating and nameless protagonist of his short story "En la popa hay un cuerpo reclinado" (1956), who confesses to the naked corpse of his murdered wife: "And my hunger for love since childhood, which the girls from the old house did not satisfy . . . remained inside of me so that you could satisfy it . . . and after all of that, there you are, still, on the bow of the boat" (*Cuentos*, 139–40).

But it was Marqués's foundational essay "El puertorriqueño dócil" (1960) that gave the Puerto Rican colonial subject its most memorable sadomasochistic and perverse form.[5] In an old debate about colonialism in Puerto Rico, Marqués polemically added the term *docile* to a constellation of terms describing the colonial subject, including *irrational, twisted, morbid, deviant,* but also *infantile, impotent,* and *queer.* He placed the Puerto Rican national subject in a sadomasochistic psychic economy, and fixed him in a position that was "submissive" to the point of self-destruction. Marqués argued that this position was the cause of a "psycho-social" problem: "the Puerto Rican's notorious self-destructive impulse, his suicidal tendency" (*Docile*, 40).

Drawing from earlier studies of the so-called traumatized nature of the Puerto Rican subject, but also from works such as Fanon's *Black Skin, White Masks* (1952), Marqués diagnosed the psychological problem of the Puerto Rican subject as a "queer" symptom of colonialism.[6] According to Marqués, the condition was "queer" in the sense that it contained "obscure and buried anxieties" (*Docile*, 67), mysterious and dangerous aspects of docility that went "unaltered from the hands of the woman to the hands of the man" (ibid., 48). Briefly put, Marqués argued that the Puerto Rican subject was psychologically queered by a repeated and sustained colonial experience. That is, the otherwise virile Puerto Rican subject was perverted, emasculated, and feminized into a masochistic suicidal subject who directed "the normal aggressive impulse . . . morbidly toward [him]self" (ibid., 40).

The Puerto Rican condition was "queer" also in the sense of "strange" or foreign since it was partly the result of the "Anglo-Saxon-style matriarchal pattern [prevalent] in 1940" (*Docile*, 47). Marqués argued that these external matriarchal influences were responsible for imposing similarly perverse external "poses" and "affectations" on the Puerto Rican subject. He deployed a ubiquitous metaphor for homosexuality in Latin America to describe the so-called docile Puerto Rican as an ostentatious bird, foolishly displaying "his mended colonial plumage" (ibid., 130 n.42). But most memorably, he referred to this behavior with a word (*ñangotamiento*), which in Puerto Rican Spanish describes the squatting position of domestic animals, a humiliating obedient submission to a powerful master, and an archaic birthing position. This part of Marqués's argument closely followed the psychological colonial structure described by Octavio Paz (1914–1998) in his influential *Labyrinth of Solitude* (1952), where the Nobel Prize winner explained Mexican consciousness as both defensive and haunted by the foundational rape of an intrinsically "open" feminine body: the abject maternal body of La Malinche.[7]

Similar to Paz, Marqués also described a raped and "open" feminine body at the center of a troubled Puerto Rican subjectivity. Unlike the "defensive" masculine national subject of Paz's essay, however, Marqués's account of the Puerto Rican national subject was masochistic. In other words, instead of protecting himself from the abject openness of the founding mother, the Puerto Rican male identified with her maternal openness and willingly (and perversely) assumed her so-called submissive position. If Paz's book led to the popularization of the term *malinchismo* to mean a predisposition to foreign (principally Spanish) influence, Marqués coined the similar term *entreguismo* for a parallel obsequious attitude of total surrender by Puerto Ricans toward the United States.

According to Marqués, the Puerto Rican masochist subject willingly assumed the obedient, docile, "open" position of "total surrender" to the point of welcoming more raping violence from the United States. Seduced by his colonial master, the maternal, open, Puerto Rican subject offered himself "without resistance" to him in order to "incorporate" his superiority. Marqués wrote,

> [I]n order to tolerate his humiliating condition [the Puerto Rican] has to . . . admit that he is inferior to the North American. . . . This unconscious admission . . . cannot help but hurt his ego, often provoking extreme compensatory reactions such as . . . total surrender. . . . [By] surrendering he is able to . . . open himself up, without resistance, to all that is North American. He hopes . . . to incorporate the "superiority" of that feared and envied being. (*Docile*, 54)

For Marqués, as for other writers of his generation, this pathological perversion amounted to a repulsive colonial disease that needed urgent attention and called for a caustic cure. But Marqués's cure did not call for abandoning the so-called repulsive, perverse psychological structure. Instead, Marqués prescribed a sadistic regimen to straighten the "twisted" mind of Puerto Ricans as if by force. He saw his essay, for example, as providing a "healthy" dose of "bitter pills," an emetic or as an antidote for the "sugar-coating" of colonialist discourse. He saw it as part of a new literature that "penetrated" the ethical conscience of Puerto Ricans with "barbs" in language such as *aplatanao* and *ñangotao* (*Docile*, 37), "punishing" (62) Puerto Rican society into facing its "traditional *ñangotamiento*" (45). In the essay, he similarly advocated for an educational system rich with "virile" and anticolonialist discipline for Puerto Rican youth (129 n.39).[8]

Paradoxically, this "cure" also suggested that all writing in Puerto Rico—including not only the new literature, but also Marqués's own caustic and punishing essay—played a structural role in the perverse dynamics of a widespread, and even normative, psychological colonial structure. "The new literature which chastises and punishes society . . . seems to be a psychological escape valve, a sublimation of a collective guilt complex through the frank and audacious comments of the writers," Marqués wrote (*Docile*, 62). In other words, even the aggressive nature of the new literature played a facilitating role in the psychological structure of colonized Puerto Ricans according to Marqués. Punishing literature served to ease the social pangs of conscience, and in this way helped to make possible the otherwise unbearable docile position of the Puerto Rican subject, he argued.

Marqués also suggested that the aggression contained in his own essay was but a symptom of a deeply rooted sadomasochistic chokehold. In an essay written just before the publication of "El puertorriqueño dócil," Marqués wrote, "It seems that what some Americans have resented most is Mr. Kazin's statement about Puerto Rican's being docile. But aren't we? Needless to say, as a Puerto Rican, I hate to admit it. But being honest, I have no alternative but to accept it" (*Docile*, 29). "El puertorriqueño dócil" was but a poignant example of this ambivalent admission of a guilty docility. It was Marqués's own literary contribution to a constitutive perversion that he suggested could not be denied. In fact, Marqués suggested that it was the responsibility of the Puerto Rican writer to confess this docility out loud rather than to deny it.

From this perspective, "El puertorriqueño dócil" becomes a founding text for a new modality of the long-standing discourse about the pathology of the Puerto Rican subject. The essay described Puerto Ricans as psychologically colonized to the point of occupying a position in a symbolic sadomasochistic embrace that provoked "the ethical man's sacred horror," but that was also inescapable (*Docile*, 44). Marqués suggested that the Puerto Rican subject had internalized his sadomasochistic perversion to the point of being constituted by it. Indeed, he suggested that Puerto Rican subjectivity was predicated on the Puerto Rican's ability to occupy both positions in the sadomasochistic embrace. The condition was so pervasive for Marqués that the Puerto Rican subject could symbolically occupy (in literature) the position of victimizing master while simultaneously guaranteeing his position as a submissive slave. The condition was identical to the awkward and aporetic position of the colonial subject described by Fanon and analyzed in chapter 1 of this book: the simultaneous identification with the position of the good subject and the evil object.

Marqués's poignant description of this psychosocial structure had the effect of making an external colonial master unnecessary and even superfluous. He replaced the colonial master with colonized, caustic, and bitter writers who would not only lash out against women (*Docile*, 48) but would willingly and deliberately take on the instruments of the sadist, and aim them squarely at themselves. And in this way, he refused to display a bashfulness or modesty that he considered to be "strange" (ibid., 44). Taking on the position of the master was the responsibility of the new writer, according to Marqués, because only his sadistic writerly practice would expose the masochistic perversion at the center of the Puerto Rican psychological structure, a "painful truth" that should not be sugar-coated or denied. "An essential part of [the writer's] labor," Marqués wrote in 1962, "if not the very essence of his never-ending search, is to break through the surface appearances, to bring to light what is true, and to rip away the veils which conceal the authentic" (*Docile*, 115).

Marqués's account of the masochistic psychosocial structure of the Puerto Rican subject, and his justification of the sadistic role for the Puerto Rican writer did more than add a new monstrous figure to the menagerie of racially and sexually abject figures that crowded discourses about Puerto Rican subjectivity. It also normalized the perverse nature of a similarly naturalized Puerto Rican colonial subject. Moreover, Marqués's heroic therapeutics were more than an extension of what Martin Stabb described as a "surgical engagement" of Latin American writers in another context.[9] Marqués's medical metaphors inaugurated a mode of colonized writing modeled after the perverse illness he found so repulsive.

In *Literatura y paternalismo en Puerto Rico* (1993), Juan Gelpí argues that Marqués's intensification of defensively violent and repressive literary practices against a nevertheless insistent eroticism brought the patriarchal literary canon to a crisis (135–36). Gelpí suggests that the desperate and strident tone of Marqués's essay (including his reactionary defense of a *machista* or *macho* literature and his suffocating metaphor of the closed and condemned house or closet) is but the last gasp of a patriarchy that lay in ruins in the 1950s. Gelpí suggests that the next generation of writers, including Ferré, abandoned Marqués's writerly practices, his strident tone and familiar figures, and openly challenged the defensive structures of the patriarchy in their own texts.

While preserving Gelpí's account of the oppositional nature of the writers that followed Marqués, I would like to argue something slightly different. An examination of a volume of the literary journal *Zona. Carga y Descarga*, edited by Ferré, suggests that her works were not so much a break as they were a development of the writerly practice performed by Marqués in his essay, even if an examination of her work also reveals important differences in her approach to the perverse.[10] Arguably, the generation of writers that followed Marqués performed a negative mode of the perverse writing as laid out in "El puertorriqueño dócil." If Marqués called for embracing the sadistic position in the sadomasochistic structure, writers like Ferré instead suggested a practice by the colonized subject that openly and aggressively embraced the "subordinate" position, in an effort to gain a new perspective, a critical, and also an empowering new vision.

Ferré's Roughhouse Aesthetics

The eighth volume of the influential literary journal *Zona. Carga y Descarga* famously included a letter by Marqués written in response to a request by Ferré for a literary contribution. The letter twice performed the perverse sadomasochistic writerly practice described by Marqués in his earlier essay. "I am sending you a copy of "Sólo un incidente," a mini-short-story, not-yet-published, which is not pornographic, stays away from words like damn and fuck, and does not spit on the grave of the yanqui's mother, like most everything that you publish. But I think it delivers a punch, even if it is a smaller *descarguita*.[11] I think you can use it in the journal. You decide" (*Zona* 8: 26). Marqués ironically used part of the name of the journal (*Descarga*, in Spanish) to describe his submission to the journal as a diminutive, smaller, less strident version of the journal's explosive contents ("a small cathartic act"). Ironically taking a submissive position—Marqués says, "You decide [whether to publish me or not]"—he also used his submission to the journal as a pretext to criticize the scandalous rhetoric that made the journal famous. And to do it, he characteristically turned its aggressive rhetoric against the journal and its director.

Marqués repeated the same gesture at the end of the letter. He again turned the explosive title of the journal (this time using the words in Spanish for "unloading and loading") against the journal in order to question the feminism of its editors. "Would you make women carry sacks of sugar and rice on their backs at the piers? That would go well with your loading and unloading zone. And what about a mighty blow to the jaw, if you think she deserves it? Will women feel offended if stupid men (*pendejos*) pay them a compliment?" (*Zona* 8: 26). Simultaneously assuming the diminished position of the castrated male (*pendejo* literally means pubic hair), while rhetorically punishing Ferré, Marqués again turned the title of the journal she edited against her. Can the women of the journal really take the load (*la carga*) like men, he asked? Does this also mean, he added, that men can "bust their jaw" (*la descarga*) when women deserve it?

In an insightful article about the remarkable anger driving *Zona. Carga y Descarga*'s editorial content and the format of the journal, Sonia Labrador-Rodríguez provocatively suggests that the title of the magazine offers a window into what she calls its aesthetics of anger.[12] The title, Labrador-Rodríguez points out, refers to an area of a warehouse where merchandise is both loaded and unloaded from trucks, but also to a cathartic act of aggression contained in an expression with origins in popular Puerto Rican slang. " 'We take off a load' and happily vent in an act that is cathartic and cleansing for us but insulting to the other" (Labrador-Rodríguez 2007, 250). According to Labrador-Rodríguez, *Zona* was both a place of dialogue with and a place of aggression against a foreign other. In the end, she concludes that the journal's overwhelmingly aggressive format undermined its dialogic intention, and was ultimately self-destructive and self-consuming (ibid., 256).

But Labrador-Rodríguez also remarks that this self-destruction was an unwanted side effect of a puerile reaction that she appears to criticize (and minimize) by comparing it to a "not-very productive childish tantrum" (Labrador-Rodríguez 2007, 257). That metaphor, together with Labrador-Rodríguez's gleeful description of the cathartic and similarly infantilized act of catharsis, suggests that the journal's aesthetics of aggression were also linked to, and driven by, a paradoxical, playful, and childish discharge of pleasure. One could in fact interpret the gleeful aggression and cathartic discharges of *Zona* as a mode of writing modeled after the roughhousing of children at play. In other words, the editors of *Zona* played rough, and in their roughhousing fully expected, and even desired, to get similar treatment from their readers. From this perspective, it comes as no surprise that the editors responded negatively to praise from a literature professor at the University of Puerto Rico, which they refused to accept, let alone publish. "We plainly reject his attempt to assimilate the antagonistic content of *Zona*," the editors wrote (*Zona* 3: 2). Similarly, it does not come as a surprise that they would respond very differently to Marqués's letter, which they accepted, published, and answered in kind.

The editors published Marqués's letter rather than the short story he submitted with it, and added insult to injury by placing it somewhere inside the journal, near its end, as if hiding it in a game of hide-and-seek. The response by *Zona* was as much a reaction against Marqués as it was a parodic tribute to the self-punishment he advocated for the Puerto Rican writer. On the one hand, *Zona* made public his low opinion of the literary journal and its editor. They went so far as to repeat (even as they also exposed) his sadistic references to punching women in the face, and to spitting on the grave of the yanqui's mother. On the other hand, they also returned the blow and gave Marqués a visual knockout punch by publishing his letter as one column of text, set on its side, inside a coffin-like stark rectangular space, at the bottom of the page, and bearing the visual weight of three columns of preceding text. In this way, *Zona* repeated Marqués's perverse writing while also "turning" it into an uncanny textual body that revealed (even as it discharged) Marqués's sadistic impulses against the feminine and the maternal body. Moreover, *Zona*'s editorial practice also suggested a willful and deliberate embrace of the now rhetorically empowered subordinate position of the rebellious child (Marqués addresses his letter to the infantilized "Rosarito") who effectively hits back against this abusive and sadistic father figure.

A Zone of Incestuous Impulses

Zona 8 also contained a review by Ferré of *Octaedro*, which was nothing short of a theoretical meditation on the incestuous impulses driving her own writerly practice. *Octaedro* was a book of short stories published a year earlier, in 1974, by the Argentinean Julio Cortázar, a writer famous, among other things, for his playful use of collage and formatting in his writing.[13] The review titled "Las ocho caras del miedo" ("The Eight Faces of Fear") was a reference to the eight-sided figure of the title, and an interpretation of the central role that maternal discharges played in the eight stories that together made up the collection of short stories. Ferré also reflected on the role that these maternal discharges played in the fantastic mode of writing that the collection as a whole represented for her. In it, Ferré described a radical vision developed in an incestuous play with the drives (or bodily affects or discharges) of the maternal body.

Ferré began her review with words from Genesis, followed by a birthing scene that provocatively suggested that the reproductive body was the source of a bodily discharge, which in turn was the origin of the Biblical text: "Woman gives birth; the child is born into the shadows" (*Zona* 8: 11). The separation from the maternal body was the first trauma, she stated, and this trauma provoked an archaic anguish, according to Ferré. Her description also emphasized a symbolic blindness that accompanied birth. Together, blindness, vulnerability, and anguish described the state of the newborn. The newborn emerged without protection and without eyes to see or to know what awaited it. The newborn was also discharged from the maternal body with a terrific sense of loss. To be born also meant to lose the protection of an early form of symbolic vision, a mode of maternal vigilance, she suggested.

Ferré then described a second trauma following the first. "Both blind and radically vulnerable, the confrontation with a strange reality is her second trauma," she wrote (*Zona* 8: 11). The second trauma was the blind confrontation of the newborn with a strange reality, but it was also a paradoxical protection from the first trauma. In an illustration of the saying "One nail takes out another," the anguish and terror of the first separation became, with the second trauma, a different mode of vision and a strange form of protection. If terror accompanied the shock of the newborn's sudden collision with reality, this discharge also gave both a permanence and a shape to the reality with which she collided. In giving a shape to this darkness, terror worked as a new form of vision for Ferré.

So, the two primal shocks or traumas received by the newborn, first her separation from the vigilant maternal body, and second her collision with a strange darkness, were also simultaneously, the origins of a bodily discharge, of a fear, of a terror, that doubled as a cure, a therapy, an answer, and a mode of seeing and writing, according to Ferré. In other words, fear, terror, and anguish became forms of knowledge, a paradoxical or blind mode of seeing, if you will, a mode of protection that was a form of negation, or negative writing. Following Ferré's argument to its logical conclusion leads the reader to speculate whether this negation was not only of the original blindness she described, but whether it was also a demystification of the idealized maternal body at the center of the traumatic birthing scene.

According to Ferré, fear, terror, and anguish were the negative form of the protection, the cover, and the vigilant knowledge that were lost after the newborn's separation from the maternal body, a loss that followed the dissolution of her archaic union with that body. Fear, terror, and anguish were then the negative form of that utopian union. To embrace them as a form of life, as Ferré suggested in this review, was also to embrace the negative force of the maternal bodily discharge or abjection of the newborn.[14] The embrace amounted to a deliberate refusal to sugar-coat the archaic origin with the utopian fantasy of an original cover, protection, and comfort. To embrace fear, terror, and anguish, to reject the so-called protective nature of the origin, provided a form of cover and a comfort from the double source of the trauma, first from the separation and then from the collision with a strange reality. "Fear is her first barrier. It is also opens the gates to the kingdom," Ferré wrote (*Zona* 8: 11).

Claiming fear, terror, and anguish, as a new mode of seeing, as a new vigilant form of knowledge, was to base knowledge and vision on the negation, the negativity, and the disavowal represented by that fear, terror, and anguish. This disavowal based on fear, terror, and anguish was also most importantly the negation of the original trauma. It was a disavowal of the archaic separation, and in this sense it was an incestuous position. It involved the active construction of a precarious fantasy of incestuous union with a body that separated from the newborn. It was also the fantastic identification with a body that was more than the maternal, with a body that was constituted by an excess of bodies, a body that was supplemented by another body, a body that was as monstrous, as terrific, as terrifying, and as fantastical a form of life as the painting of Arcimboldo that accompanied the review.

This fantastical body that generated a negative discharge against the traumatic separation and subsequent collisions with strange realities was also the negative of a body. It was a body made of a vacuum of bodies, constituted by the absence of bodies. More than a body, it was a space, a place for energy charges and discharges, a zone for loading and unloading bodily impulses. This fantastical zone was also a symbolic body, a textual body. In fact, this zone of maternal discharges was another meaning of *Zona. Carga y Descarga*, which the first editorial of the journal significantly described as a birthing zone: "a body zone of holes that we collectively and patiently open as we fall through them" (*Zona* 1: 2). Indeed, *Zona. Carga y Descarga* was a mode of incestuous symbolic production, of colonized writing modeled after the bodily impulses that constituted this birthing zone (the birth canal?) according to Ferré. Arguably, *Zona* was modeled after the negative discharges that generated fear, terror, and anguish themselves sublimated to the category of art (*Zona* 8: 11). I dedicate the next chapter of my book to the sublimation of bodily impulses in the journal.

Zona was also modeled after the terrifying short stories of *Octaedro*, which contained a radical form of vision similar to Oedipus's incestuous blindness, according to Ferré: "[His stories] take us back to the possibility of seeing radically," she wrote (*Zona* 8: 31). Ferré also wrote that the short stories from *Octaedro* were made of discharges, of abjections, of injunctions even, that pushed the subject into the kingdom of life through the gates of fear (*Zona* 8: 31). These maternal discharges at the origin of *Octaedro* were represented by the zone of exchange or transit that was *Zona*, according to its editors, whose first number famously opened with a recipe for "Monstrous Egg" on the front cover. The recipe was remarkable for the violence of its culinary instructions, which suggested a creative practice modeled after the intimate handling, but also the perverse torture, of a bladder-like sac holding the monstrous egg: a symbolic violence done to the reproductive body. At the end of the instructions, in capital letters and without diacritical marks, the editors wrote: "Take a large bladder-like sac, put in the egg whites, placing the curdled yolk in the center; tie it into a knot and cook again, until you think they might be hard, then take it out, cracking open the sac and the monstrous egg is done" (*Zona* 1: 1).

In her review of *Octaedro*, Ferré distinguished between two principal and interrelated modes of writing modeled after the bodily affects of the maternal body, its energy and its discharges, modes that referred back to Marqués's account of the perverse positions occupied by the Puerto Rican sadomasochistic subject. She described the first mode as a sadistic kind of writing. The sadistic writer, she argued, transformed his fear into sangfroid, a distance, and even a perverse mode of pleasure and joy. She argued that some of the stories in *Octaedro* suffered from this mode of perversion. In them, terror was similar to a discharge (*Descarga*) that was projected and displaced onto the reader and onto a plane that was external to the subjectivity of the writer, who examined this plane as if he were a doctor.

The position allowed the writer to "observe the supernatural event . . . to examine it, dissecting it, interiorizing it, with an always-brutal intensity that is often sadistic" (*Zona* 8: 11).

However, in other stories of *Octaedro*, Ferré also found a mode of writing that suffered from the opposite mode of perversion, a mode that was more compelling to her: a melancholy masochism perhaps. This form of writing was perverse in its familiarity with fear, in its direct understanding of anguish, in its immediate encounter with terror, in other words, in its identification with an abject birthing zone. This incestuous identification also provoked a cruel mode of writing, but its cruelty was not aimed outward, at somebody else. Its cruelty was based on the writer's knowledge of her imminent and inescapable death brought about by the identification with the maternal body and its discharges. The deadly force of this cruelty was the result of a wish for revenge provoked by the writer's own tragic fate, and it produced the "powerful autobiographical charge" of a writer "who judges and destroys herself" (*Zona 8:* 31). In other words, the violence of this melancholy mode of writing was principally aimed at the self. It was a twisted version of the masochistic and even suicidal mode of writing described by Marqués in his essay, and by Fanon in his analysis of decolonized literature.

In her writing in general, and in this review in particular, Ferré repeated Marqués' psychosocial mode of analysis while taking it in a psychosexual direction that he clearly resisted, as was evident from his antifeminist letter. She subjected Marqués's model for Puerto Rican subjectivity to a series of inversions that together amounted to a reversal of Marqués's perverse model. Like Marqués, who turned *Zona*'s scandalous rhetoric against it, *Zona*'s editor turned the similarly scandalous bodily drives contained by Marqués's letter against him and his writing. If Marqués's model evoked what was for him a repulsive symbolic sadomasochistic relation between two males figures, Ferré developed a similar sadomasochistic model based on an incestuous struggle with the maternal body. If Marqués's homoerotic model was execrable to him because it reproduced affects that kept the Puerto Rican subject in a submissive position, Ferré's incestuous model was instead empowering because its perverse impulses offered the same subject a radical, revolting, but also a revolutionary perspective. If Marqués's role for the writer was to perversely and violently reveal the painful and humiliating hidden face masked behind an artificial reality, Ferré's account of this role involved a similarly perverse process of separation, but this time from the body, and from the utopian account of the caring maternal body, in order to reveal a terrifying (oedipal) way of seeing. Put in yet another way, Ferré turned Marqués's text from a model for patriarchal social politics into a feminist mode of body politics.

Ferré's negative account of Marqués's perverse model for Puerto Rican subjectivity offered a perspective that was also similar to her predecessor's in its concern with colonial relations and with the mode of writing such relations produced. Unlike Marqués, however, Ferré's point of departure for geopolitical commentary was the body in general and the feminine and reproductive body in particular. She modeled her social analysis of Puerto Rico's colonialism after the intimate and even incestuous relations with the maternal body, and this helped Ferré make crucial distinctions between Latin American and Caribbean subjects, specifically between the utopian and liberal fantasies of the former, and the dystopian fantasies of the latter. For example, in a second review of *Zona* 8, Ferré criticized *Persona non grata* (1974), a controversial memoir by the Chilean writer Jorge Edwards (1931–), who worked for the government of Salvador Allende as a diplomat in Cuba from 1970–71. She applied her psychosexual model inflected by symbolic maternal discharges to geopolitics in that review.

Indirectly joining the debate framed by Marqués regarding the social and political role of the colonized writer, Ferré argued that the criticism leveled by Edwards in his book against the Cuban Revolution in general, and against Fidel Castro in particular, was symptomatic of a liberal fantasy that was not possible in Caribbean nations with vexed colonial histories such as Cuba or Puerto Rico. Edwards's misguided critique of Castro, she wrote, was the result of his nostalgia for a utopia, a fantasy for a perfect place, which nostalgic fantasy was in turn the symptom of privilege, and the effect of the rhetoric of the liberal Latin American state. In other words, the colonial history of the Puerto Rican reader did not give Ferré the luxury of taking the moral high ground against Castro. Instead, she occupied a compromised position that was always vexed and contradictory. She saw things differently from Edwards, and could only read against the grain of his critique. She wrote,

> The Puerto Rican reader finds it hard to believe in the nostalgia of Edwards (a member of one of Chile's most aristocratic families, even if he [did] not share their wealth) during a sit-down dinner served, on board the Esmeralda, by the "waiters who passed around glowing silver trays, and fine bottles of wine from the aged reserves of Macul, and who preserved the submissive and

> Creole attitudes of a strictly hierarchic world, even as the ship was docked at the piers of a classless society." (*Zona* 8: 28–29)

Puerto Rican readers, she suggested, identified with the submissive attitude of the servants inside the school-ship *Esmeralda*, not with its captain or passengers, as Edwards seemed to do in his book. Caribbean colonial subjects were united by a familiar separation from a symbolic, abundant, and nurturing origin. Their origins were distinctly impoverished and abject. Not surprisingly, Edwards, accustomed to the fine taste of the Macul wine, felt repulsed and nauseated by Castro's taste for milk, in an episode described in detail by Ferré. But milk was for a Castro-identified Ferré the thick and raw discharge of a nation historically constituted (like Puerto Rico) by colonial abuse, lack, poverty, and constant police surveillance.[15] Cuba, like Puerto Rico, was made of material and symbolic want and poverty. There was an absence of basic freedoms in both islands, according to Ferré, and therefore she suggested that Caribbean writing and politics should be characterized by a similar negativity. She warned that to miss this tragic condition, as Edwards did, was to be blind to the colonial history of the region and to its ambiguous effects.

Ferré was not sympathetic to the plight of Chileans such as Edwards, who wrote nostalgically in his memoir about the government of President Salvador Allende after the military coup by Augusto Pinochet (carried out by the same Navy and by the same *Esmeralda* that Edwards idealized). She refused to sympathize with the melancholy plaints of writers such as Edwards for a lost origin that was misogynist in the end. For her, these writers were Latin American subjects that arrogantly projected mystified utopian fantasies on their Caribbean peers. They deceived themselves, she argued. But worse than that, by insisting on utopian fantasies that were profoundly matricidal, by ignoring and denying the perverse processes that constituted the colonial experience of Cuba and Puerto Rico, Latin American liberals such as Edwards remained blissfully blind to the great injustices suffered by the women and the writers (and by the women writers) of some of these Caribbean nations. She wrote that she could not believe what she read when "the captain of the Esmeralda wanted to ask 30 to 40 women to the formal ball on board and Edwards wrote that he did not need to emphasize they should be 'society ladies' because 'such details were understood'" (*Zona* 8: 27).

Ferré modeled the colonial experience that was invisible to Edwards after an incestuous mode of perversion, but she used it to her advantage as an empowering source for the colonized subject. Like Marqués, Ferré pointed to a perverse core of colonial subjectivity, but unlike Marqués, she also argued that the perverse identification of the colonized subject with the symbolic discharges of the maternal abject gave her a radical vision that protected her from the mystifications of the liberal Latin American State.

Foundational Matricide

Montero's novel *El capitán de los dormidos* can be interpreted as an extension of, as well as a shift away from Ferré's diagnosis of the matricide at the center of colonial masochism or self-violence. Like Ferré, Montero suggests the central importance of the social abjection suffered by the maternal figure, represented by Estela's suicide and rape in the novel. In fact, the novel is woven from a set of memories that, like a train heading for a wreck at full speed, drives the reader relentlessly forward to the scene where the body of the suicide is raped. In this sense, Montero is explicitly critical of the sadistic fantasy of control of a figurative master who rapes the maternal corpse, even as he eroticizes her suffering and pain. But Montero is equally critical in her novel of the masochistic fantasy of control by the figurative slave that Ferré describes and appears to embrace in her work. Ferré's account of colonial perversion unwittingly repeats a form of symbolic matricide by identifying the maternal birthing zone with a fear that must be embraced, a fear with which she then goes on to identify in order to gain a radical form of vision. Montero both dramatizes but also criticizes this mode of masochistic identification with the maternal abject in her novel. In the novel, this mode of identification is associated with the character of Frank Yasin, the Nationalist father of the protagonist, as well as with Andrés, his son. And Montero takes the analysis of colonial symbolic matricide farther by suggesting its intensification by the next generations of writers. Finally, Montero also expands her analysis of the foundational matricide at the origin of perverse colonial relations beyond the geographic limits imposed by Marqués or the Caribbean boundaries set by Ferré.[16]

In this sense, the novel displaces to a secondary position the two fantasies of control over the slave and over the master represented by Marqués and Ferré in their respective works. So far, we have seen these fantasies brandished against one another by colonial subjects that struggle to occupy the symbolic position of the master and the slave respectively. In Montero's novel, these fantasies of control by the master and the slave are revealed to be the foundation for a new figure in the catalogue of colonial perversions. Going beyond the perverse sadomasochistic and incestuous figures screened by Marqués and Ferré, Montero offers us a character who identifies with the foundational matricidal fantasy in a new way, in a spectacular way, intensifying its power. This new figure (represented by Andrés Yasin in the novel) becomes involved in a love triangle that extends, complicates, and shifts the sadomasochistic binaries set up by Marqués and Ferré.[17]

El capitán de los dormidos tells the story of Andrés Yasín, the son of a Nationalist couple (Estela and Frank) who once smuggled guns and helped to organize and supply a revolutionary uprising from their small hotel in Vieques. The couple recruited Jonathan Timothy Bunker (J. T. in the novel) to help them in their cause because of his skill as an airplane pilot, and because his background put him above suspicion during a time when Puerto Rican Nationalists were persecuted.[18] The triangular relationship between Estela, Frank, and J. T. becomes very complex. It leads to two related traumatic events, one factual the other invented. First, the novel describes the Nationalist insurrection in late October and its aftermath in early November 1950, when armed groups of members of that political party unsuccessfully tried to violently take over the island, and in so doing also tried to stop the new direction of colonial relations between Puerto Rico and the United States.[19]

Andrés's father, Frank, is both a melancholy idealist involved in the political struggle and Estela's estranged husband. At the end of the novel, Frank leaves his unhappy wife at home and travels to the main island of Puerto Rico to help the uprising of the Nationalists. The uprising is a resounding failure, but Frank survives its defeat and returns home to Martineau.[20] Frank's return after the failed insurrection is then followed by the explosive ending of the novel. Before the uprising, Estela breaks off an adulterous romance with J. T. And after the Nationalist uprising is squelched and her childhood friend (Roberto) is killed in the lethal counterattack by the government, she commits suicide. Estela's suicide sends J. T. on a jealous rampage and a drunken binge that culminates with the necrophilic rape of her corpse, witnessed by her son, Andrés.

The Master's Fantasy

The novel, structured as a set of long monologues by Andrés followed by short confessions by J. T., suggests an explanation of what led to these two related traumatic events (the counterattack by the government and the rape by J. T.), and it places the love triangle between J. T., Frank, and Estela at their origin. The shape of this particular triangle, however, is unique. Passion does not make a perfect and linear circuit that moves from one acute angle to the next in one direction. In the words of J. T., the triangle is "kind of imperfect and quivering whose outline sometimes disappeared against a background of secret shadows" (*Captain*, 35). This "imperfect" and "quivering" love triangle is best represented in the novel by a scene also described by J. T. It happens close to the end of the novel, between the two traumatic events that change the lives of the characters forever. After the government's counterattack against the Nationalist uprising, J. T. helps Andrés's parents—who are literally worried to the point of sickness and are still reeling from the experience—by dropping off their son at school the next morning. On his way back to the hotel, J. T. is confronted with an "unreal scene."

J. T. sees an elderly but corpulent man, barechested, holding up and strangling an enormous dog that frantically struggles and helplessly kicks as its life ebbs away. He also notices a second dog, seated next to the imposing man, watching the gruesome scene. The half-naked figure of the man, together with the fact that he appears to kill the dog with his bare hands, suggests an eroticized sadistic scene involving the old man's necrophilia. J. T. slows down the car to take a closer look and the old man returns his gaze in a moment of identification. The scene becomes for J. T. the beginning of a nightmarish realization. He realizes the "delicate horror" of his life; that his role is to be a shadowy figure in analogous dreamlike fantasies, a similar "lunatic" driven by darkness. He realizes that, like the old man, he too is a lost soul "without a compass," controlled by his dark dreams and perverse fantasies. And these fantasies, like the violent passion suggested by the scene, always involve a denial of limits and an excess of desire; a desire not only beyond what is "proper," or beyond what is properly one's own, but a desire beyond life itself. The old man in the scene appears to be driven by a passion without limits to the point of death. Significantly Gerónimo (the gardener) warns Andrés that this is what happens "when devils are let loose" (*Captain*, 193) when Gerónimo drives by the scene with Andrés in tow.

J. T.'s desire is without limits, and gradually grows out of control in the novel, going from adultery to necrophilia, and from desiring the wife of his best friend to desiring the dead Estela. At the end of the novel, J. T. abandons himself helplessly to the power of an unbound desire that possesses him. He allows himself to be driven by Eugene (a toy-like jeep that mysteriously takes on supernatural powers), back to the hotel where yet another version of the unreal scene awaits him. In this version, J. T. takes the place of the sadistic old man, as he rapes Estela's corpse. Also, in the new scene, Andrés takes the place of the small dog as he watches the senseless violence. It is in this morbid sense that J. T. becomes the "captain" of the novel's title. Frank originally gives J. T. this nickname in order to hide from young Andrés the fact that his friend sometimes has the gruesome task of flying back the corpses of Viequenses who want to be buried in their homeland.[21] And indeed, J. T. is the would-be pilot of a machine of denial and fantasy also represented in the novel by his Cessna "Parakeet," which takes on powers similar to Eugene the jeep (*Captain*, 169). In this sense, J. T. is the "captain" of sleeping suicides, or sleepwalkers driven by the power of denial and by their own defensive and perverse fantasies. J. T. denies Estela's marriage to Frank, her refusal to accept him, and her death. He even twice denies the rape ever happened: he says to Andrés, "[T]here's no madness that can justify what you saw, or what you thought you saw. No, nothing justifies it, because it didn't happen" (ibid., 36).

Montero suggests that J. T. Bunker's sadistic fantasies are the result of his denials of the limits imposed by a reality that hurts him as well as others. In an essay about Montero's early novels, Antonio Vera León argues that death is the motor for the unhinged form of desire so prevalent in Montero's fictions. J. T. and his metaphorical army of sleeping suicides allow neither propriety, nor rejection, nor death itself, to get in the way of satisfying their unhinged and unquenchable desires, to the point of denying and eroticizing death itself. And their violence is not limited to the rape of Estela's body. J. T.'s sadism is also an allegorical sign for the violence that comes with the occupation of Vieques by the U.S. Navy. At one point in the novel, Braulia, the hotel's manager, asks Andrés whether he knows what a pervert is after warning him that there is sure to be one "running loose" among so many soldiers (*Captain*, 30). Braulia's fears prove to be well founded when her niece is raped and sadistically murdered in the novel.

J. T. Bunker's fantasy also suggests that he is the metaphorical captain of an army of occupation in a phantasmatic struggle with Frank and the Nationalists for the control of Estela and the land where she was born. In other words, the rivalry between J. T. and Frank mirrors the public struggle for political control between the Puerto Rican Nationalists and the United States government in 1950, and between the neo-Nationalists and the United States Navy in 2003. Significantly, J. T.'s last name (Bunker) is also the word for an underground defensive position with a fortified projection for gun emplacements, a protective chamber also made for attack. And indeed, J. T.'s bellicose denials are similar to those of the Navy as described by Jesse Jackson during the struggle for power over the control of Vieques in 2003: "The Navy reminds me of a man . . . who desperately wants a beautiful woman. . . . The woman keeps saying 'No,' and you keep insisting you have to have her" (quoted in Jiménez 65).

Most importantly, J. T. follows his denials of his sadistic violence against Estela with a gesture that transforms her into a powerful martyr that haunts him. Indeed, J. T. Bunker attenuates his guilt by turning Estela into a powerful memory and himself into a haunted man. In other words, he turns Estela into a phallic figure that punishes him for his guilty desires. He says that, unlike him and unlike Frank, Estela had the "balls" to kill herself (*Captain*, 169). Her suicide, he adds, was no act of desperation. It was a logical and deliberate act, planned after the outcome of the revolt. He concludes that her suicide preserved her virtue and dignity. It was better for her to be dead than to live under the new political regime. She died the death of a martyr, defending both her honor and the honor of the motherland. J. T. says to Andrés that he thought "that Estela would do something crazy, which is the easy way to say she'd do exactly what was expected of her" (ibid., 167). In other words, J. T. turns Estela into an idealized martyr that puts him and Frank to shame. Unlike them, she gives her life for the cause that she believed in.

The Slave's Fantasy

Like J. T. Bunker, Frank Yasín suffers from disturbing colonial fantasies, but unlike J. T. who identifies with the master, Frank identifies with the slave. In other words, the novel is not only a study of the psyche of the colonizer that drives the fantasy of the phallic mother. It is also a study of the psyche of the colonized that drives the fantasy of the abject mother. Briefly put, if J. T. lives a life of desire without limits, Frank lives at the limits of a life without desire.

As such, *El capitán de los dormidos* contains a critique of the perverse fundamentalism at the origins of the Nationalist movement. It is an exposé of the process of perverse identifications that hide behind its politico-religious ideal of perfection. Moreover, Montero also suggests that the self-sacrifice of the Nationalists is a drama, a theatrical performance, meant to provoke moral outrage from a sympathetic audience, even as it hides the grab for power and the gratification at its center. From this perspective, Frank Yasín is far from being frank about his beliefs. In fact, during a visit to a movie theatre in the capital city of San Juan, where the character of Urbano (a Hunger Artist) is performing, Frank tells his son that what the actor really wants is to eat a good steak.[22] Similarly, Frank is anything but honest with himself about his real desires. His hunger for the American "way of life" is betrayed by his second marriage to an American woman, and by his move to Georgia, where he lives troubled but comfortably until the end of his days.

Frank is the son of a Lebanese merchant, Khalil Yasín, and his last name contains a rich set of references that link Frank's ideals to the fundamentalist fantasies that are partly to blame for the conflict in the Middle East today. Yasin is one of the names given to the apostles, or messengers of the prophet in the *Qur'an*. Indeed, Yasin is a figure similar to that of the Archangel Gabriel. The Archangel blows his trumpet to warn those who are blind to the teachings of the prophet, and to wake the sleepers, the dead, as the day of Final Judgment approaches.[23] Like that biblical figure of Gabriel, Yasin is an avenging and punishing figure that blinds the heedless.[24] Yasin is also both the name for a weapon, and it has become synonymous with suicidal attacks. Abdul Rahman Yasin, for example, helped to make the bombs used in the 1993 attack on the World Trade Center. He appeared in the list of the FBI's top twenty-two most wanted terrorists, released in 2001 by President George W. Bush. Also, the Yasin is an antitank weapon developed by Hamas. The weapon is named after Ahmed Yasin, the founder and spiritual leader of Hamas, now a political party. After his assassination in 2004, the Brigades of Martyr Ahmed Yasin claimed responsibility for the abduction and execution of four U.S. security contractors in Fallujah, Iraq.

Frank's surname also connects him with Albizu Campos, the Puerto Rican Nationalist hero and martyr, whose Arabic-sounding surname and dark features make him a "moor," according to Frank. In the novel, Albizu Campos is compared to Urbano, the Hunger Artist, and both suffer from a constitutive lack, a great void that nevertheless gives them both great power. The chest of Urbano is collapsed as if from a blow that leaves a disturbing "hollow" covered over only by a thin layer of skin (*Captain*, 64). Similarly, Albizu's sunken eyes remind Frank of Urbano, and his lips remind Frank of the mouth of a woman (ibid., 70). These two small, fragile, and soft-spoken characters (Urbano and Albizu) have a strong effect on their respective audiences, provoking unrest and rebellion. They both represent the paradoxical power that the emasculated slave wields over his emasculating master in the novel. A power that is based on the blows he receives in a fluid master-slave dialectic.

Frank has never known his father, Khalil, and Apollonia (Frank's mother) covers over his absence with a romantic story. She substitutes the missing father with Águila Blanca (a mythical outlaw credited with armed resistance against the U.S. invasion in 1897 (*Captain*, 116)), and also with stories about Albizu Campos, "another Lebanese" (ibid.). But for Frank, Apollonia is not only the source of consoling stories that hide his father's absence. She also reacts to her abandonment by taking up the Nationalist cause. Indeed, Frank describes her as the Nationalist ideal of self-sacrifice. She turns her husband's absence and betrayals into ammunition against the government. Appolonia raises Frank to believe in her political cause, and she provides the protective "lair" where Frank waits for news about the revolutionary assault (ibid., 149).

Appolonia returns to haunt Frank years after Estela's death, and after Frank relocates, remarries, and reinvents himself as a real estate broker. Frank imagines his mother as a corpse turning over in her grave from shame at her son's escape, and at his desire for a different life. (Frank tells Andrés how much he enjoys his comfortable life in Georgia [*Captain*, 151]). Significantly, when Andrés visits Frank years later, his father is dying of lupus. Could the disease be a metaphor for psychological defenses that are running amok in Frank's body, for Frank's simultaneous idealization and denial of the abject, which turns against him in the end?[25]

Montero suggests in her novel that the fantasies of the master and the slave are different in an important way. If the master denies his perverse fantasies, the slave identifies with them. J. T. denies raping the beautiful Estela, while Frank identifies with the suffering of Appolonia. But the master and the slave are also similar insofar as both J. T. and Frank share the same matricidal fantasy. Both Estela and Appolonia become phallic and castrating mothers that haunt J. T and Frank for the rest of their lives.

Spectacular Matricide

Montero also suggests that these specular struggles, competitions, or confrontations develop into a third form of colonial fantasy that is not bound to the fantasy of the master or to the fantasy of the slave. This fantasy is founded instead on the absolute denial of the matricidal fantasy shared by both the master and the slave. In the novel, Andrés is the character that suffers from this fantasy to the third power. He is the sleeping suicide of the title, the insomniac, but also the voyeur who wants it all. He might be also an allegorical representation of the Commonwealth for Montero. The greedy and childish Andrés can be interpreted as a figure for a contradictory political solution characterized by the proverbial desire to have one's cake and eat it too.

Montero's grotesque figure for his spectacular defensive fantasy is the image of the scarred "third eye" of Vidal, one of the fighters of the Nationalist uprising who suffers a wound to the head but miraculously survives the killing rampage that follows the assaults. When Andrés recognizes him and tries to remind him of the events, Vidal refuses to recognize him and turns his back on Andrés. Before he turns around, however, Andrés sees the scar on his forehead left by a bullet wound, now transformed into a deep purple third eye, an eye that is closed shut and keeps out the memory of the attack (*Captain*, 179). The wounded eye of Vidal suggests that the vision of the colonized subject is traumatically foreclosed, according to Montero. Like the wounded Vidal and his closed eye, the colonized eye is first sutured, and then scarred shut by the spectacle of Nationalist and imperialist subjects fighting each other for control over a "motherland" twice "killed" by their complementary fantasies. Vidal's wounded eye is a screen for this matricide to the third power. And Andrés carries a similar psychological scar that is also a monstrous defense against the absence of his mother, Estela.

Estela is the woman-turned-memorial, stele, or slab of stone by the patriarchal narratives designed to protect us against her haunting figure. But Estela nevertheless returns in the novel, and her returns are like the hold of the Kristevan abject, they are similar to the effect of Lita in Ferré's poem "Necrofilia."[26] Estela is an explosive symbolic device, a figurative bomb that turns all the characters in the novel into wounded subjects. In this sense, Estela is also the explosive material that remains, a reproductive body that is still free from the traumatic fantasies of a patriarchal law. Her living corpse throughout the novel is the abject and unstable material that blows up in everybody's face, as it is caught in a repeating and endless cycle that everybody tries to control to no avail. The explosion briefly opens Andrés's eyes. He sees himself as the stunted imaginary child, and as the sleeping suicide that he has become (*Captain*, 181). Montero appears to forgive his perversion with the ambiguous maternal words that end the novel: "—Sweet dreams, Andrés. Sleep tight!" (ibid.).[27]

The Defensive Erotization of the Abject

Montero's fiction is remarkable for its representation of perversion. Necrophilia, sadomasochism, and voyeurism are but a few examples of perverse behavior exhibited by central characters of many of Montero's novels, including (but not limited to) *La trenza de la hermosa luna* (1987), *El rojo de su sombra* (1992), and *Son de almendra* (2005). But Montero's work does not merely represent an imaginary world filled with outlandish sexual behavior. Her repeated representation of perversion in her novels elaborates a literary discourse that is widespread in Puerto Rico. This discourse, suggests that perversion is more than an obligatory rite of passage marking the complex construction of personality, as Freud suggested in his *Three Essays on the Theory of Sexuality* (1905). If Freud understood perversion as a defensive deviation of the sexual instinct, writers from Puerto Rico suggest that perversion is also a defensive erotization of a body abjected by colonial relations. They also suggest that perversion might be a necessary defensive social structure under a colonial regime.

Montero's novel *El capitán de los dormidos* adds three elements to the discourse of colonial perversion in Puerto Rico. First, it adds a third element to its psychological structure, moving from Marqués's binary model of a struggle between a master and a slave to a triangular one that intensifies the power of the original psychological structure. Second, she moves away from the earlier emphasis on sadomasochism and incest as defensive or empowering inversions of the sexual instinct in a colonial society. Instead, Montero explores the possibility that necrophilia, voyeurism, and disavowal are symptoms of a compromised psychological agency that offers little control to colonial subjects. Finally, Montero confirms in her novel that despite the changing nature of psychological responses to colonialism, a symbolic matricide remains firmly in place at the center of all of its forms.

4

Zona. Carga y Descarga

MINOR LITERATURE IN A PENAL COLONY

> The critic is the guardian appointed to follow the insane everywhere he goes, trying to bring order to the chaos he leaves behind . . . the explosion of a star that later the critic will spend years ordering with astrolabe and compass. After he is finished with his careful measurements, the critic will say: Alpha Centauri is a star. But millions of years will have passed by the time its light reaches him and by then Alpha Centauri will have exploded into the fragments of a new constellation. Alpha Centauri will be no more.
>
> —The editors. *Zona. Carga y Descarga*

The authors of the few articles, conferences, and essays dedicated to the short-lived *Zona. Carga y Descarga* seem to agree when they describe the journal (published from 1972 to1975) as an important contribution to the history of Puerto Rican literature, and particularly to a moment of crisis and rupture in that history when a young generation of writers violently broke with an earlier generation by challenging its moral and aesthetic values. To some degree, all these critics describe *Zona* as an unusual and sudden moment of openness in the literary history of Puerto Rico when new modes of reading and writing were tried, and out of which emerged what Gelpí calls "the three fundamental texts of Puerto Rican narrative during the seventies: *Papeles de Pandora* by Ferré, *La guaracha del Macho Camacho* by Sánchez and *La novelabingo* by Ramos Otero" (1984, 134). The comment of another critic highlights the strict limits set by many of the readings the journal has received: "[F]rom the beginning Zona was intrinsically a university phenomenon and was never able to find a reading public beyond the walls of the University of Puerto Rico" (Ibáñez 1992, 333). In an interview with *Zona*'s editor Ferré, Donna Perry further reduces the range of the journal by referring to it as a "graduate school publication" (1993, 89). The emphasis on the limited and local audience that the journal commanded is ironic if one considers the journal's insistence on a broad, hemispheric, Latin American perspective, and if one further considers what may have been its main effect: the very openness that the critics hail as the journal's contribution to the history of Puerto Rican literature.

In what follows, I will go beyond the binary reading that governs these interpretations of the limited reach of *Zona* and of its impact on Puerto Rican culture, and their characterization of the journal as a sudden break in a local literary history. Instead, I would like to place the journal in the context of what Gilles Deleuze and Félix Guattari call a minor literature, which has a better chance of returning meaning, signification, and sense, to a journal and to a cultural expression that the critics continue to minimize.

In their influential work on Franz Kafka, Deleuze and Guattari identify three characteristics of a minor literature. It is impossible in practice (its writers find it impossible to write both inside and outside a major literature), political in range, and collective in value (Deleuze and Guattari 1985, 16–17). While I think that their description of the collective value of minor literatures is somewhat romantic, I find that their diagnosis of the impossible situation facing the writer of a minor literature, and their description of its inherently political range applies to *Zona*. But what I find most compelling about their analysis (and what I will focus on in this essay) is not so much their definition of a minor literature as it applies to the journal, but their metaphorics and what these metaphorics suggest. Deleuze and Guattari insist on describing minor literature as a mode of "techne," as a machine, or as what they call an "assemblage" (ibid., 18). With these metaphors, Deleuze and Guattari approximate what I believe to be crucial about minor literatures in general and about *Zona* in particular: to wit, the objectification of minor literatures by moral, cultural, and literary majorities on the one hand, and the reanimation by minor literatures of the material that is rendered inert and machinelike on the other (ibid.).

Deleuze and Guattari help me to place the literature, the language, the writers, and the writing of *Zona* in the context of a minor literature. *Zona* contains the work of similarly "minor writers" (Latin American, Portuguese, Puerto Rican, Nuyorican, but also women and homosexual writers) who return signification, who learn to write in a zone (both literal and imaginary) of "booms," explosions literary or otherwise,[1] in a context where all writers (but the minor writer in particular and most intensely) are sometimes literally, but most often symbolically, burned to a crisp of unrecognizable meaning, in a zone of conflict of almost apocalyptic proportions best represented by the most marginal of places of both Latin America and the United States: Puerto Rico's Kafkaesque penal colony during the seventies.

By penal, I refer to the carcelary nature of social relations at that time, when Puerto Rican society and culture can be said to have been held in a veritable state of siege by the effects of the Cold War in the Caribbean. But by penal, I also refer to the sexually repressive nature of the penal code of the colony which still contained a so-called sodomy clause until 2003 when the U.S. Supreme Court declared unconstitutional the sodomy law of Texas, which led to a revision of the Puerto Rican Legal Code. Finally, I also refer here to Kafka's compelling short story "In the Penal Colony" (1919), where a character turns the carcelary instrument of torture against himself, as an apt symbolic representation of the effects of the Cold War on Puerto Rico, its culture, society, and government, during the seventies, and of a self-violent form of defense against these effects.

In the context of a penal colony, minor writers do not break with, or leave, the majority culture that always to some degree incarcerates them. To the contrary, they come closer to its center. They often travel to, and/or return from, their capitals (Paris, New York), and they learn to write in a parallel (if insistently imaginary and symbolic) mode. As such, their writing takes the form of erasure, marking, tensing, torture, which in *Zona*, and for reasons that I will discuss below, takes the form of a slow-burning, a stretching, and an inversion of the materials of signification. In the context of *Zona*, what is most important to understand, however, is that these inversions are a necessary repetition of the abjections of the penal colony, even as they transform and change them. From this perspective, Kristeva helps me to better define the crucial symbolic operation of reanimation suggested by the metaphorics of Deleuze and Guattari, as a repetition and transformation of perversion: a turn or return to the material (and for Kristeva also maternal) object, a turn or return that brings signification back to the place where signification and sense are erased, pulverized, and destroyed, back to where the subject has been perverted, or reduced and minimized to a revolting and meaningless object. Kristeva calls this symbolic turn to the object (and concomitant return of the abject) a transmuting *père-version*, or better yet a *mère-version* (2002, 13).[2] In this essay, I will trace the development of this peculiar practice and minor mode of writing, and will call it a *merversion.*

The term is a version, in English, of Kristeva's neologism. I mean the term to evoke several things, ranging from the turn to the materials of the journal, to the parallel with, and the difference from perversion.

The effect of *Zona*'s merversion or its far-reaching, slow-burning, stretching, and inverted/inverting mode of writing is simultaneously reanimating to the minor literature of Puerto Rico and disturbing to the majority of the so-called Latin American Boom. In order to better visualize this effect, to describe *Zona*'s disturbing energy, or force, I will borrow two phenomena from the field of astrophysics: black-body radiation, and fossil light. According to Max Planck (1858–1947), "the surface of a body never emits rays, but rather it allows part of the rays coming from the interior to pass through" (Planck 1959, 4). In 1860, Gustav R. Kirchhoff (1824–1887) stated that a cavity without any source of radiation inside was a black body: an object that absorbs all electromagnetic radiation, or "heat radiation," being purely nonreflective and opaque (Kangro 1976, 134). However, its thick and unreflective surface still emitted what Max Thiesen (1849–1936) called black radiation, and its peculiar properties posed problems for the laws of thermodynamics (ibid., 184).[3] Fossil light refers to a similarly disturbing emission. It describes the potent but diffuse irradiation that remains after the explosion that gives origin to the universe: the Big Bang. It is a light that appears to break the laws of perception by suggesting the presence of a star to the astronomer, when in fact it bears witness to the absence of all stars.

The effect of *Zona* on its political and literary contexts (on the penal colony of Puerto Rico and on the Latin American Boom) is similar to the disturbing effect of black-body radiation and fossil light, both of which appear to liberate us from the laws governing physics, perception, and common sense, through a peculiar inversion of these very laws. From this perspective, the journal and its effect is not a rupture but a reaccommodation, a shift, or better still an inversion even of the function of mainstream or major literatures of the seventies, of which the Boom was perhaps the most spectacular example. The Argentinean art critic Marta Traba suggested just such a connection between Latin American writers and Puerto Rican artists when, in her polemical book on Puerto Rican art, she wrote that "current Latin American literature is different from its North American and European counterparts and the difference is in the way they have loaded the signifiers and have reestablished a dear or beloved relation between the word and what it signals and explains; and its value comes from this difference, which is an indisputable fact, even in the developed world" (Traba 1971, 68–69). *Zona* similarly reestablished a relation between the word and what it signals, though I would not describe the nature of its load as dear or beloved, like Traba does. Instead, I would describe *Zona*'s load or discharge as a form of black-body radiation or fossil light that inverted and transformed (perhaps even imploded) the laws and violent governing practices that rendered colonial subjects mute by reducing, minimizing, and turning their bodies of cultural expression into irrelevant literatures. *Zona* also inverted and transformed the literary forces that threatened to exhaust reading and writing practices with their emphasis on transparent communication, mimetic representation, and realism, magical or otherwise.

Zona's minor writing as merversion not only developed out of a violent, repressive, and penal context, but it also grew out of the influence and lessons of Cuban exiles Zilia Sánchez and Severo Sarduy. More specifically, writing as a mode of merversion developed out of the close relations between the stretched canvases of Sánchez's *Topologías eróticas* (1970) and the pages of the journal; and between Sarduy's concept of writing as a form of self-violence, a tortured, wracked, or martyred mode of signification described in *Escrito sobre un cuerpo* (1969), and the inscriptions and columns of the journal's writing. In each case, these two series of works and essays from two Cuban exiles were contained inside (even as they troubled) the still strangely nationalistic *Zona*, and both artists were paradoxically responsible for the turn of the journal to its object, to its materials, to the page and to what Derrida calls the graft.[4] Indeed, both Sarduy and Sánchez were responsible for giving *Zona*'s turn a distinctively corporeal and erotic dimension, a "homotextuality," to borrow a term from art critic Rudi Bleys.[5] And both are also at least partly responsible for the journal's effort to make signify again what appeared as ancillary, supplementary, in short, minor, to the surrounding culture of moral majorities, to the major writers from the Boom, and to the critics that followed them.

Zilia's Zone

Many if not all of the references to Zilia Sánchez in the criticism and testimonials about *Zona* give the impression that her contribution was perhaps limited to the technical aspects of production (Gelpí 1993, 173; Ibáñez 1992, 334). The criticism seems to echo the words of one of the journal's co-founders (and perhaps its central figure), Ferré, who states in an interview that Sánchez taught the members of the journal how to use color, how to move the type in the typesetting machines, and how to do the layout (García-Pinto 1988,

90, 93). Moreover, Sonia Labrador-Rodríguez correctly points out that the name of Sánchez disappears after *Zona* 5, when the photographer Gabriel Suau is credited with the graphic design and with the journal's cover (Labrador-Rodríguez 2007, 251).[6] But the criticism has missed the meaning of Sánchez's long-lasting technical contribution, which meaning Ferré suggests in a conference talk that she gave during a congress celebrated in her honor in 2005. She writes that "among the first to be recruited, Zilia Sánchez, a Cuban vanguard artist arrived to Puerto Rico one year earlier, was of the greatest importance. And it was Zilia who taught us how to make the journal, because she had been involved in similar projects in Cuba" (R. Ferré 2005).

The fact that Sánchez's principle of design outlasted her participation in the first three or four numbers of the journal also suggests her profound influence on its editors. This principle can perhaps be summarized as the notion of the page as both a tactile and visual art object and agent, as something more than a neutral and passive space that merely contained the more important writing and images. Instead, *Zona*'s page was a signifying space in itself; it gave support to the intersecting and parallel planes of color, type, and image; and it stretched the possibilities of the materials. This principle was never abandoned, as is evident from its gradual stylization until the last number of the journal. Arguably, even the decision to take the journal from Puerto Rico to New York for its last three issues can be traced back to Sánchez's influence. She had not only been involved in similar projects in Cuba (one of her works was featured on the cover of the journal *Ciclón*), but also in New York, where she was involved in the production of Dolores Prida's journal (*La Nueva Sangre*). Indeed, Sánchez had strong links to that city where she lived, studied, and worked for nine years before her arrival in Puerto Rico in 1971.[7] She studied printmaking at the Pratt Institute of New York, learned art restoration techniques at the Herbert E. Feist Gallery, and exhibited her work in some venues in the city including Galería Zegrí, Herbert E. Feist Gallery, and the Sarduy Gallery.

In fact, there is a connection between Sánchez's experience in New York and the importance of the page in *Zona*. In a prologue to the catalogue of an individual exhibit from 1970, Severo Sarduy gives an account of the development and progress of Sánchez's work. He identifies three stages. The third is marked by an emphatic turn to the canvas, which becomes both the object and subject of Sánchez's work, a turn that Sarduy traces to the New York minimalist school of art, and particularly to Robert Morris, Sol Lewitt, and Don Judd (Sarduy 1970). Her exhibits from 1970 and 1971 in New York and San Juan generated a number of critical assessments of her work by critics both from New York and from Latin America that confirm Sarduy's assessment.[8] All the critics also agree on the remarkable difference of Sánchez's frameless and modular constructions in wood and canvas from the formal abstractions of minimalist art. Like the latter, Sánchez's large format structures stress abstraction, numbers, and sequences. But unlike minimalist art, they also simulate heroic, even mythological, feminine body parts, and suggest an epidermal notion of desire with titles such as *Topología erótica* (1969), *Antígona* (1969), *Lunar III* (1970), and *Nacimiento de Eros* (*Topologias*) (1971). Prida suggests this difference in Sánchez's canvases when she signals a strange form of agency contained by her works: "There is a challenge in the silent lunar forms, in the undulating gray curves of bodies sensitive to a caress—woman" (quoted in *Zilia Sánchez: tres décadas*). In his prologue, Sarduy describes the difference of Sánchez's constructions in relation to the latest trends in writing, in Continental philosophy, and in literary theory as they appear in the French journal *Tel Quel*.[9] Sarduy implicitly criticizes minimalist art and the deconstructive codes of the French *nouveau roman* for their obsession with a pure and abstract object, and for abandoning the space that Sánchez's topologies insist upon: a tactile space supported by desire, voluptuousness, and erotics (*Zilia Sánchez: tres décadas*).[10]

Perhaps a discussion of Sánchez's works from this period, particularly of her *Topologías eróticas*, can shed some light on the meaning of her contribution to *Zona*. The word *topology* carries different, almost opposite meanings in the fields of physics and medicine. In physics, it describes the study of the properties of geometric figures or solids not normally affected by changes in size or shape, suggesting a formulaic, sequential system of signification or mathematical language. By contrast, in medicine topology refers to the anatomical structure of a specific area or part of the body, suggesting highly organic, if still somewhat abstract (structural) forms. In several of his essays from *Escrito sobre un cuerpo*, Sarduy takes advantage of this ambiguity in the word to signify a plane of existence (he calls it a zone) characterized by the flexibility necessary to maintain a certain tension, by the ability of this zone to sustain inversions, changes, and transformations. The motility of this zone is in contrast with the apparent rigidity of the economic or political reality of a fixed world determined by concepts such as class struggle, when reality is in fact nothing more than an unstable surface for Sarduy. Indeed, for him, topology is another word for the zone of signification, for the plane of language whose lines of force between its parts, whose tension between its signifiers, whose amatory violence, he describes as erotic (Sarduy 1969, 46). Sánchez turns this zone, metaphorically described by Sarduy, first into the canvases of her *Topologías eróticas* and then into the pages and general design of *Zona*.

Sánchez's Merversion

Sánchez works from the seventies and early eighties materialize this erotic zone: the lines of force and the horizontal and vertical planes that intersect it and give it form, according to Sarduy. Sánchez's series *Topologías* is defined by a minimal use of materials belonging to the visual arts and sculpture (canvas, acrylic paint, and wood). She stretches the materials out, up, down, and forward beyond the plane of an always frameless modular form. Many of her works reach heroic dimensions, some of them standing vertically seventy-two inches tall, and stretching out to what is often a fine point from a flat surface (Fig. 4.1).

The works function as screens for a complex and invisible skeleton, a wooden and angular support structure that stands behind the canvas, pushing up against its flexible surface, combining rigid with malleable planes, softening the rough texture of the wood. The surface is stretched and extended to simulate folding, caressing, and touching feminine sexual body parts (highly abstract and stylized details that suggest nipples, labia, navels, vulvas, urinary tracts, anuses, clitoris, and the end of the urethra), which in turn project into, and enter, another space, both laterally and frontally, sending out imaginary lines or rays or even tendrils that seem to go in all directions, reaching and touching the contiguous canvas and the viewer. The colors of the works are muted, subtle shades of white, gray, and silver, but also radiant, as if meant to reflect blindingly the bright light of the Caribbean sun.[11] Colors are often arranged in round forms or concentric circles that surround the projecting and radiating surfaces, adding another degree of tension to the already tensile structure of the work, suggesting an irritation on the skin of the canvas, pain, but also contrast and beauty, brought about by the intensity of the stretch. When joined together, the modular pieces create a negative space between them, an imaginary folding plane that is perpendicular to the mostly vertical surface of the canvas, and an invisible plane that complements the imaginary lines projected out from the end of the pointed protuberances. This perpendicular, negative, invisible plane is like a flat curving horizon that stretches out from the work to touch, surround, and then leave the viewer, going beyond him, to the infinite.

FIGURE 4.1. Zilia Sánchez. *Topología erótica (Serie las amazonas)*. 72" × 42". 1978. Reproduced with permission from the artist.

The meaning of the language of Sánchez's *Topologías eróticas*, its homotextuality, if you will, is the effect of this system of signifying materials, of the tension or amatory violence between its components, of the signifying force of the canvas, the wood, and the color. This effect is a tactile motility that is transformative in nature. It is a touch or point of contact between the components of the work of art, between the artwork and the viewer; a point of contact that changes both the space of the canvas and of the viewer. It is nothing less than a transformation and opening of an otherwise empty, closed, and neutral space. It is a resignification of the until-now invisible and inert space between the materials of the work, between the work and viewer, as well as a transformation of the space of the viewer who is touched and contaminated by the radiating topologies of the work. In other words, the meaning of the topologies is an inversion of the truths that common sense and convention dictate, truths that order the space of contact with, and the rules that govern, the encounter with the work of art. Truths and rules that establish the principle of distance and separation not only between the different materials but also between the art work and the viewer. Sánchez's works interrogate these truths, including the question of the meaning and value of the material origin of the work of art. The viewer of Sánchez's works leaves the scene of the encounter asking whether canvas, wood, paint—in short, the objects or so-called materials of art—have meaning, and whether they have meaningful value in and of themselves, whether they are alive. It is no wonder that Prida asks, "Who is watching whom?" when she is faced with these topologies (*Zilia Sánchez: tres décadas*).

Sánchez's tactile inversions are a particular form of merversion—the inversion of the perverse practices of master subjects who reduce others to mere objects of their fantasies and pleasures. Her canvases signify a return to the fetish, to the maternal abject, to the overdetermined and violent Freudian fantasy of the phallus (Freud 1963, 215). But a return that brings with it a difference and comes with an inversion, a turn, a revolt, a negativity, perhaps an invagination, which aims to bring back signification to the place where signification is erased. One finds the peculiar force of Sánchez's mode of merversion, the unique strength of her repetition and inversion of the tensile, tortured, erased, surface of the maternal abject, in its minor key. The force of her canvases is located in their subtle glow, in their inverse and intense heat, or what I called earlier their black-body radiation. This zone or topology of negative radiation is perhaps most visible in *Nacimiento de Eros* (*Topologias*), a work from 1971 (Fig. 4.2), and its effect is acutely felt and contained by the pages of *Zona*. But a careful study of the radiation

FIGURE 4.2. Zilia Sánchez. *Nacimiento de Eros*. 90" × 116.5". 1971. Collection of the Museo de Arte de Puerto Rico. Reproduced with permission from the artist.

coming from Sánchez's canvases and its effect on *Zona* must be preceded by a description of the artistic context where the journal (as art object) is first imprinted with an aesthetic of ironic self-violence.

Myrna Báez's Negatives and Dark Humor

Labrador-Rodríguez's careful examination of the first layer or topology of color, image, and editorial content of the journal reveals what she is right to call an "aesthetic of violence" (2007, 248). Such an aesthetic makes sense from the perspective of a minor literature trying to make meaning by repeating and inverting the direction of the explosive forces going off in the highly politicized context of Puerto Rico's penal colony. It is as if the handling of the "loads" but also the "energy discharges" of its title were a symbolic reaction to the shocks, and a resignification of the radiation from the literally explosive

Cold War fought in Puerto Rico during the late sixties and early seventies.[12] These traumatic shocks included systematic bombings of territories of Puerto Rico (Culebra and Vieques) by the training forces of the U.S. Navy in preparation for the bombing campaigns of Vietnam; bombings of U.S. and Puerto Rican retail stores, hotels, and Federal properties by Nationalist terrorist groups in protest and opposition to the Vietnam War and to the political status of the island; burnings by student protesters (probably infiltrated and agitated by undercover government agents) of the R.O.T.C. buildings on university grounds; persecution and police brutality against university students leading to deaths among the students and police; burnings of the headquarters and newspaper of the opposition political party, and bombing of the cars of their leaders by right-wing anti-Castro Cuban terrorist groups; and even the first accident in the history of nuclear power in Latin America (Baralt 1998, 112–14, 116–21).[13] In the words of a character from a novel reviewed by *Zona* and described as required reading (*Zona* 1: 20): "Things [in Puerto Rico] are getting hot, real hot!" (Díaz-Valcárcel 1972, 351).

In her polemical review of Puerto Rican painting and visual arts, Traba reminds us that we should not consider this period in the history of Puerto Rican cultural production as a unique and singularly violent moment of irruption, subversion, or transition, tempted as we might be to do so. Instead, Traba makes the compelling point that there is a valuable and highly individualistic tradition in Puerto Rican artistic production that expresses obliquely and never belligerently a somber, melancholy, and even morbid tone of anxiety, a troubled and troubling aggressive passivity, sometimes represented in painting as an uncanny zone of contact with a monstrous vegetation, and by a "defective illumination," a peculiar light that she describes as "unrefined, blunt, and beaten" (Traba 1971, 55, 58). Traba traces this longstanding tradition back to Lorenzo Homar and Rafael Tufiño, famous Puerto Rican printmakers, engravers, woodcut and silk screen artists established during the forties and fifties who were inspired by (even as they transformed) Mexican muralist art from the thirties and forties. She finds the best expression of this tradition in the canvases from the sixties by Puerto Rican painter Francisco Rodón, and particularly in the ghostly light invading a pair of paintings representing a mother and her daughter (the sister and the niece of the artist): the *Primera Inés* and the *Tercera Inés*, respectively (ibid., 58). She also suggests that Myrna Báez, the youngest member of the seventies generation of painters, transposes this sustained and eerie beaten illumination into a painterly technique that also marks her works with a reversing tradition analogous to that of the minor writers. Traba compares Báez's paintings to "anti-bodies" that reverse, from the very inside of the diseased social body, the effect of the antigen or of the invasive surrounding culture (ibid., 62, 67). Traba suggests that Báez similarly torments her subjects (Traba describes Báez's representation of her subjects as *supliciadas* or "tormented") with her innovative version of this familiar negative light: her own and uniquely reversible "cut" (ibid., 129, 131).

This peculiar light is well represented in Báez's series of negatives that follow her 1970 collograph *El juez*, winner of the Prize for Graphics at the Pratt Institute of New York for that year.[14] The series dates between 1970 and 1976 and it includes similar experiments with negative light including *La espera* (1971), *Afuera el verde* (1971), *Fuga* (1972), *Sombra y celaje* (1973), *Positivo-negativo* (1973), *La lámpara Tiffany* (1976), and *Sin título* (1976). The series ends with *Noviembre 1976*, but perhaps the best example of its negative light is an acrylic painting on canvas of Báez's mother from 1972 titled *Tríptico (Retrato de América Báez)* (Fig. 4.3), which intensifies the beaten illumination of an earlier portrait of Báez's mother from 1961.

FIGURE 4.3. Myrna Báez. *Tríptico (Retrato de América Báez)*. 40" × 48.5". 1972. Collection of the Museo de Arte de Puerto Rico. Reproduced with permission from the artist.

Significantly, the triptych also changes the serious tone of the earlier maternal portrait to a more irreverent commentary and representation of what could perhaps be described as a form of maternal straying.

The triptych is an almost literal example, or a visually spectacular simulacrum, of the symbolic operation that I have been calling here a merversion. The relatively large canvas (40 inches by 48 ½ inches) is divided into three zones. The central panel shows the maternal subject sitting quietly, hands folded, legs crossed, on a chair, wearing a simple dress. The colors are washed-out grays, blues, and greens. The features are vague as if worn out. América Báez looks out calmly from the painting with eyes that look more like dark sockets. The central panel is framed by two others, both of them painted to simulate negative versions of the positive portrait at the center. They show the same subject sitting down on one side, standing up on the other, in a negative of the color spectrum on one side (where blues become reds and orange), and a simpler black and white version simulating a photographic negative on the other. The painting can be interpreted to make visible, even literal, the symbolic merversions (oblique, and indirect) so characteristic of the tormented tradition of Puerto Rican art, its revolting attention and abject return to the exhausted materials of Western art, resisting the move toward abstraction, insisting on a superannuated figurative language, outmoded and inverted, dramatizing the force of the double negative perhaps, an eerie positive created from the contact with two negatives.

Art critic Rudi Bleys rightly points out that "repression and censorship clearly nurtures Báez's work," further suggesting that her visual language screens models of erased identities including homosexual identities (2000, 110). And Báez's attention to the exclusion and erasure of abject figures that fall through the cracks (both in terms of technique and subject matter) is perhaps best represented by the dog, front center, head down, averting eyes, that strangely inhabits both the negative and the positive zones of the painting. Dogs, cats, and animals in general are recurring figures in the work of Báez. Here, the dog is stray in many senses of that word. It strays in the sense that it inhabits an interstice, an in-between space between the planes of the painting. It is stray also in the sense that it appears to have no collar, no identifying mark, no owner, and no name. Finally, the dog makes the painting stray from its seriousness of purpose. Its pose intensifies the mother's calm and sedate composure despite the symbolic fire that consumes her. Beaten but also vibrant with the negative light that Traba found so peculiar to Puerto Rican art, the dog is surrounded by a paradoxical aura of strength that comes from its passive character, from a surrender or "submission" (Traba 1971, 62). Indeed, the dog sits as a double of the spectral image of América Báez, who in turn sits behind the dog, "cut" and beaten (but also glowing) with a similar negative light. The posture, colors, and illumination of the figures screen the paradoxically self-sacrificial nature of this mode of merversion so peculiar to Puerto Rican artists, where the stab at the mother is also a stab at the self.[15]

There is a danger, however, in taking this reading too seriously and too far. A quick review of Báez's paintings reveals a tendency to joke and play, though it is significant that many of her jokes are dark both in content and in form. There is, for example, an ironic, if also playful, quality in her repeated juxtaposition of human and animal subjects, adding a layer of levity to her otherwise serious compositions. Beginning with *El roble blanco* (1963), many of her human subjects share their portraits with animals that seem to be just passing through, including an acrylic titled *La perra sata* (1981) and her self-portrait from 1986.[16] She also shows a preference for stark representations of subjects at play, beginning with works such as *Ciclistas* (1963) and *Juego de cartas* (1970). Finally, with *La Gioconda* (1973), Báez begins a long series of irreverent appropriations of classical works that transpose them to tropical and often quite funny settings, the best of which might be her version of Susanna and the Elders set in a bathtub (*Susana después del baño*, 1994). As we shall see below, *Zona* also contains and redeploys the dark humor that is characteristic of Báez's works.

Indeed, focusing on the negative series of paintings by Báez and on their mode of merversion or self-undoing, which is characterized by the negative light of burnt (rather than burning) figures, reveals that the first topology of *Zona. Carga y Descarga* has much in common with this light. Through the lens of these paintings, or transparencies, from Báez's negative series, *Zona* comes strangely alive. It comes alive as a transposition or application of Báez's painterly practice to the page, the images, and the type of the journal. One could call it *Zona*'s "eclipse effect," best represented by a photograph illustrating Ramos Otero's story "Pilgrimage for an Eclipse," which dramatizes in its narrative the inverted, mysterious, and ominous light that marks Puerto Rican reality for him (*Zona* 3: 12–13). The photograph shows the negative shadows (in white) of two bodies lying flat on a black bedcover, as if their silhouette were the remains of an atomic explosion. More examples of this use of almost radioactive photography are found in the later issues of *Zona*, as Ramos Otero (1948–1990) becomes more involved as editor of the journal (*Zona* 4: 20–23; *Zona* 7: 29, 30; *Zona* 8: 5, 9, 15; *Zona* 9: 2, 25).

The use of black pages inscribed with brightly white type in *Zona* is a literal representation of these negative inversions, or of this negative light. It gives the page the appearance of burnt paper and the print the appearance of an element that burns through it, like the material remains from an exploded star (*Zona* 3: 18; *Zona* 4: 17). There is a similar deployment of the negative quality of the color of Báez on the cover and centerfold of *Zona* 6, which lists the famous Puerto Rican engraver Homar as a consultant for this number. The editors take this negative effect to an extreme in the inverted cover of *Zona* 7, which not only places the white type on black background on its front page, but also places the front matter (title and contents of the journal) on its last page. Similarly, the use of an almost radioactive color in the covers and centerfolds of *Zona* is less indebted to the experiments of Pop Art, than to the experiments with self-undoing of a long Puerto Rican tradition of painting and printmaking. Together, these effects bring the merversions of the Puerto Rican aesthetic tradition to the page of *Zona*: its tormented art, its beaten light and punished subjects, its peculiar mode of surrendered and passive resistance, and its self-sacrifice.

Labrador-Rodríguez points to the ultimately limited and perhaps counterproductive effect of this topology of *Zona*. Its self-violence threatens to become a repetition of the revolts and revolutions of the political and artistic context, leading even to an imaginary or literal auto-da-fé. It threatens to loose the levity and humor contained in Báez's maternal stray dog, for example. Indeed, it is not surprising that Ferré remembers the widespread tendency to burn either *Zona* 7 or *Zona* 8 soon after it reached the newsstands and bookstores (García Pinto 1988, 91; Perry 1993, 92). From this perspective, Labrador-Rodríguez provocatively suggests that *Zona*'s explosive mixture of art and politics ultimately led it to close itself off from its readers, and to implode into what can perhaps be described as an example of self-combustion. However, *Zona* is intersected by more than one plane of signification or typology, and while one cannot dismiss the presence and the ambiguous (both troubled and troubling) effect on *Zona* of the self-sacrificial and melancholy tradition of Puerto Rican art, it is also true that Sánchez's presence and contributions insisted on an erotic topology that opened up the journal to a sensual mode of wracked, inverted, writing that together with a dark humor characteristic of Puerto Rican art was perhaps the journal's most lasting effect. A description of Sánchez's *Nacimiento de Eros* will take us some distance in this direction.

Overexposures

Nacimiento de Eros (*Topologías*) is a large, even monumental stretched canvas on wood from 1971, one year before the publication of *Zona* 1. Its heroic dimensions are 90 inches tall by 116 ½ inches wide. Like many of Sánchez's works from this series, it is rectangular in shape, it has no frame, and contains two geometric details, off-center, to the right of the canvas. The title of the topology, *Nacimiento de Eros*, suggests that the details might simulate parts of the maternal reproductive body: a navel and labia rarified, stylized, and abstracted almost beyond recognition. The title also gives a particular meaning to the stretch of the canvas that slopes gradually up from the sides of the rectangle to the top of the subtle protrusions. The canvas creates the illusion of a negative space behind the taut skinlike surface, a tensile space that pushes the canvas out, a hidden and invisible support that gives the work a subtle topographic complexity, a gentle curve, that is intensified by the slightly off-kilter location of the protruding details. The work also creates the illusion of warmth, a slow burning heat emanating from the canvas itself, the simulacrum of an irritation, a skin rash, a boil even, emanating from inside the pores of the canvas, an illusion created by the light that reflects off its silver white surface, and by the washed-out gold frames that shadow with subtle color the space surrounding the two protuberances. Eros is here far from its classical depiction as an angelic figure with bow and arrow, with a blindfold, and sometimes as a baby. Eros is instead an amatory violence, a passion represented by a form of heat, a negative heat, invisible, radiating out from, and through, the stretched, tortured, body-like canvas, at the very moment when the canvas threatens to burst, to rupture, to open painfully into a combusting flame.

It is instructive to study the pages of *Zona* through the lens of these canvases by Sánchez. The pages of *Zona* are a similarly privileged space made evident by their size, weight, and color. Indeed, Sánchez emphasized all of these properties when she was in charge of its design. Perhaps under the influence of her large canvases, *Zona* grows from a slightly yellow, thinner and lighter paper 16 ½ by 11 inches in *Zona* 1, to a whiter, thicker, heavier, and bigger paper 17 by 12 inches in *Zona* 2.[17] And its large dimensions remain the same until the end. A quick review of the pages of *Zona* also shows that it is cleverly and creatively manipulated to create the feeling in the reader of a topographical landscape, of a tattooed skin, and even of a living body. The editors achieve this effect with images and drawings of eyes, feet, pores, ears, and beating hearts, sometimes complemented with onomatopoeic writing like "PUM PUM PUM PUM PUM PUM PUM PUM" (*Zona* 3: 22). The journal's large dimensions, combined with its unusual arrangement of the type and images, also calls attention to the spine, the texture, the surface, and more importantly constitutes the primary motor for the movement of the page. The reader of *Zona* needs to fold and turn the unwieldy pages around in an effort to read the journal. But *Zona*'s strongest and perhaps its surviving "life" comes partly from the subtle and vibrant spaces created in between the plane of the page and the other signifying layers of the journal (color, type, and images).

Arguably, these intermediary spaces, planes, zones, or typologies give the journal its most significant depth and movement, and also its supporting and malleable structure. They are the zones of contact that give materiality and meaning to an otherwise invisible, marginal, and transparent layer of the journal. They are as invisible and as far-reaching as the radiating heat and slow-burning topologies that project out from Sánchez's canvases. Rather than containing the harsh, punished, and punishing light of *Zona*'s negatives, these zones instead hold and reflect a different light. This light can be compared to the illumination or negative heat provided from overexposure in photography. The gold and gray cover of *Zona* 2, and other similar experiments in the first three numbers of Zona with overexposed photographs (cf., *Zona* 1: 10–11, 18; *Zona* 2: 4, 14, 24; and *Zona* 3: 11) contain and emit this negative heat also similar to black-body radiation. And its function is to retrieve a lost (closed or invisible) space between the page and the print of the journal. It does so through a process that is similar to the pentimento effect in painting, where an older image bleeds through the canvas and reappears, gradually inverting not only spatial binaries (what is in front, and what is in back), but also temporal ones (what was in the past, and what is in the present), slowly changing, transforming, and interrogating our basic assumptions about the stability of reality (Fig. 4.4). From this angle, *Zona's* effect is also analogous to the fossil light from Alpha Centauri that begins this essay, and that Sarduy compares to the residue and to the remains of bodies, whether human, animal or stellar, in his 1974 book *Big Bang* (1999, 168–69).

Zona's process of radical inversion and its revelations can be traced back to the emissions from Sánchez's overexposed canvases, to their heat or black-body radiation, and to their effects on the viewer. So far, I have mostly explored the effect of an overexposure similar to the photographic technique of leaving open the aperture of the lens in order to allow an excessive amount of light to enter. However, both *Zona* and Sánchez's canvases are overexposed in yet another sense. They also double or triple the exposure of a naked body, and they bring into view, front and center, sexualities considered either minor or invisible by the moral majorities and by the major writers of the Latin American Boom: feminine sexuality and homosexuality. On the one hand, *Zona* and Sánchez overexpose this sexualized body as a tormented system of signification and as a minor language. On the other, they suggest the far-reach

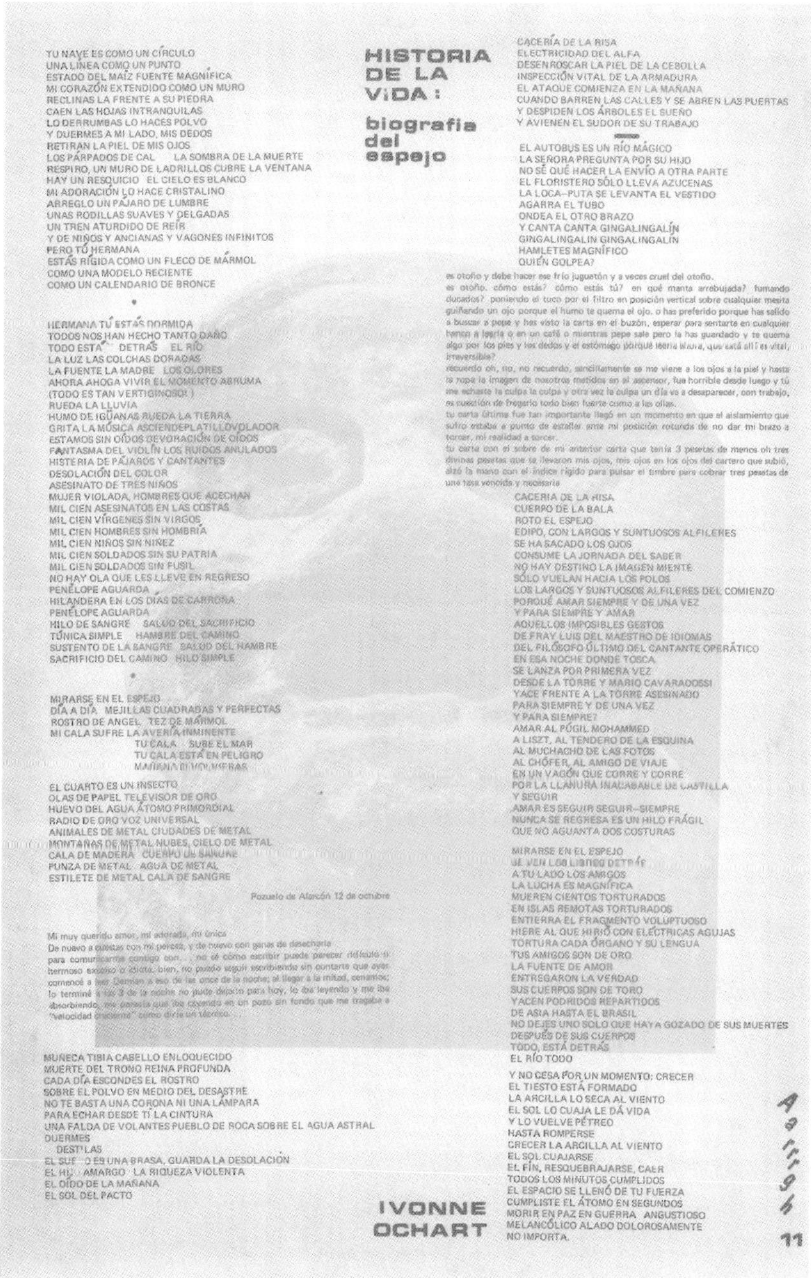
HISTORIA DE LA VIDA: biografia del espejo

TU NAVE ES COMO UN CÍRCULO
UNA LÍNEA COMO UN PUNTO
ESTADO DEL MAÍZ FUENTE MAGNÍFICA
MI CORAZÓN EXTENDIDO COMO UN MURO
RECLINAS LA FRENTE A SU PIEDRA
CAEN LAS HOJAS INTRANQUILAS
LO DERRUMBAS LO HACES POLVO
Y DUERMES A MI LADO, MIS DEDOS
RETIRAN LA PIEL DE MIS OJOS
LOS PÁRPADOS DE CAL LA SOMBRA DE LA MUERTE
RESPIRO, UN MURO DE LADRILLOS CUBRE LA VENTANA
HAY UN RESQUICIO EL CIELO ES BLANCO
MI ADORACIÓN LO HACE CRISTALINO
ARREGLO UN PÁJARO DE LUMBRE
UNAS RODILLAS SUAVES Y DELGADAS
UN TREN ATURDIDO DE REÍR
Y DE NIÑOS Y ANCIANAS Y VAGONES INFINITOS
PERO TÚ HERMANA
ESTÁS RÍGIDA COMO UN FLECO DE MÁRMOL
COMO UNA MODELO RECIENTE
COMO UN CALENDARIO DE BRONCE

•

HERMANA TÚ ESTÁS DORMIDA
TODOS NOS HAN HECHO TANTO DAÑO
TODO ESTÁ DETRÁS EL RÍO
LA LUZ LAS COLCHAS DORADAS
LA FUENTE LA MADRE LOS OLORES
AHORA AHOGA VIVIR EL MOMENTO ABRUMA
(TODO ES TAN VERTIGINOSO!)
RUEDA LA LLUVIA
HUMO DE IGUANAS RUEDA LA TIERRA
GRITA LA MÚSICA ASCIENDEPLATILLOVOLADOR
ESTAMOS SIN OÍDOS DEVORACIÓN DE OÍDOS
FANTASMA DEL VIOLÍN LOS RUIDOS ANULADOS
HISTERIA DE PÁJAROS Y CANTANTES
DESOLACIÓN DEL COLOR
ASESINATO DE TRES NIÑOS
MUJER VIOLADA, HOMBRES QUE ACECHAN
MIL CIEN ASESINATOS EN LAS COSTAS
MIL CIEN VÍRGENES SIN VIRGOS
MIL CIEN HOMBRES SIN HOMBRÍA
MIL CIEN NIÑOS SIN NIÑEZ
MIL CIEN SOLDADOS SIN SU PATRIA
MIL CIEN SOLDADOS SIN FUSIL
NO HAY OLA QUE LES LLEVE EN REGRESO
PENÉLOPE AGUARDA
HILANDERA EN LOS DÍAS DE CARROÑA
PENÉLOPE AGUARDA
HILO DE SANGRE SALUD DEL SACRIFICIO
TÚNICA SIMPLE HAMBRE DEL CAMINO
SUSTENTO DE LA SANGRE SALUD DEL HAMBRE
SACRIFICIO DEL CAMINO HILO SIMPLE

•

MIRARSE EN EL ESPEJO
DÍA A DÍA MEJILLAS CUADRADAS Y PERFECTAS
ROSTRO DE ANGEL TEZ DE MÁRMOL
MI CALA SUFRE LA AVERÍA INMINENTE
TU CALA SUBE EL MAR
TU CALA ESTÁ EN PELIGRO
MAÑANA EL VOLVERÁS

EL CUARTO ES UN INSECTO
OLAS DE PAPEL TELEVISOR DE ORO
HUEVO DEL AGUA ÁTOMO PRIMORDIAL
RADIO DE ORO VOZ UNIVERSAL
ANIMALES DE METAL CIUDADES DE METAL
MONTAÑAS DE METAL NUBES, CIELO DE METAL
CALA DE MADERA CUERPO DE SANGRE
PUNZA DE METAL AGUA DE METAL
ESTILETE DE METAL CALA DE SANGRE

Pozuelo de Alarcón 12 de octubre

Mi muy querido amor, mi adorada, mi única
De nuevo a cuestas con mi pereza, y de nuevo con ganas de desecharla para comunicarme contigo con. . . no sé cómo escribir puede parecer ridículo o hermoso excelso o idiota. bien, no puedo seguir escribiendo sin contarte que ayer comencé a leer Demian a eso de las once de la noche; al llegar a la mitad, cenamos; lo terminé a las 3 de la noche no pude dejarlo para hoy, lo iba leyendo y me iba absorbiendo, me parecía que iba cayendo en un pozo sin fondo que me tragaba a "velocidad creciente" como diría un técnico. . .

MUÑECA TIBIA CABELLO ENLOQUECIDO
MUERTE DEL TRONO REINA PROFUNDA
CADA DÍA ESCONDES EL ROSTRO
SOBRE EL POLVO EN MEDIO DEL DESASTRE
NO TE BASTA UNA CORONA NI UNA LÁMPARA
PARA ECHAR DESDE TI LA CINTURA
UNA FALDA DE VOLANTES PUEBLO DE ROCA SOBRE EL AGUA ASTRAL
DUERMES
DESTILAS
EL SUEÑO ES UNA BRASA, GUARDA LA DESOLACIÓN
EL HIJO AMARGO LA RIQUEZA VIOLENTA
EL OÍDO DE LA MAÑANA
EL SOL DEL PACTO

CACERÍA DE LA RISA
ELECTRICIDAD DEL ALFA
DESENROSCAR LA PIEL DE LA CEBOLLA
INSPECCIÓN VITAL DE LA ARMADURA
EL ATAQUE COMIENZA EN LA MAÑANA
CUANDO BARREN LAS CALLES Y SE ABREN LAS PUERTAS
Y DESPIDEN LOS ÁRBOLES EL SUEÑO
Y AVIENEN EL SUDOR DE SU TRABAJO

EL AUTOBÚS ES UN RÍO MÁGICO
LA SEÑORA PREGUNTA POR SU HIJO
NO SÉ QUÉ HACER LA ENVÍO A OTRA PARTE
EL FLORISTERO SÓLO LLEVA AZUCENAS
LA LOCA–PUTA SE LEVANTA EL VESTIDO
AGARRA EL TUBO
ONDEA EL OTRO BRAZO
Y CANTA CANTA GINGALINGALÍN
GINGALINGALIN GINGALINGALÍN
HAMLETES MAGNÍFICO
QUIÉN GOLPEA?

es otoño y debe hacer ese frío juguetón y a veces cruel del otoño.
es otoño. cómo estás? cómo estás tú? en qué manta arrebujada? fumando ducados? poniendo el tuco por el filtro en posición vertical sobre cualquier mesita guiñando un ojo porque el humo te quema el ojo. o has preferido porque has salido a buscar a pepe y has visto la carta en el buzón, esperar para sentarte en cualquier banco a leerla o en un café o mientras pepe sale pero la has guardado y te quema algo por los pies y los dedos y el estómago porque leerla ahora, que está allí es vital, irreversible?
recuerdo oh, no, no recuerdo, sencillamente se me viene a los ojos a la piel y hasta la ropa la imagen de nosotros metidos en el ascensor, fue horrible desde luego y tú me echaste la culpa la culpa y otra vez la culpa un día va a desaparecer, con trabajo, es cuestión de fregarlo todo bien fuerte como a las ollas.
tu carta última fue tan importante llegó en un momento en que el aislamiento que sufro estaba a punto de estallar ante mi posición rotunda de no dar mi brazo a torcer, mi realidad a torcer.
tu carta con el sobre de mi anterior carta que tenía 3 pesetas de menos oh tres divinas pesetas que te llevaron mis ojos, mis ojos en los ojos del cartero que subió, alzó la mano con el índice rígido para pulsar el timbre para cobrar tres pesetas de una tasa vencida y necesaria

CACERIA DE LA RISA
CUERPO DE LA BALA
ROTO EL ESPEJO
EDIPO, CON LARGOS Y SUNTUOSOS ALFILERES
SE HA SACADO LOS OJOS
CONSUME LA JORNADA DEL SABER
NO HAY DESTINO LA IMAGEN MIENTE
SÓLO VUELAN HACIA LOS POLOS
LOS LARGOS Y SUNTUOSOS ALFILERES DEL COMIENZO
PORQUÉ AMAR SIEMPRE Y DE UNA VEZ
Y PARA SIEMPRE Y AMAR
AQUELLOS IMPOSIBLES GESTOS
DE FRAY LUIS DEL MAESTRO DE IDIOMAS
DEL FILÓSOFO ÚLTIMO DEL CANTANTE OPERÁTICO
EN ESA NOCHE DONDE TOSCA
SE LANZA POR PRIMERA VEZ
DESDE LA TORRE Y MARIO CAVARADOSSI
YACE FRENTE A LA TORRE ASESINADO
PARA SIEMPRE Y DE UNA VEZ
Y PARA SIEMPRE?
AMAR AL PÚGIL MOHAMMED
A LISZT, AL TENDERO DE LA ESQUINA
AL MUCHACHO DE LAS FOTOS
AL CHÓFER, AL AMIGO DE VIAJE
EN UN VAGÓN QUE CORRE Y CORRE
POR LA LLANURA INACABABLE DE CASTILLA
Y SEGUIR
AMAR ES SEGUIR SEGUIR–SIEMPRE
NUNCA SE REGRESA ES UN HILO FRÁGIL
QUE NO AGUANTA DOS COSTURAS

MIRARSE EN EL ESPEJO
SE VEN LOS LIBROS DETRÁS
A TU LADO LOS AMIGOS
LA LUCHA ES MAGNÍFICA
MUEREN CIENTOS TORTURADOS
EN ISLAS REMOTAS TORTURADOS
ENTIERRA EL FRAGMENTO VOLUPTUOSO
HIERE AL QUE HIRIÓ CON ELÉCTRICAS AGUJAS
TORTURA CADA ÓRGANO Y SU LENGUA
TUS AMIGOS SON DE ORO
LA FUENTE DE AMOR
ENTREGARON LA VERDAD
SUS CUERPOS SON DE TORO
YACEN PODRIDOS REPARTIDOS
DE ASIA HASTA EL BRASIL
NO DEJES UNO SOLO QUE HAYA GOZADO DE SUS MUERTES
DESPUÉS DE SUS CUERPOS
TODO, ESTÁ DETRÁS
EL RÍO TODO

Y NO CESA POR UN MOMENTO: CRECER
EL TIESTO ESTÁ FORMADO
LA ARCILLA LO SECA AL VIENTO
EL SOL LO CUAJA LE DÁ VIDA
Y LO VUELVE PÉTREO
HASTA ROMPERSE
CRECER LA ARCILLA AL VIENTO
EL SOL CUAJARSE
EL FÍN, RESQUEBRAJARSE, CAER
TODOS LOS MINUTOS CUMPLIDOS
EL ESPACIO SE LLENÓ DE TU FUERZA
CUMPLISTE EL ÁTOMO EN SEGUNDOS
MORIR EN PAZ EN GUERRA ANGUSTIOSO
MELANCÓLICO ALADO DOLOROSAMENTE
NO IMPORTA.

IVONNE OCHART

Aarrigh

11

FIGURE 4.4. Rosario Ferré et al. *Zona. Carga y Descarga* 3 (1973): 11.

(and the liberating promise) of its language of erotic inversions, which are often playful and irreverently funny. On both accounts, Sarduy's study of the sadistic origins of writing, and his concept of a self-violent, wracked, or martyred form of writing developed in *Escrito sobre un cuerpo*, are central to fathom this topology of *Zona* both as a self-undoing or a self-sacrificial practice which nevertheless returns meaning to what has been reduced to meaninglessness by the surrounding culture and its explosive languages.

Sarduy in *Zona*

It is likely that Sarduy's long-lasting friendship with Sánchez helped to bring her to *Zona*. In her "Notes about *Zona de Carga y Descarga*," Ferré writes that "Zilia was friends with Severo Sarduy and I knew Severo. Severo gave me her address and we contacted her" (R. Ferré 2005). Sánchez and Sarduy had met in Cuba, nineteen years before, in 1953.[18] They were both involved in the Cuban journal *Ciclón*, and Sarduy wrote positively about Sánchez's work in the 1956 catalogue of her second individual exhibit at Galería Cubana (Sarduy 1970).[19] In 1969, Sánchez was part of a group exhibit of Cuban Painting in New York at Galería Sarduy, owned by Severo Sarduy's cousin Rosa María Sarduy. A year later, in 1970, Sánchez also had an individual exhibit at Galería Sarduy, favorably reviewed by Stephen Spector of *Arts Magazine*. That same year, Sarduy again praised her work in the prologue to the catalogue of Sanchez's exhibit at the University of Puerto Rico Museum, titled "*Estructuras en secuencias*." Curiously, these last two documents share a misspelling of both of their first names (Zilia Sánchez is called Cecilia Sánchez by Spector, and Severo Sarduy appears as Sevedo Sarduy in the catalogue), suggesting that beyond sharing some success in their respective crafts, they were also united by a misrecognition owning perhaps to their relative obscurity and invisibility as minor artists.

In his essay on Sánchez, Sarduy gives a compelling account of the phases of Sánchez's work up to 1970. Most importantly, however, he describes the scriptural quality of her work as a denunciation of the naturalistic, mimetic, conventions of art. More specifically, he finds a theoretical intuition in Sánchez's bas-reliefs, and in her modular and sequential canvases. For Sarduy, Sánchez's canvases embody the theoretical principles that he develops in his book of essays, *Escrito sobre un cuerpo*. Modular, stretched, and tactile, the canvases are arranged in arbitrary sequences, and they exemplify the recuperative (if also vexed) force and practice of language for Sarduy. They actualize in space (and in the skin of the canvas) what constitutes the prime mover for Sarduy: the ludic meaningfulness of language, as both a tense, a wracked, and a martyred system of differential signs (like Traba describing the subjects of Báez's painting, Sarduy describes representation in language as *supliciado* or "tormented"), and as a related erotic display of desire and voluptuousness. Sánchez's emphasis on the paradoxical nature of the materials of art, and in particular on the monochromatic canvas as both a supporting topology, and as a stretched layer that experiences the tensing effects on it of an invisible rack, coincide with Sarduy's similar emphasis on the paradoxical building blocks of art as both a support for a disseminating practice, and as a blank and wounded space constituted by a radical loss.[20] *Zona*'s tortured page, taken to the limit of what it can handle, not only coincides with Sánchez's topologies (similarly stretched to their limit or *supliciadas,* martyred), but also with Sarduy's account of both literary and artistic production as a process of inversion, sublimation, and refinement of the Enlightenment's sadistic violence.[21] Given their friendship, and the similarities both theoretical and otherwise contained in their artistic production, it is not surprising that Sarduy was featured prominently in *Zona*, particularly in the journal's third number, when Sánchez was still responsible for its design.

Sarduy's theoretical appeal for the designer and for the editors of *Zona* was complemented by his position at the margins of the so-called Boom of the Latin American novel. *Zona's* editors had made it plain that their intention was to establish connections in literature between the writers of the island and their counterparts in Latin America during the intense literary production and visibility of the Boom. To do so, the editors structured the journal as a space where their readers got to know writers from Puerto Rico and from Latin America from three separate but related perspectives. To carry out its mission, and justify its appeal, they featured their work; they also interviewed some of them; and finally they reviewed some of their books. However, Mario Vargas Llosa was the only recognized writer belonging to the Boom who contributed unpublished material to *Zona*.[22] Perhaps the fact that he had been a professor at the University of Puerto Rico prompted him to do so. He contributed a fragment from his novel *Pantaleón y las visitadoras* (1975) which was included in *Zona* 4. Notably, while many of the writers featured in *Zona* wrote letters of encouragement and gratitude to the editors, Vargas Llosa delegated this task to his wife Patricia, who conveyed her husband's enthusiasm and gratitude to "Rosario and Olguita" (*Zona* 2: 2).

Lesser-known writers and novelists such as Sánchez, Jorge Aguilar Mora, José Luis González, Héctor Manjarrez, Edgardo Rodríguez Juliá, and Eduardo Gudiño Kieffer also appeared in the journal (cf. Ibáñez 1992, 341).[23]

And only a select few received preferential treatment in *Zona*. The journal published the work of these preferred writers, and complemented the selection with book reviews and interviews. Of the three writers who received this treatment, only Sarduy received all three forms of attention in one number of the journal.[24] The treatment these writers received was not only evidence of the editors' personal preferences. The marginal status of these writers relative to the Boom also suggested a political statement by the editors who supported authors who were relegated to minor positions in a vexed publishing context. Extraordinary recognition was showered on some authors who wrote from similar metaphorical penal colonies, and who wrote about their troubled and troubling effect on sexuality and the body.[25] The choice also reflected the obstacles that the editors faced given their comparative invisibility and their marginal location in relation to the rest of Latin America.

An Anti-Boom Zone

Sarduy's relatively minor position in relation to the greater visibility of writers from the Boom of the Latin American novel (e.g., Julio Cortázar, Carlos Fuentes, Gabriel García Márquez, and Mario Vargas Llosa) was complemented by the very nature of his work, which according to critic Roberto González Echevarría was a "kind of anti-Boom" from its very beginnings (1987, 47). González Echevarría further states that it was the *Tel Quel* group that "gave Sarduy the necessary methodological impulse to think the novel and literature in general in a different way" (ibid., 43). There is clearly much truth in both of these claims, and González Echevarría is sensitive to the different way in which Sarduy deploys his lessons from *Tel Quel* (ibid., 46). But the question remains, what is it about the role of the body in Sarduy's approach to literature that makes his thinking about writing so different from *Tel Quel*, and from the Boom? The answer to this question is important because it is this aspect, captured by the fossil light of his poems, which made Sarduy's writing so compelling to the editors of *Zona*.

Sarduy turned away from the commonplaces of the Boom writers both theoretically and in his writing. He implicitly criticized what remained invisible (while giving support) to their literary work: a sense of mastery based on a series of exclusions, erasures, and negations of the vexed, tortured, and meaningful body of language. In other words, Sarduy implicitly criticized what could be referred to as the Boom's theatre of cruelty. Sarduy criticized the reduction by the writers of the Boom of the possibilities of language to a mere object for the pleasure of the subject. The mimetic drive and representational imperative of the Boom writers were equivalent to a subtraction, an emptying out of the value and life of language for Sarduy. They engaged in a mode of writing that was akin to perversion: they reduced the subject of language to an eroticized object.[26] Sarduy wrote that "to pervert one is not only to amplify the gestures of sexuality, it is also to reduce them" (1969, 13). Mainstream, realist language in general, and the writing of the Boom writers in particular, were for Sarduy a mode of violence, a reduction and a torture of the body of language, of its martyred skin, wracked by its users to a form of mimetic representation, doing great violence to its flexible nature and porous surface. More importantly for Sarduy, insofar as it was subjected to this self-violence, language lost its ability to support the life of the subject.

By opposition, Sarduy practiced a minimalist mode of writing that transformed this self-aggrandizing perversion into an inverted or "transvestite" form of writing, in essays such as "Cubos" (1989, 82–83). This form of writing also represented a spectacular expansion, elaboration, riff, or a mode of overexposure of the minor object or material of artistic expression. The cube was a minor object because it was the minimum level of signification for artistic expression, but it also was minor because it represented important material that was minimized. From this perspective, Sarduy practiced a minimalist art in his writing, minimalist in the sense that it sought to establish the primary and necessary relation between playing (both as a system of signification and as a source for pleasure) and meaning (cf. "*Las topologías*"). Minimalist also insofar as he focused on the disavowed and disturbing body as a troubled and troubling origin of, and support for, writing. In this way, he inverted, that is redeployed, repeated, appropriated, and redirected the effect of perversion on the remainder of the martyred body-object of language, on its traces, on its fossil light. In this way, he also returned motility, movement, transit, back-and-forthing, signification, in short, life to language. Sarduy stretched the once-reduced (wounded) skin of language, placing it again on a rack, submitting it to a form of self-violence, but this time to take its material to its limits, and in order to make it mean again (1969, 53). In this, Sarduy's writing might have been the model for Sánchez's stretched (or martyred) canvases, and (in turn) for *Zona*'s self-undoing pages.

Sarduy was featured in *Zona* 3, published in January and February 1973. Three of the twenty-four pages of this number of the journal were dedicated to his work: pages 6 and 7 and page 22. The first two pages, viewed together (Fig. 4.5 and Fig. 4.6), constituted one large rectangular

SEVERO SARDUY: POEMAS INEDITOS

I

Mete!
Y si ardor o pudor o amor ay, saca!
Lamida maruga, mojada matraca
entra mejor. Si en este brete
se te
cae, recobra su natura de estaca:
hueso embadurnado de laca,
de perro mascado tolete.

Foutez allegrement! La vida es eso:
darle hasta que se caiga a la sin hueso
untada con "K.Y."(sabor a menta).

Considerar sin fin el fin de cuenta:
uñas y pelo y sobre la osamenta,
blanda corona, derramado el seso.

COBRA, tercera novela de Severo Sarduy, cuya traducción francesa realizada por Philippe Sollers apareció hace ya varias semanas en París, acaba de ser publicada, en su versión original, en Argentina (Ed. Sudamericana). El éxito de la edición francesa no tiene precedentes en la literatura de vanguardia: **Le Monde** dice: "Sarduy divierte, arrastra, provoca, asombra, seduce... El más representativo, el más dotado y también el más humorístico de los 'nuevos novelistas' "; **L'Express** dice que "Cobra" es un "salto de felino, una aparición que marca una fecha"... y en ese tono hablan los otros periódicos... El talento del autor tiene múltiples facetas, de modo que aproveché la ocasión de esta entrevista para que se nos presente de la manera más completa posible tanto el Sarduy autor de teatro, como el poeta, el ensayista y el editor... También (¿por qué no) el hombre que se pierde (¿se encuentra?) en ese extraño mundo subterráneo de París (o de Amsterdam, ciudad que Sarduy frecuenta), donde tantas veces se mezclan, hasta confundirse, lo maravilloso y lo monstruoso... Empecemos con un dato periodístico notable: Francia será representada al Premio Italia, el más importante de teatro radiofónico, con una pieza de Sarduy: "Relato", que ha sido difundido recientemente acompañada de un texto de Philippe Sollers y de otro de Maurice Roche. Algunos críticos, por cierto, han asociado a Sarduy, Sollers y Roche con el americano William Burroughs (el autor del Festín Desnudo, **Naked Lunch**) para formar lo que ellos llaman "la generación invisible", dada la afinidad de procedimientos literarios y aun de temas (entre Sarduy y Burroughs, por ejemplo) que une a estos cuatro autores de vanguardia...

JMF. — Empecemos pues, Sarduy, con tu teatro, que es de lo que menos se ha hablado a pesar del éxito de sus difusiones en Alemaniá...

SS. — Tanto **La Playa,** que se representó en Kassel, como **Relato,** como **La Caída,** actualmente en curso de traducción para Stuttgart, tratan de practicar lo que yo llamo el **Teatro de la Fijeza:** en mi teatro no hay ni entrada ni salida de personajes, ni carreras en escena, ni navajazos, ni acción ninguna en el sentido tradicional de la palabra "acción". En **La Playa,** por ejemplo, tal y como se representó en Alemania, los actores están insertados en paneles de plexiglás, desnudos o pintados o con trusas fluorescentes, como si fueran enseñas publicitarias. Es como si se contemplara una foto en colores o un grupo escultórico de la escuela hiper-realista (más verdaderos que los seres de verdad)... De pronto, los reflejos en el plexiglás se multiplican y las voces se van escuchando, van formando dúos, tríos, coros...

JMF. — Se trata en suma de una esp...ie de ópera de cámara, ¿no es eso?

6

SS. — Si se quiere. Lo que cuenta —y de allí la importancia de la noción de fijeza— es partir de un detalle mínimo, inmóvil, de cuya **contemplación activa** se deriva un saber sobre una totalidad, aunque éste no se encuentre formulado. Los escultores del llamado **minimal art,** como Robert Morris, Larry Bell, Judd, Flavin, Smith, etc., conocen bien la importancia generativa de las estructuras primarias de un volumen. **La Playa** da a ver, si así puede decirse, estructuras primarias gramaticales... Pero también los budistas (en Oriente) y los drogados (en Occidente) conocen muy bien este ejercicio: los monjes tibetanos que vi en los monasterios del norte de Nepal (viven allí en exilio) pasan el día ejecutando plegarias repetitivas y monocordes o contemplando mandalas, reducciones del universo, a veces muy simples (círculos concéntricos, por ejemplo, con una divinidad central); sabemos, por William Burroughs, que los adictos a la morfina pasan semanas, a veces, mirándose los pies, o "estudiando" un detalle anodino de la habitación que agrandan... Pero, en fin, la fijeza interviene, además, para mí, como un elemento erótico: inmovilizar totalmente al "partenaire", poseer su imagen pura, sin que la contamine el movimiento, la imperfección...

JMF. — Este pues, el erótico, es el origen de la fijeza en ti... ¿Hay otro?

SS. — Sí. En la literatura. Cito a los maestros: la fijeza es una de las obsesiones de Lezama: el símbolo de su obra sería un escarabajo atrapado en un pisapapeles: la vida apresada, detenida en un instante preciso, para siempre. La fijeza es también importante en la obra de Octavio Paz cuya obsesión, como puede verse en el espléndido **Simio Gramático,** su último libro, es la negación del tiempo: el "presente es eterno" y el camino de Galta (una ciudad india abandonada) no conduce más que al hecho de recorrerlo; no hay significado último (esta noción de Paz es muy búdica, por cierto), no hay centro (como en el mundo cristiano), sólo caminos (o palabras) que desembocan en otros caminos (o palabras).

JMF. — Bueno, esto, en cuanto a su teatro. Pero este año apareció en Pauvert un libro tuyo de poemas con ilustraciones de Leonor Fini (**Merveilles de la Nature**); las ediciones Fata Morgana anuncia para fin de año otro libro tuyo de poemas (**Big bang**) con ilustraciones de Alejandro. ¿Con qué articulas tu poesía? ¿Qué soporte teórico tiene?

SS. — La teoría que me interesa ahora (ya veremos cómo eso nos lleva a la poesía) es la de la Cosmología actual. Creo que en nuestros días hay algo totalmente cierto y es que la Astronomía y la Cosmología se han confundido. La Astronomía, antes, era la observación de los cuerpos celestes y la formulación de las leyes que regían sus movimientos, etc.; la Cosmología era el preguntarse sobre el universo. Cada época (en religión o en ci a esa pregunta su respuesta. Hoy en día nomía se ha confundido con la Cosmolo no podemos ya hacer observaciones que fieran, que no nos remitan al origen del simplemente, por un hecho muy banal podemos ver (o al menos detectar) el universo. Como tú sabes, mientras más observa más atrás se va en el tiempo... podemos observar lo que los astrónom **rayos fósiles,** es decir, residuos de la inicial que dio origen al universo... Un del equipo Meudon-Nancay me dijo el otr radio (como sabes, trabajo en la radio fran periodista científico) cosas tan aterradora pués de muchos años de oficio me dier de abrir la puerta del estudio para huir. N de hipótesis, ni de teorías vagas, sino de perfectamente observables. El universo ese astrónomo es **pulsante**) se originó quince billones de años. La parte del uni se observa actualmente y cuyo diámetro mente inconcebible en los límites de la humana (las cifras no dicen, a esas esca está en expansión. Las galaxias huyen una a velocidades muy próximas a la de la lu que se alejan a 210.000 kilómetros por se decir que el universo es como un globo superficie (de la cual conocemos algo 600 billones de años luz) se encuentran las cada una con un promedio de 100 billon trellas mucho más grandes que nuestro so astrónomo llamó el Monsieur Dupont, el del universo), esa superficie pues... se hecho de que el universo esté en expan pensar que es el resultado de una gigante sión inicial, el célebre Big Bang, y que **tod** ria estuvo concentrada en un volumen cido... una habitación, dicen algunos, un densidad infinita, dice el abate Lemaitr en fin... verás cómo con un salto acrobát a caer en la poesía... ¿Qué imagen debe página? A mi juicio, la del universo. Se de establecer un sistema verbal en exp página tiene que estallar o que haber est palabras (o sus sentidos) tienen que hui otras, creando un sistema de galaxias sig o como dice Paz, de signos en rotación. no hay que olvidarlo, tiene **tres** dimensi dos, como se piensa, y aun **cuatro,** pues interviene. La página sintetiza la historia del universo, pero esa síntesis, que total junto, no le es exterior sino una simple del mismo. En fin, ves cómo surge el libro **Big Bang** y qué soporte teórico tiene... Q trate de dar... Ves también en lo que días (a parte de hacer el amor y tomar jugo de tomate, que así hace menos dañ todo lo que encuentro sobre el Big Bang.

FIGURE 4.5. Rosario Ferré et al. *Zona. Carga y Descarga* 3 (1973): 6.

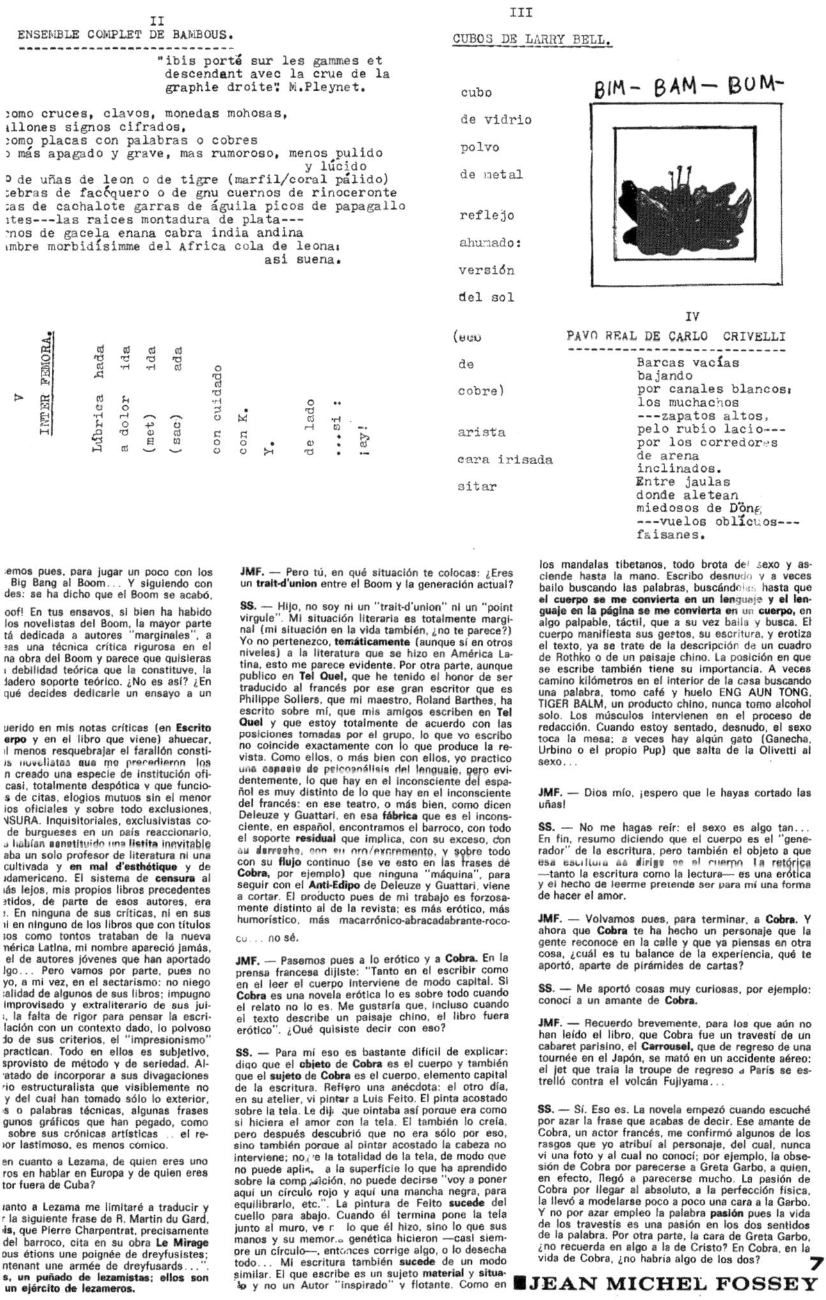

II

ENSEMBLE COMPLET DE BAMBOUS.

"ibis porté sur les gammes et
descendant avec la crue de la
graphie droite": M.Pleynet.

:omo cruces, clavos, monedas mohosas,
illones signos cifrados,
:omo placas con palabras o cobres
) más apagado y grave, mas rumoroso, menos pulido
y lúcido
o de uñas de leon o de tigre (marfil/coral pálido)
:ebras de facóquero o de gnu cuernos de rinoceronte
:as de cachalote garras de águila picos de papagallo
ites---las raices montadura de plata---
:nos de gacela enana cabra india andina
imbre morbidísimme del Africa cola de leona:
así suena.

V

INTER FEMORA.

Lúbrica hada
a dolor ida
(met) ida
(sac) ada
con cuidado
con K.
Y.
de lado
...sí:
¡ay!

III

CUBOS DE LARRY BELL.

cubo
de vidrio
polvo
de metal
reflejo
ahumado:
versión
del sol
(eco
de
cobre)
arista
cara irisada
sitar

BIM- BAM- BUM-

IV

PAVO REAL DE CARLO CRIVELLI

Barcas vacías
bajando
por canales blancos:
los muchachos
---zapatos altos,
pelo rubio lacio---
por los corredores
de arena
inclinados.
Entre jaulas
donde aletean
miedosos de Döng
---vuelos oblícuos---
faisanes.

:emos pues, para jugar un poco con los Big Bang al Boom... Y siguiendo con des: se ha dicho que el Boom se acabó.

oof! En tus ensayos, si bien ha habido los novelistas del Boom, la mayor parte tá dedicada a autores "marginales", a eas una técnica crítica rigurosa en el na obra del Boom y parece que quisieras debilidad teórica que la constituye, la dadero soporte teórico. ¿No es así? ¿En qué decides dedicarle un ensayo a un

uerido en mis notas críticas (en **Escrito erpo** y en el libro que viene) ahuecar, il menos resquebrajar el farallón consti- os novelistas que me precedieron los n creado una especie de institución ofi- casi, totalmente despótica y que funcio- s de citas, elogios mutuos sin el menor ios oficiales y sobre todo exclusiones, NSURA. Inquisitoriales, exclusivistas co- de burgueses en un país reaccionario, habían sanstituido una **listita** inevitable aba un solo profesor de literatura ni una cultivada y **en mal d'esthétique** y de idamericano. El sistema de **censura** al iás lejos, mis propios libros precedentes etidos, de parte de esos autores, era :. En ninguna de sus críticas, ni en sus ni en ninguno de los libros que con títulos sos como tontos trataban de la nueva nérica Latina, mi nombre apareció jamás, el de autores jóvenes que han aportado lgo... Pero vamos por parte, pues no yo, a mi vez, en el sectarismo: no niego :alidad de algunos de sus libros; impugno improvisado y extraliterario de sus jui- :, la falta de rigor para pensar la escri- lación con un contexto dado, lo polvoso do de sus criterios, el "impresionismo" practican. Todo en ellos es subjetivo, sprovisto de método y de seriedad. Al- atado de incorporar a sus divagaciones rio estructuralista que visiblemente no y del cual han tomado sólo lo exterior, s o palabras técnicas, algunas frases gunos gráficos que han pegado, como sobre sus crónicas artísticas .. el re- oor lastimoso, es menos cómico.

en cuanto a Lezama, de quien eres uno ros en hablar en Europa y de quien eres tor fuera de Cuba?

uanto a Lezama me limitaré a traducir y r la siguiente frase de R. Martin du Gard, **is,** que Pierre Charpentrat, precisamente del barroco, cita en su obra **Le Mirage** ous étions une poignée de dreyfusistes; ntenant une armée de dreyfusards...". **s, un puñado de lezamistas; ellos son un ejército de lezameros.**

JMF. — Pero tú, en qué situación te colocas: ¿Eres un **trait-d'union** entre el Boom y la generación actual?

SS. — Hijo, no soy ni un "trait-d'union" ni un "point virgule". Mi situación literaria es totalmente marginal (mi situación en la vida también, ¿no te parece?) Yo no pertenezco, **temáticamente** (aunque sí en otros niveles) a la literatura que se hizo en América Latina, esto me parece evidente. Por otra parte, aunque publico en **Tel Quel,** que he tenido el honor de ser traducido al francés por ese gran escritor que es Philippe Sollers, que mi maestro, Roland Barthes, ha escrito sobre mí, que mis amigos escriben en **Tel Quel** y que estoy totalmente de acuerdo con las posiciones tomadas por el grupo, lo que yo escribo no coincide exactamente con lo que produce la revista. Como ellos, o más bien con ellos, yo practico una especie de psicoanálisis del lenguaje, pero evidentemente, lo que hay en el inconsciente del español es muy distinto de lo que hay en el inconsciente del francés: en ese teatro, o más bien, como dicen Deleuze y Guattari, en esa **fábrica** que es el inconsciente, en español, encontramos el barroco, con todo el soporte **residual** que implica, con su exceso, con su derroche, con su oro/excremento, y sobre todo con su **flujo** continuo (se ve esto en las frases de **Cobra,** por ejemplo) que ninguna "máquina", para seguir con el **Anti-Edipo** de Deleuze y Guattari, viene a cortar. El producto pues de mi trabajo es forzosamente distinto al de la revista; es más erótico, más humorístico, más macarrónico-abracadabrante-rococu... no sé.

JMF. — Pasemos pues a lo erótico y a **Cobra.** En la prensa francesa dijiste: "Tanto en el escribir como en el leer el cuerpo interviene de modo capital. Si **Cobra** es una novela erótica lo es sobre todo cuando el relato no lo es. Me gustaría que, incluso cuando el texto describe un paisaje chino, el libro fuera erótico". ¿Qué quisiste decir con eso?

SS. — Para mí eso es bastante difícil de explicar: digo que el **objeto de Cobra** es el cuerpo y también que el **sujeto de Cobra** es el cuerpo, elemento capital de la escritura. Refiero una anécdota: el otro día, en su atelier, vi pintar a Luis Feito. El pinta acostado sobre la tela. Le dije que pintaba así porque era como si hiciera el amor con la tela. El también lo creía, pero después descubrió que no era sólo por eso, sino también porque al pintar acostado la cabeza no interviene; no ve la totalidad de la tela, de modo que no puede aplicar a la superficie lo que ha aprendido sobre la composición, no puede decirse "voy a poner aquí un círculo rojo y aquí una mancha negra, para equilibrarlo, etc.". La pintura de Feito **sucede** del cuello para abajo. Cuando él termina pone la tela junto al muro, ve no lo que él hizo, sino lo que sus manos y su memoria genética hicieron —casi siempre un círculo—, entonces corrige algo, o lo desecha todo... Mi escritura también **sucede** de un modo similar. El que escribe es un sujeto **material** y **situado** y no un Autor "inspirado" y flotante. Como en los mandalas tibetanos, todo brota del sexo y asciende hasta la mano. Escribo desnudo y a veces bailo buscando las palabras, buscándolas hasta que **el cuerpo se me convierta en un lenguaje y el lenguaje en la página se me convierta en un cuerpo,** en algo palpable, táctil, que a su vez baila y busca. El cuerpo manifiesta sus gestos, su escritura, y erotiza el texto, ya se trate de la descripción de un cuadro de Rothko o de un paisaje chino. La posición en que se escribe también tiene su importancia. A veces camino kilómetros en el interior de la casa buscando una palabra, tomo café y huelo ENG AUN TONG, TIGER BALM, un producto chino, nunca tomo alcohol solo. Los músculos intervienen en el proceso de redacción. Cuando estoy sentado, desnudo, el sexo toca la mesa; a veces hay algún gato (Ganecha, Urbino o el propio Pup) que salta de la Olivetti al sexo...

JMF. — Dios mío, ¡espero que le hayas cortado las uñas!

SS. — No me hagas reír: el sexo es algo tan... En fin, resumo diciendo que el cuerpo es el "generador" de la escritura, pero también el objeto a que esa escritura se dirige es el cuerpo. La retórica —tanto la escritura como la lectura— es una erótica y el hecho de leerme pretende ser para mí una forma de hacer el amor.

JMF. — Volvamos pues, para terminar, a **Cobra.** Y ahora que **Cobra** te ha hecho un personaje que la gente reconoce en la calle y que ya piensas en otra cosa, ¿cuál es tu balance de la experiencia, qué te aportó, aparte de pirámides de cartas?

SS. — Me aportó cosas muy curiosas, por ejemplo: conocí a un amante de **Cobra.**

JMF. — Recuerdo brevemente, para los que aún no han leído el libro, que Cobra fue un travestí de un cabaret parisino, el **Carrousel,** que de regreso de una tournée en el Japón, se mató en un accidente aéreo: el jet que traía la troupe de regreso a París se estrelló contra el volcán Fujiyama...

SS. — Sí. Eso es. La novela empezó cuando escuché por azar la frase que acabas de decir. Ese amante de Cobra, un actor francés, me confirmó algunos de los rasgos que yo atribuí al personaje, del cual, nunca vi una foto y al cual no conocí; por ejemplo, la obsesión de Cobra por parecerse a Greta Garbo, a quien, en efecto, llegó a parecerse mucho. La pasión de Cobra por llegar al absoluto, a la perfección física, la llevó a modelarse poco a poco una cara a la Garbo. Y no por azar empleo la palabra **pasión** pues la vida de los travestís es una pasión en los dos sentidos de la palabra. Por otra parte, la cara de Greta Garbo, ¿no recuerda en algo a la de Cristo? En Cobra, en la vida de Cobra, ¿no habría algo de los dos?

7

JEAN MICHEL FOSSEY

FIGURE 4.6. Rosario Ferré et al. *Zona. Carga y Descarga* 3 (1973): 7.

space spatially divided into four other rectangles containing an interview, five unpublished poems from the last section of *Big Bang* (published one year later, in 1974), and two images. The first image is of Sarduy in triplicate, arranged in a composition that reminds the reader of a fan-like sequence of three tarot or playing cards. The second image is of a series of concentric squares with a dark form inside, and the letters BIM-BAM-BUM handwritten and on top. The facing page stood apart from these, both physically in the journal, but also from a visual perspective (Fig. 4.7). The page contained two columns of text, each visually mimicking an upright rectangular body, with images of tattooed feet and of texts (that look like feet) supporting them from the bottom. This section is dedicated to a review of *Cobra*, Sarduy's novel from 1972. The fact that the journal published a recycled interview by Jean Michel Fossey—a review that appeared relatively late after the publication of the book—with what can appear as a miserly number of unpublished poems, is perhaps symptomatic of some of the difficulties the editors faced in publishing new material in the journal.[27] Despite these obstacles, or better yet taking advantage of them while stretching them to their limit, Sánchez and the editors of *Zona* made the best of the sparse, recycled, and superannuated material with which they were left. They even turned their abject situation into a bitter joke. The review of *Cobra* was visually supported by a beauty tip: a call to recycle waste (the cotton balls found in medicine bottles) as nail polish remover (*Zona* 3: 21).

These three pages of *Zona* are representative not only of Sarduy's anti-Boom and transvestite mode of writing, or of his redeployment and inversion of the Boom's violence now toward the practice of writing itself, but they are also examples of the merversion contained in Sanchez's tactile and sensual topographies, and in the herethical tone or dark humor of Báez's canvases.[28] The three pages turn to the abject, to the signifier made object, to the sign turned mere communicative and mimetic signal, and give it a different sense, a meaning in itself, a life of its own. From this perspective, the square, the cube, and the rectangle are icons for Sarduy, and for Sánchez. They represent the minimum and minimized common denominator of representation. And also they are the privileged compositional figures of *Zona*. The two supporting pages are of course divided by the spine of the journal into two rectangular squares, which are divided into two sections each forming two other rectangular spaces, which in turn contain other rectangular forms and concentric squares, either drawn or made by the disposition of the print and the images on the page. The rectangular page is here made visible as the primary compositional principle, and as such as

severo sarduy

COBRA

Editorial sudamericana, Buenos Aires, 1972, 263 p.

Sin con Gestos (1963), De donde son los cantantes (1967), y Escrito sobre un cuerpo (1969), Severo Sarduy había ingresado de forma determinante en la literatura hispanoamericana, COBRA confirma y supera su obra anterior. Pintura que se convierte en texto que se convierte en pintura, Cobra es un lienzo donde el blanco intenta ser más que sólo fondo para la letra impresa y exige dimensión estructural (ej. A Cobra. . . sigue página vacía). Como las pinturas de Pollock, que al parecer no tienen principio ni fin e implican una extensión más allá, alcanzando y rodeando al espectador, COBRA rodea al lector espectador involucrándolo en sus imágenes, apelando a las sensaciones, texturas, efectos visuales en explosiones de color y movimiento. El lector macho participa con todo el cuerpo en una compleja experiencia de intrincado barroquismo donde se recrea el mundo moderno con una pasión mística por la totalidad que lo lleva a incorporar la totalidad del deseo de los ritos tántricos hindúes y los bordes del universo en expansión. Objetiva sus preocupaciones cosmológicas en personajes (las enanas blancas).

Cobra ⟶ Pup
(estrella) (estrella en su máximo desarrollo
(animal mítico de India) o condensación)

y funde la tradición religiosa hindú, la sociedad tecnológica y los conceptos de la crítica estructuralista.

Literatura- filosofía (astrofísica), mística tántrica y pintura, Cobra se articula estructuralmente con el vocabulario de los expresionistas abstractos (El maestro Albers, Pollock, De Kooning, Kline, Gottlieb, Rothko) y como algunos diagramas místicos hindúes es una construcción de cuadrados concéntricos:

p.176 "Hombres y pájaros aquí tienen su sitio (imagino los cuadrados concéntricos); los astros y sus órbitas, las nieves, las piedras ciegas y las que arman un templo, todo aquí vendrá a contemplar su identidad, ascenderá a su centro. (Esas líneas negras soportan mi pensamiento, su diagrama lo estructura y lo aclara, de esa armazón no escapa) . . .en los cuadrados interiores van apareciendo las casas; escuetas, las ciudades, como en un mapa (en una red otra red). Todo emana, expansión del vacío, sucesión de sílabas (repito la sílaba), doble del emblema oscuro, macizo, terroso, nevado en la cima, de una pieza, piñazo, piedra, estupa, buda, del Monte Merú."

Como los diagramas hindúes y los poderosos lienzos del expresionismo abstracto, pero colocado bajo el signo de los pintores C O B R A (Appel, Aleschinsky, Corneille, Jorn) por el grado de libertad de las formas expresivas, violencia de brochazos, orden dentro de un caos aparente y abandono sólo parcial de la figuración, que en literatura = anécdota.

Aunque COBRA está cuidadosamente equilibrado en dos partes con cinco secuencias dos de éstas subdivididas a su vez, o sea, que es evidente el trabajo consciente por alcanzar exactitud en los volúmenes, Cobra II, por lo amplio de sus imágenes y el vuelo de su libertad, envuelve y comprende a Cobra I. Simplificando:

Cobra II
Cobra I

(comprobamos esta impresión plástica con el detalle literario:
el travestí, sombrero rojo y pintarrajeado, aparece marginalmente en Cobra II)

Cobra I narra la historia de un travestí apasionado por la fijeza del rostro- totem de Greta Garbo quien recorre el mundo en busca del mago (Dr. Ktazob) que haga realidad su deseo. En un lenguaje mágico cargado de ironía y humor asistimos a las penurias que su pasión obliga. La anécdota intenta ser sólo un pretexto, mero soporte transparente por parte del autor aunque su personaje lo increpe: p. 28 "la literatura aún necesita temas" y éste responda: "Cállese". Pretexto para la fiesta del lenguaje y observaciones críticas sobre el ser de la literatura, lo que Barthes llama la literalidad de la escritura, texto que se cita a sí mismo continuamente. El travestí Cobra puede entenderse como una metáfora de la escritura si releemos las observaciones de Sarduy refiriéndose a Lugar sin límites de Donoso: "Manuela muestra la coexistencia, en un solo cuerpo, de significantes masculinos y femeninos, la [illegible], la repulsión, el antagonismo que entre ellos se crea. . . Los planos de intersexualidad son análogos a los planos de intertextualidad que constituyen el objeto literario." Es evidente que Sarduy en su personaje intenta algo análogo y el desarrollo de Cobra I sigue bastante de cerca el pensamiento expuesto en sus ensayos. Así, Sarduy ha dicho que la literatura es un "texto que se repite, que se cita sin límites, que se [illegible] a sí mismo" y en COBRA no sólo se cita a sí mismo (aparecen Auxilio y Socorro -De Donde son los cantantes-) sinó que la [illegible] es un plagio directo del texto de Giancarlo Marmori (Storia di Vous). "Está maquillada con violencia, la boca de ramajes pintada. . .etc." – frase que es repetida a modo de estribillo o epíteto épico.

Cobra II continúa siendo un mundo de ficción consciente de sí mismo, pero mientras las metamorfosis progresivas o sorprendentes de unos personajes mueven Cobra I, los personajes evolucionan orgánicamente al bifucarse en sucesivos desdoblamientos, desde un centro, (Cobra) hacia afuera, en Cobra II las imágenes unitarias (lezamescas) son la puerta giratoria y el acuario. Si Cobra es omnipresente en la primera parte, en la segunda es una ausencia, poco asoma o dice y la acción gira alrededor de su vacío. Recordamos a Roland Barthes: "El fondo de la obra considerado como una ausencia, la metáfora como un signo sin fondo, es esa lejanía del proceso del significado lo que el proceso simbólico designa".

S S S S S S T

En la segunda parte deben destacarse como logros estéticos los fragmentos La Iniciación y Eat Flowers. El primero narra la iniciación del protagonista en una secta compuesta por tipos estilo Scorpio Rising (film underground nortsamericano) – machos de motocicleta y chaqueta de cuero negro que frecuentaban el paisaje urbano de U.S.A. y sus films comerciales de los 60's. Pero es la forma en que la acción se desenvuelve lo que convence e impacta, porque Sarduy trabaja el texto en contrastes violentos entre la simbología urbana (Bar, motoras, flechas de tránsito, carteles POP) y paisaje oriental utilizando recursos líricos (los de vencedores), dramáticos (cada personaje es narrador independiente que increpa agresivamente) y cinematográficos (superposición de imágenes, velocidad del lente óptico). La variedad de técnicas y saltos del punto de vista espacial y temporal resultan deslumbrantes. Eat Flowers reitera esta técnica con violencia creciente y funciona como metáfora de la estructura. Se segundo apartado es una parodia de la subcultura de la droga organizada en preguntas y respuestas en ocasión de la visita de un gurú payaso. Esta escena se repite dos veces más con variaciones en el resto del libro y tiñe de burla brutal la obra completa. Me parece un acierto por el humor —la risa estalla sin remedio— y porque envuelve el todo con una ambigüedad esencial.

Obra seria que incluye su propia contradicción, precisa en el detalle y la nitidez de sus contornos y barroca y abigarrada al mismo tiempo, reconcentrada y dispersa, filosofía y chacota (choteo cubano), cursilería y exquisito gusto, COBRA es realmente la unidad en la dispersión e irrumpe como un vendaval en el panorama literario. Alucinante, su lectura es una experiencia de libertad en el lenguaje y evidencia la erradicación de los deslindes convencionales entre los géneros literarios. Ante una obra de tamaño impulso, la crítica convencional se encuentra desarmada. COBRA, provocadora, es:

TOTEM "Cobra: para que envenene, Para que ahogue, Para que se enrosque alrededor de sus víctimas y las asfixie. Para que hipnotice con el aliento y sus ojos brillen en la noche, enormes, de oro." ¡TIGRE "Para que repte y se confunda entre las piedras. Y muerda en el tobillo. Y de un zarpazo, escamas afiladas, hiera."

Me confieso herida por la fascinación de tu veneno. COBRA. Silbas, peligrosa y amenazante, en el corazón del lenguaje.

Olga Nolla Conde

Aproveche todo

NO tire el algodón que traen dentro los frascos de píldoras, cápsulas y tabletas. Es justamente lo que usted necesita para limpiarse el barniz de las uñas.

No me confunda con otras
MADAME CARMEN
Incienso Mágico
Bola de Cristal * Cartas
La Mano Espiritual
*La Mente

22

FIGURE 4.7. Rosario Ferré et al. *Zona. Carga y Descarga* 3 (1973): 22.

the all-important support structure giving form, or the first layer or topology of depth, movement, and meaning to the content of the journal: the square or cube, is the least common denominator of the page, is the prime mover of *Zona.*

Layered onto the page, and interacting with its rectangular topology, the reader of *Zona* finds numerous connections between the text and the body dramatized in the same pages. The connections are made visible and explicit by the turn of Sarduy's image toward his poem, by the flowing nature of the text that appears to come out of his eye, and by the tattoo-like quality of the poem, whose title (roman numeral "I") takes the place of Sarduy's eye on the page. Moreover, both the tattoo as writing on the body, and conversely the body as a mode of writing, are represented on the review by a tattooed set of feet, by the location of these feet at the bottom of the column of text, as well as by its mirror-like composition, repeated and inverted next to it, by the image of a Hindu woman with feet of text (two small fake advertisements in different print). Finally, the pages also make visible the invisible and abject life and meaning of the object of language, by making multiple references to the sensorial quality of the signs on the page, and by extending these sensory signs to the signifiers of language. Indeed, all five senses combine in these pages to suggest the material and living nature of language. The pages refer and appeal to its acoustic dimension through onomatopoeia (BIM-BAM-BUM), to its visual dimension through the differences in the type of the letters (typewriter type, handwriting, typographical), to its tactile dimension through its rotating text and images, to smell through the burnt quality of the negative signs or overexposed images, and even to taste in the visual and onomatopoeic references to the tongue (see for example the content and visual form of the poem "Inter Femora" and the curves of the SSSSST running between the columns of text of the review [*Zona* 3: 22]).

The compositions also suggest another dimension of the journal's merversion or amatory violence in a herethical mode: a disturbing, macabre, but also irreverent, funny mode of joking, that reminds the reader of the dark humor of the film *Dr. Strangelove or How I Learned to Stop Worrying and Love the Bomb* (1964), and that can be traced back to the visual jokes of Báez's radioactive paintings. The signs of *Zona* display an erotic life that is both tortured (martyred) but also pleasurable in a unique, distinctive, and profoundly dark-humored and funny way. These combined erotic topologies of *Zona* also turn against Sarduy, and call attention to the exclusions of his own sometimes overly serious, strictly homoerotic, and meager contributions to the journal. Significantly, during the published interview, Fossey tries to make Sarduy laugh after he describes himself typing away in the nude while his cat jumps on a typewriting machine that Sarduy also identifies with his sexual member. "My god [Fossey exclaims], I hope you had its nails cut!" To which Sarduy replies, "Don't make me laugh: sex is something so—," censoring himself and cutting himself off (*Zona* 3: 7). The playful manipulation of, and violent cuttings done to Sarduy's image; the caustic and ironic onomatopoeic references to the blows of his sadomasochistic theory, and to the universal claims of his poetry (BIM-BAM-BUM); and the ironic mock advertisements simultaneously making fun of his Orientalism, and of his male-oriented writing, all point to a desacralizing topology of *Zona*, the herethical dimension of its merversions. This dimension of *Zona* makes light of the serious image of Sarduy, as turtlenecked and tweed jacket–wearing French-looking intellectual and critic, impassive, arms crossed, looking out at the reader like a father waiting in judgment.

Zona's Herethical Abjection

The first number of *Zona* published the transcript of a university conference on the state of Puerto Rican literature that was celebrated in 1972. It was a rallying point for the journal. At this conference, the Uruguayan critic Angel Rama insisted on the importance of establishing the conditions of possibility for a writing life that clearly resonated with the editors of the journal. Calling attention to the explosions of the moment (literary and otherwise), Rama deployed the heroic, military, suicidal, and self-sacrificial rhetoric so prevalent among Puerto Rican nationalists (see chapter 2 of this book). He states that there is no mission more important for the writer than creating a literary work in which he believes blindly, without any doubts whatsoever, no matter if the world goes up in flames around him.[29] Rama paraphrases Faulkner to argue that writing must be the first and foremost concern of the writer, and also that the writer (like Calibán) must be free to steal from his burning environment the tools of his craft. Rama uses a striking matricidal metaphor to illustrate his point: he says, "Faulkner's phrase 'One can steal anything necessary; one can even kill one's mother, in order to write' is but an exaggerated way of putting what is an absolute truth for the writer" (*Zona* 1: 7).

Regardless of their ideological differences (and there were many) Rama, Traba, and Sarduy were all in agreement about the resignifying potential of the violent reductions and inversions of a minor art and literature generated in (and by) an explosive environment. Where Rama spoke of a Calibanistic reappropriation of the tools of the master, Traba spoke of an individualistic art behind the barricades. From this perspective, Sarduy's theoretical writings were another turn in the screw of this critical tradition trying to return meaning to exhausted systems of modernist, avant-garde, or magical and otherwise realistic modes of signification. This critical tradition tried to reanimate what Traba described as the anomie of a fatigued cultural expression, or the despair represented by the black flags of the French student revolts in May 1968 (Traba 1971, 67, 76–77). This tradition criticized the perverse reductions of existentialist writing, which Sarduy ridiculed as merely playing at being empty ("Las *Topologías*"), and sought to make words recover their meaning again through what Sarduy described as a self-wounding process (1969, 52). Nothing was sacred to this revolting tradition, not even the matricidal matriarchy paradoxically invested with an aura by Rama, the self-appointed spiritual guardian of the journal.[30] And indeed, Rama's metaphorics (the matricide, the tropical girl, and the blessing) illustrate the intractable and insistent nature of the problem *Zona*'s critics and writers also set out to solve.

Zona's merversion had an effect on this critical tradition that was similar to the fossil light from an exploded star that was measured, ordered, diagnosed without success by the guardian of the epigraph. Like the literary body of a minor literature, the meaning of *Zona*'s merversion is ultimately lost to the master critic who tries to inform and order the journal, giving it a distinctively reduced and domestic range. From its radiant pages, however, *Zona* still energizes, activates, animates, and represents a mode of erotic writing that screens the loss of its own abject body to the Cold War and to the pyrotechnics of the Boom. *Zona* transforms all of this debris into its own distinctive, symbolic, and meaningful explosions. Sánchez, Ferré, Nolla, Luis César Rivera, and Ramos Otero followed Rama, Traba, and Sarduy, as they burned, stretched, and irradiated *Zona*'s pages, and its type to their limit, pages that in turn gave support to an analogous mode of writing. In so doing, the makers of *Zona* recovered the signifying promise of a language, in a gesture that is analogous to the reanimating effects of a minor literature according to Deleuze and Guattari. They infused their language and their writing with passion and desire, and returned to its surface the supportive quality denied them by their explosive colonial contexts. They made apparent the violence done to them by the master writers and critics they were trying to approximate, emulate, and address. And ironically in this way, and perhaps only for a brief moment, the page of the journal was able to once again bear its abject load, even as it inverted that load into a mode of writing similar to the black-body radiation and fossil discharge from an exploded star.

5

Colonial Sublimations of a Noir Eros in "El Josco" and Two Detective Novels

> Juan, Pedro, Gratitud,
> who farted? It was you!
> Don't blame me, blame Teté,
> beat her beat her, it was her!
>
> —Puerto Rican nursery rhyme

Abelardo Díaz Alfaro's 1948 short story classic "El Josco" marks an important shift in the expression of a collective imaginary in Puerto Rico. It substitutes the parricide that Freud placed at the center of the story of civilization with self-sacrifice in the form of a paternal suicide. And this fundamental substitution has dramatic consequences for the development of Puerto Rican culture and language, particularly as it negatively affects the necessary sublimation of a Noir Eros that according to Kristevan psychoanalysis is found at the origins of all subjectivity and national identity. Also from this perspective, "El Josco" dramatizes a Puerto Rican version of the Freudian fantasy represented by the phrase "a child is being beaten." But instead of a father beating a child, in the Puerto Rican version of this fantasy it is the father who is being beaten, and whose self-sacrifice points to an oedipal complex that is far from optimal in Puerto Rico, partly due to its colonial history. In fact, "El Josco" sets the stage for the entrance to the cultural stage of the figure of the Big Mother, which will take the form of *El alacrán* ("The Scorpion"), a repeating character in the police novels of Edgardo Rodríguez Juliá. And this repeating figure, I will suggest, is in turn a version of the symbolic matricide at the center of the Puerto Rican scene of self-sacrifice that I have been tracing throughout this book.

The Erotic Fantasy in the Christian Passion

Trying to throw light on the causes at the origin of the clash of religious fundamentalisms at the beginning of the third millennium, and drawing from Freud's *Totem and Taboo* (1912–13) and from the essay "A Child Is Being Beaten" (1919), Kristeva interprets the biblical story of the Christian Passion as a lasting and influential two-thousand-year-old fantasy that works through, displaces, and sublimates the insistent Noir Eros (or the primal incestuous sadomasochism) both at the center of the archaic myth of the primal horde and at the origins of all subjectivity, law, culture, and language ("A Father Is Beaten to Death").[1] Kristeva argues that the climax of the story of the Christian Passion contains the fantasy represented by the phrase "a son-father is beaten to death," which does more than reinforce the foundational prohibitions against parricide and incest contained in the story of the primal horde and its aftermath.[2] Paradoxically, she argues, the fantasy also "assumes [parricide and incest], it displaces them and clears the way for their perlaboration or sublimation" (2009, 59). In other words, the fantasy in the Christian Passion prepares the guilty, prohibited, incestuous, and parricidal love and hate at the origins of the story of the primal horde for their transformation into a different affect, a passion that is beyond resentment, a love that is both sublime and worthy for Kristeva.

The sublimation of these dark feelings depends on what Kristeva calls an "optimal oedipal complex." In other words, they depend on the success of the appeal that is at the center of stories such as the Christian Passion: an appeal to the shadow (or to the double) of the punishing father of the law, what Kristeva calls the loving father or the "paternal function." She describes the paternal function as a center that is unfixed, similar to the support for the Brownian motion, the serial music, or the improvised dance that produces works of art such as *One* by Jackson Pollock: an open order that produces an undecidable identity. Without recourse to a similar symbolic order (one that is open to its own dissolution and recomposition) and without access to a symbolic father that is willing to join the subject in what Kristeva calls a traversal of the death drive, stories like the Christian Passion can instead bring both abuse and permissiveness. Such defensive unwillingness can lead to erotic confrontations that begin by abolishing paternal and symbolic power, and end by replacing the Dead Father with compensatory punishing figures such as the Big Mother. Indeed, this is the state of things as Kristeva finds them at the beginning of the third millennium, when political and paternal authority has collapsed, when perversions and merversions (see chapters 3 and 4 of this book) are encouraged, and when our minds, our societies, and even our bodies have become dangerously disorganized by the failure of our appeals to the symbolic father. In what follows, I will apply Kristeva's analysis of the Noir Eros (and its ultimately forgiving agency) to three texts written by Puerto Rican writers under the American Century.

"El Josco," A Colonial Sublimation of the Erotic Fantasy

As critics have noted, "El Josco" contains foundational myths regarding Puerto Rican national identity internalized by many Puerto Ricans (Lugo-Ortiz 1998, 79). It is the story of the vexed colonial relations in Puerto Rico turned into an allegorical fable. Among other things, the story famously dramatizes the conflict between two representative Puerto Rican male characters and their misguided solution to the colonial problem. Don Leopo, the patrician Creole landowner, believes in the whitening of the race, and wants to bring in a white bull from North America as the new and improved stud for his cattle. Marcelo disagrees. He is the *jíbaro* or iconic peasant who is meant to represent authentic Puerto Ricanness within the logic of the story.[3] He wants the local bull (the melancholy animal of the title) to remain as the stud for the cattle, despite his surly and sullen disposition, brown skin, smaller bulk, and wily ways. It is significant that Marcelo himself loads the bull of the title with a negative charge, even as he simultaneously questions the decision of his master to replace it with the white, larger, and stronger, American bull.

The story goes on to describe a duel between these two bulls (and the ideologies that the bulls represent) that ends with the melancholy bull's triumph over the white bull despite all of its disadvantages. His success, however, is not enough to change the mind of Don Leopo. Clearly, the bull is still polluted, and it is its duplicitous nature, its sullen disposition, and its brown skin that justify his sacrifice for the sake of the improvement of the breed in the eyes of Don Leopo. Marcelo, all of the inhabitants of the region, as well as the narrator disagree and are distraught, but they don't do anything to stop Don Leopo, except warn him repeatedly that the melancholy bull was not born to live under a yoke. Finally, the bull goes missing and is found at the bottom of a hill, with its neck broken. Don Leopo's silence at the end of the story suggests that from his perspective, the bull's accident confirms his decision to sacrifice him by beating the glum nature and sullen disposition out of the breed. However, Marcelo's repetition of the warning at the end of the story offers a different interpretation of the so-called accident, which nevertheless does not contradict Don Leopo's judgment of the bull. In a voice that trembles with the disturbing rage and sadness that makes the bull so abject for Don Leopo, and that similarly inflects the bull's melancholy bellows, Marcelo produces the phrase "My poor dear Josco, he broke his neck in a rage" (Díaz Alfaro 1984, 63). The phrase expresses his compassion for the bull, and it suggests his interpretation of the death of the bull as the effect of a suicidal rage.[4]

Marcelo's phrase is significant for many reasons. One reason is the ambiguity with which it places blame for the bull's death. Guilt depends on how you interpret the word *rage* in the phrase "he broke his neck in a rage." On the one hand, Marcelo uses a word that means an intense form of anger (*rabia* in Spanish), perhaps a reaction to the decision of the master to castrate the bull and put it under the yoke. On the other, the word for anger in Spanish is also the word for rabies, an animal disease and its contagious symptom, a foaming at the mouth. From this perspective, and by calling attention to a condition that might be internal to the bull, the story emphasizes the suicidal nature of the bull's rage. This aspect of the rage is also contained in the use of the Spanish reflexive verb *se esnucó,* which, literally translated, would mean that the bull broke his own neck, although in the context of the story the expression is clearly also meant to suggest that the bull broke his neck by accident.[5]

Sacrifice and suicide are the competing meanings given to the story, depending on the position of the reader who might take the perspective of the "master" Don Leopo, or the "slave" Marcelo. As such, the story is also a colonial version of the totem in the Freudian story, and its Christian elaboration in Kristeva's account of the Passion. In other words, the story of "El Josco" represents a sublimation and a perlaboration of an original totemic figure that is similar to (but also far from) the optimal Christian elaboration as Kristeva imagines it. Arguably, "El Josco" can go so far as to represent an inversion of the story of the Christian Passion.[6] The bull at the center of the story is a Christ figure that the author inverts to tell the story of the passion or suffering brought by colonialism. The story opens with a representation of the shadow of the melancholy bull, head raised with horns in the shape of a cross, on top of the hill where he will die, evoking the place where Christ was crucified with an image that reminds the reader of Golgotha. Later on, the bull is described as the only son of Marcelo, the peasant that raises him. Later still, he is crowned with the signs of his martyrdom, the branches, wild flowers, and reeds that reappear at the site of his death. At the height of his Passion we hear his uncanny bellow, evoking the moment on the cross that Kristeva has described as Kenos: the descent into nothingness signified by the all too human reproach, "Father, why have you forsaken me?"[7] But Christ's phrase, his resentful appeal to his Father leaves open the possibility of a sign or a response from a loving father, while the hermetic untranslatable bellows of a melancholy animal preclude a similar response. In the same way, by the end of the tale, the bull is found at the bottom of the hill, body upside down, with its back (not his front) legs sticking out, suggesting a particularly gruesome, inverted, eroticized and sadistic crucifixion that makes the possibility of rebirth or resurrection almost hopeless. "And we saw the Josco inert, the back legs open and rigid; the head buried under the weight of its muscular body," writes the narrator (Díaz Alfaro 1984, 63).

In this inverted elaboration of the Christian Passion, there is never a realization that the bull (both the symbolic father of the Puerto Rican colony and the son of its iconic peasant) is an animal to kill, as in the Christian fantasy represented by the phrase "a father-son is beaten to death." Instead, here the melancholy bull is always represented as a victim. It is either represented as a scapegoat, as an animal to sacrifice for others, for another life, so that others can survive in its place, or it is represented as a victim of its diseased rage, as an animal that commits suicide. From the perspective of Don Leopo, the symbolic father is loaded with the sins of his sons, with their sullenness and duplicity, and his sacrifice shields future Puerto Ricans from their stigma and from their abject influence. In other words, Don Leopo's sacrifice whitens the race in more than one sense. The bull as scapegoat leaves the officiants clean and free from sin, without offensive traits. From the perspective of Marcelo, the symbolic father is loaded with the melancholy sadness, the rage, and the duplicity produced by the colonial situation, feelings also experienced by the sons. But despite Marcelo's compassionate identification with the bull, his suicidal interpretation also displaces these dark and abject feelings to the bull, and turns them into an explosive weapon that the bull turns inward, against itself as a dire warning for, and as a disturbing lesson to the colonial master and its slaves. If we understand the story as an inverted elaboration of the story of the

Christian Passion, then both the sacrificial victim and the suicidal victim are ultimately means to displace and even disavow Noir, dark, feelings away from the Puerto Rican self. In short, by representing the *Josco* as a victim, the responsibility for its death never falls in the hands of the sons.[8]

If Marcelo isn't guilty, he sure acts as if he were. Marcelo is the character in the story who finds the dead bull, but the narrator of the story insists that Marcelo is not to blame for the death of the bull. However, the implicit denials can't help but provoke a suspicion of guilt in the reader. Marcelo never openly contradicts Don Leopo, as if he were willing to go along with his master's plan; he is desperate when looking for the bull, as if he knew what had happened to the animal; he knows where to look for the bull, as if he knew where the so-called accident happened; he throws up his arms and screams in anguish when he finds the bull, as if he needed to make an exaggerated gesture of surprise and innocence; finally, the phrase he produces, "My poor dear Josco, he broke his neck in a rage," relies on the reflexive verb, a verbal form famously used in Spanish (and particularly in Puerto Rican Spanish) to deflect responsibility. From this perspective, the final phrase can also be interpreted to mean, "Don't look at me. I didn't break his neck. It broke itself, in a rage." Taken together, Marcelo's protestations of innocence have the opposite effect in the reader, suggesting, at the very least a guilty conscience, if not duplicity and outright responsibility for the death of the bull.

The duplicity and guilt associated with Marcelo are the other side of his presumed innocence. They are his dark side, and they reconnect the peasant with the bull's dark character, described as depressed, melancholy, and sad but also as angry, wily, and tricky or duplicitous. These shared character traits are the immediate cause of the death of the bull. And the logic of the story interprets them as the result of colonialism, of the imposition of the colonial yoke on Puerto Ricans, a reaction to external circumstances.

And yet, the story also suggests that these Noir or dark feelings define the Puerto Rican character in a way that precedes the recent history of colonial rule by the United States and seems embedded in the very language of the story.[9] For example, the homonymous nature of the name of the bull, "The Melancholy Bull" or *Josco,* is a sign for this disturbing darkness, a rage, a tone of voice that also inflects both the tone of the bull's lament, giving it a phantasmatic quality, as well as Marcelo's distinctive voice and trembling warning, which conveys pity, a veiled accusation and a threat.[10] The same dark rage and veiled violence found in the voice of Marcelo can be detected in the collective voice that describes the perverse crucifixion at the end of the story, as well as in the first person narrator who tells most of the tale, including the epic fight between the bulls told with obvious relish. Most importantly, however, the disturbing effect of this tone of voice punctuates the very narrative of the story, giving it the troubled form of what Kristeva calls a phantasmatic dialect. The tone of voice trembles or moves awkwardly from first person plural to first person singular, and from an impersonal collective descriptive tone to a personal intimate confessional one. Like the sound of the bull's bellows, this tone is also a scandalous scansion. It is made of noise, nonsense, disturbing and uncanny rhythms, and it does not find a sympathetic ear, partly because even the speaker is deaf to the bull's lament. This scansion remains hanging, floating in the air of the story, only reaching an ear that has been reduced to a resentful audience by a punitive colonial context. The cadence remains beyond the displacements of colonial history, beyond the original confrontation with, and embrace of the symbolic father (the animal to kill, or the totem), whose disavowed murder nevertheless continues to haunt the Puerto Rican subject.

Colonial Law, Culture, and Language

Without the foundational murder or symbolic parricide, however, there is no prohibition against incest, an inversion not only of the Christian story of the Passion but even of the outcome of the Freudian story of the primal horde. The *Josco* is the Puerto Rican totem, an animal that stands for a symbolic father, a man-beast-monster, whose story is at the foundations of Puerto Rican culture. But in this version of the primal horde, the symbolic father is killed only indirectly and for the wrong reasons. Here the brothers do not band together against the father, killing him in a ritual murder that will set the stage for his incorporation and for the prohibitions of murder that inaugurate culture, language, and society according to Freud. In this version of the primal horde, the father does not fight the band of brothers. Instead, he first fights against an other, a foreign symbolic father, an American father, brought in from the outside, to mate with the local cows, to "improve the breed." Most importantly, however, he doesn't fight, but instead surrenders to his own worst, dark, instincts. In this version of the primal horde story, the totem, the animal to kill, not only survives the first part of the story but actually prevails, proving that he, and not the competition, is better suited to be stud. Instead, the bull dies by his own hand (or hoof), possessed by his deadly instincts. Such an outcome prepares the ground for a culture and a language ruled by both abuse and permissiveness. It guarantees that language and culture will be governed by a punishing and eroticized Big Mother, who fills the void left by the suicide of the symbolic father. Such a culture and language makes an appeal to the paternal function, to its open order, both vexed and difficult.

Lugo-Ortiz has provocatively argued that despite the ideological conflicts dramatized by the tale, the story of "El Josco" has been a means for Puerto Ricans to interiorize a coherent and consistent national identity that is always gendered masculine, but at the cost of naturalizing or internalizing an archaic threat of castration, emasculation, or lack that also underlies the experience of colonialism.[11] She also argues that this masculine subject anxious about its own masculinity will set the boundaries of normative Puerto Rican sexuality in texts such as "En la popa del barco hay un cuerpo reclinado" (1956) by Marqués and "El asedio" (1958) by Emilio Díaz Valcárcel. These later texts mark the boundary separating normative heterosexual from deviant homosexual subjectivity with stereotypical figures such as the castrated father and the mannish lesbian, which paradoxically grow out of the cracks and fissures of the masculine body as it struggles against its anxieties and desires in stories like "El Josco." But such figures also could be examples of a homophobia that results from the inability of the Puerto Rican subject to listen to what I am here calling the Noir Eros, and to work through its primary incestuous and sadomasochistic drive.

From my perspective, the Noir Eros that troubles the Puerto Rican elaboration of the story of the Christian Passion sets the conditions of possibility for two familiar figures of Puerto Rican storytelling: the Victim Father and the Big Mother. This perspective also leads to a model for Puerto Rican subjectivity that is split, both guilt-ridden and free from responsibility for a primal symbolic parricide. And finally, it reveals a distinctive voice inflected by an uncanny rhythm or scansion, by the eerie sound of a strange rage and sadness. This cadence inflecting Puerto Rican, colonial, storytelling is the remainder of the unprocessed and raw Noir Eros that is not only displaced but even disavowed as a vexed (both defensive and rebellious) response to a relatively recent history of colonialism. And yet, it is also a cadence that continues to trouble Puerto Rican language, and bears witness to the disquieting effect of the colonial disavowal of the Noir Eros on contemporary Puerto Rican culture and society.

Detective Novels as Sublimations of the Language of Noir

Kristeva begins her analysis of the clash of religious fundamentalisms at the beginning of the third millennium by talking about the death of her father in 1989, two months before the fall of the Berlin wall. Kristeva says that the only way she could talk about his death or mourn it was through writing a "metaphysical detective novel," a mode of writing that, she says, seems to have found her (and not the other way around). Indeed, she suggests that two consequences of her father's death found their way (as if on their own) into the words and phrases of the police novels she has written since then.[12] She writes,

> [M]y father's death drove me to see society as the criminal pact described by Freud: "Society was now based on complicity in the common crime." The other consequence of this event is the loss of inhibition I felt that enabled me to unveil the repressed sadomasochism of the lovers surrounding the novel's "dead father." (Kristeva 2015)

She suggests that the death of her father made her aware of an incestuous sadomasochism that was anterior to the Freudian symbolic parricide. More importantly, however, Kristeva insists that her father's death also brings into writing the Noir Eros, the incestuous sadomasochism whose denials drive the murder of her biological father by the surrounding culture.[13]

She insists that the Noir Eros, the dark drive that assaults the symbolic father, has a language of its own. It is a punctuated cadence, a rhythm, a force that beats up, fragments, dissolves, or atomizes the symbolic father and his laws, that fragments the symbolic order and its language, so that it may be reborn. It is a negative of language in that it is the obverse of language, its condition of possibility. It is an obscure language, a Noir language, an uncanny language, that finds itself into her writing, that becomes the detective novels or the Noirs that Kristeva writes as a result of its appeal. For Kristeva, to write a Noir, a police or a detective novel, is to listen to the appeal of this negativity, to be open to its dissolution of language, to verbalize and to develop a story from, and out of, this atomizing cadence, but also to allow the self to become possessed by its negativity, to allow the Noir Eros to speak through her writing, and in so doing to place what she calls the psychoanalytic bet: that we can go beyond our genitors, beyond our self, and beyond our loves, and return an uncanny love. Kristeva ends her preliminary remarks by saying that her experience with detective fiction can throw some light on our dark times of religious conflict and fundamentalism. She suggests that stories such as the Christian story of the Passion operate in a similar way to the Noir novel but over thousands of years, confronting us with the disturbing drives and desires at play at the origins of culture, language, and society, repeating them, but also working through them and sublimating them. Kristeva is an atheist, but she urges us to listen again, though heretically this time, to the story of the Christian Passion.

Colonial Noir

Kristeva's provocative use of the modern detective story to shed light on the thousand-year-old Christian story, and particularly to highlight the negative language supporting its central fantasy represented by the phrase "a father-son is beaten to death," can be a model for reading Rodríguez Juliá's detective novels. In the previous section, I showed how Puerto Rican colonial experience and storytelling have changed and transformed, even inverted, the operations of confrontation and sublimation at the center of the story of the Christian Passion. I explained and described the origins of the key figures of Puerto Rican storytelling as symptomatic of the effect of a colonial context. These figures include the Victim Father, the Big Mother, and a Split Son unwilling to accept responsibility. And these figures are the result of a colonial disavowal and displacement not just of parricide but more importantly of the Noir desire at the origins of parricide. In the following section, I would like to suggest that Rodríguez Juliá's detective novels are examples of the continuing influence of that Noir Eros on the colonial subjectivity of Puerto Ricans. They are examples of the continuing attempt of this Noir Eros to speak through the language and culture of Puerto Rico, and of the bullheaded effort of this Eros to confront and work through what I call the colonial maladies of the Puerto Rican soul.

In an essay written the same year his first detective novel was published, Rodríguez Juliá answers the implicit question: Why did you write a police novel? The question appears to be loaded with an implied negative criticism. He begins his answer with an angry gesture of frustration followed by a similarly frustrated denial: "In the end or finally, I wrote a police novel, or a detective novel, or whatever you want to call it: I don't know why I wrote it" (Rodríguez Juliá 2003, 155). The denial is followed by two paragraphs where Rodríguez Juliá rehearses a number of reasons why he might have written *Sol de medianoche,* all of which are attempts to explain his first gut response, which seems guilt-ridden: "I publish a police novel, therefore I am a writer of lightweight literature, postmodern, tempted by opportunistic literature. . . . Maybe my ambition is to bring myself into an entertainment industry that has seduced contemporary literature" (ibid.). Both the angry denial and the self-punishing tone of his defensive response suggest a feeling of shame that Rodríguez Juliá experiences by writing in this so-called lightweight genre. He suggests that the shame comes from his betrayal of so-called heavyweight literature, which is defined as not opportunistic and resistant to the seductions of the entertainment industry (read Hollywood as the new colonizing power of the ruling society of the spectacle). And indeed, shame is the colonial version of the Noir Eros that defines the protagonist of Rodríguez Juliá's detective novels, that occupies the center of his inquiry, and that remains as the conditions of possibility for sublimation.

Published in 1995 and in 2004 respectively, *Sol de medianoche* and *Mujer con sombrero Panamá* can be interpreted at one level as inquiries into the violence that has been endemic to Puerto Rican society in the last three decades of the twentieth century. On the one hand, the violence is the result of a recent twist in the colonial relation with the United States that was explored and diagnosed in "El Josco." Since the eighties, that history has included Puerto Rico's role as an important site of drug trafficking and money laundering together with other border states such as Texas, Florida, California, and New York in the so-called War against Drugs of the U.S. Federal Government. In part as a result of this history, the risk of dying from homicide in Puerto Rico between 1990 and 1999 was one of the highest in the world. According to the Health Department, homicide ranked fifth in causes of death among Puerto Ricans, and it was the main cause of death among Puerto Ricans between fifteen and twenty-nine years of age in 2003 (Mirabal et al. 2010). Finally, Puerto Rico ranks only second to Washington, D.C., in numbers of murders and robberies in the United States (Montalvo-Barbot 1997). From this perspective, the novels can be interpreted as attempts to reveal the complicity of the Puerto Rican middle class in this violence, generated partly by its investment in the forces driving the colonial economy, society, and culture. The critique returns a social function to literature: a means to what Rodríguez Juliá calls an ethical imagination (2003, 161).[14]

Sol de medianoche tells the story of a murder mystery investigated, and perhaps caused, by Manolo, a former spy and traitor who both helps and then betrays his friend Carlos Ruiz by taking both sides of his case. In this story of duplicity and self-deception, Carlos, a Puerto Rican architect, hires Manolo to discover if he is being followed by the husband of his lover, Migdalia, a woman that Manolo describes as a Dominican mulatto woman with a wish to be white and blonde. Educated as a lawyer, she has given up her career to become the trophy wife of another lawyer. Manolo agrees to help Carlos while simultaneously contacting Migdalia's mother and offering his services to find out the identity of her daughter's lover, profiting in this way from both sides of what Manolo calls the "biggie-size" (*Sol*, 35). Finally, Carlos is assassinated in a hotel room. The novel ends with Manolo, in his apartment, with a woman lying in his bed (it is not certain whether she is dead or alive), looking at himself in the mirror and recognizing there the face of a murderer, but only for a fleeting instant.

Mujer con sombrero Panamá finds Manolo involved in another case of adultery, but this time he is hired by the adulteress, Arelis, to find first her lover, Jimmy Sarriera, who has suddenly gone missing, and then also to find a set of compromising love letters that she suspects may contain a winning lottery ticket. Manolo finds Jimmy in a hospital where he lies dying from a cerebral thrombosis. He finds the letters together with similarly compromising photographs with the help of Jimmy's partner, Toño Machuca, a homosexual lawyer who is assassinated by his lover after giving the letters to Manolo. Finally, the duplicitous detective gives the letters to Arelis, but also gives a set of copies of the photographs to Yvette, Jimmy's wife, letting the cat out of the bag. In this way, Manolo betrays not only Arelis's confidence, but also Jimmy, who wanted to keep everything a secret after his death. The novel ends with Manolo driving into the sunset in his vintage car, while a copy receipt, the evidence of his guilt, flies off and sinks into the murky waters of a lagoon.

Haunting Figures of Colonial Noir

Similar to the metaphysical detective novels of Kristeva, Rodríguez Juliá's police novels combine an interpretation of current and local forms of political, social, and economic violence with an inquiry into its archaic sources.[15] In the case of Rodríguez Juliá's novels, this inquiry takes the form of an investigation into the relation between the denials of responsibility of the characters and the colonial shame over betrayal and murder, a relation that is at the center of both novels, and that brings us back to the colonial phrase "a father beats himself to death," also represented by the *Josco*'s suicide. In the words of a character at the end of *Mujer con sombrero Panamá*, lying to yourself "is like bilharzia . . . it lodges in the chest, in the liver, lasts your whole life and then finally the anger kills you" (*Mujer*, 220). Bilharzia was an endemic and deadly tropical disease caused by a local parasite eradicated in the early twentieth century with the help of the new laboratory medicine brought by the United States military doctors, tasked with making the island safe for the occupying forces. With a vexed metaphor that combines the memory of a violent colonial eradication with the cure for a local tropical disease, Roberto, a friend of Manolo (the detective of both novels), makes reference to the diseased rage affecting Puerto Rican subjects as the real cause of death of the victims. He warns the detective that lying to yourself makes you so angry that it finally kills you, not unlike the *Josco*'s rabies or rage. From this perspective, the novels suggest that despite the effort of the Puerto Rican middle class to lie to itself about its innocence, it feels the consequences of the return of the repressed. The repressed Victim Father returns to haunt them down. In other words, the colonial violence that haunts these novels takes place in the shadow that begins the story by Díaz Alfaro: "Eternal shadow of the Josco on the hill that looks over the valley of the Toa river" (Díaz Alfaro 1984, 57). The violence is the betrayal of the *Josco*, and it lies at the origins of colonial shame.

The Victim Father

Indeed, at the center of the detective novels we find the story of a sadomasochistic passion (both in the sense of a grossly exaggerated Christian suffering and an unchecked desire aimed at the self), and the violent death of several failed models of Puerto Rican manhood and fatherhood, all of whom are described as victims of a rage that is, at first, leveled from outside, but ultimately is shown to be suicidal and to come from within. Carlos and Jimmy are the victims at the center of both detective novels. They are very similar characters: Puerto Rican white professionals, married with children, addicts either to cocaine or to alcohol, and both adulterers. In the words of the detective of the novels, they are perfect examples of the "Puerto Rican male" (*Sol*, 36). Carlos's role as a Christ figure is emphasized with references to Christ's Passion and crucifixion: he dies *clavado* (crucified, but also "fucked" in Puerto Rican Spanish) in a hotel, shot in the head and stabbed twice, once in the heart and then in the jugular (ibid., 146).

In the second novel, the figure of the Victim Father is represented by two characters: Jimmy, but also Toño Machuca, Jimmy's partner in their law firm who is described as a father to Jimmy (*Mujer*, 58). Like Carlos, Toño Machuca (whose last name means "to beat to a pulp" in Spanish) is a Victim Father who dies a violent death, twice run over by a Porsche Boxter driven by his greedy and jealous male lover. Like Carlos, Toño is also a Christ figure highlighted by the Calvary where he is murdered: a secluded beach dominated by a monumental stake that skewers the sand and ends in a sharp point, whose origins nobody seems to remember (ibid., 133). Also like Carlos, Jimmy is involved in an adulterous and scandalous affair, but unlike Carlos, Jimmy suffers the blows of an internal force: of a stroke that kills him. He is also described as a Christ figure by the narrator who heretically compares his adulterous affair with the Passion of the crucified Christ that hangs between the posts of his bed (ibid., 147). As in the case of the other characters, the narrator emphasizes the suicidal nature of Jimmy's lifestyle and describes his desires as an appetite for self-destruction (ibid., 147, 197).

Significantly, all of these figures are nothing if not versions of the detective's father, Tite Pérez: the Victim Father buried under the sadomasochistically crucified characters of both novels. Tite is the local, Puerto Rican, colonial version of the Freudian totem: the animal that kills itself. For Manolo, the unhappy cases of murder and adultery that he investigates are also reminders of his past, and they become simultaneous anamnestic journeys back to the life of his father and his mother. He describes his father as a man with the ambition to be a creole colonial master, but who ends up a slave to his castrating wife (*Mujer*, 183, 187). Tite, charming, charismatic, and with the gift of gab, likes to wear the costume of the colonial master: the wide Truman ties, the two-toned Oxford shoes, and the Panama hat from the title of the second novel (ibid., 183–84). But, like Carlos and Jimmy, Tite gradually becomes a sacrificial victim to his own inherent lack, to the void behind the screen of his ambitious but only apparent mastery (ibid., 187). He is a slave to the fear of causing harm, to the so-called virtue of commitment, to his unremarkable and obedient nature, all contained in his unassuming last name, Pérez, the opposite of the ostentatious family name his wife would have wanted for herself, and the source of her disappointment and great resentment against him (ibid., 185). In the end, Tite dies like all the victims of the novels, a victim of self-consuming rage. Self-deluded about his identity, Tite dies bitter and resentful, full of bile, his liver filled with rage, convinced that his life was a mistake (ibid., 186).

Tite, the Victim Father, is also represented in the novels as a Minotaur that is as haunting as the *Josco*. Rodríguez Juliá has written of his debt to the Argentine writer Jorge Luis Borges, and he considers the voice that emerges from his first police novel as a voice possessed by the return of an uncanny "other Borges" (Rodríguez Juliá 2003, 215). Rodríguez Juliá describes this voice as the blind spot in the stories of this famously blind seer: a first person narrative whose realism can only reveal the perplexity of an "ideé fixé, an obsession . . . the ideal limits of human experience" (ibid.). Rodríguez Juliá draws his Minotaur from the famous short story by Borges: "La casa de Asterión" (1947). But, if Rodríguez Juliá's Minotaur is a form of Borges's obsession, it is an abject mode of that obsession that becomes melancholy and even suicidal at the hands of the Puerto Rican writer.[16] The Minotaur in Rodríguez Juliá's novels is a thing that comes in and out of memory as an experience that cannot be looked at squarely in the face, an event that cannot be seen directly, like the midnight sun of the title, and like the Black Sun that is the abject for Kristeva.[17] More specifically still, what appears and disappears and haunts the detective is the strange way the Minotaur has of looking at him: the estranging and devouring look of the other; a stone-faced look; a paradoxical, perplexing, blind and blinding stare that also suggests the fundamental innocence of children to the narrator (*Sol*, 156).[18] And the perplexing, blind, innocent stare of the Minotaur is the same look that the detective's father had on his face when he died: "Father died seventeen years later, looking at us without affection, like one who stares at a wall," says Manolo (ibid., 186). The Minotaur's look and Tito Cáceres's stare are modes of a look that seems to put the father beyond the appeal of his sons. They are forms of an inward-looking stare that is the sign of the victim's innocence but also of the father's radically depressed and melancholy condition. They are the stigmata from the *Josco,* the signs of the suicidal Victim Father, the Puerto Rican version of the Christian Passion, and the central figure in the colonial fantasy represented by the phrase "a father beats himself to death." The narrator remembers his father telling him, "Shit, Manolo, everybody thinks that I fucked up her life, that [your mother] is the victim here; but it is the other way around, the other way around, I promise you" (ibid., 99).

The Big Mother

According to Kristeva, the lack of a paternal function (the loving and forgiving father open to its own dissolution and recomposition at the hands of its children) and the presence of a less-than-optimal Oedipus complex lead to the punishing figure of the Big Mother.[19] In Puerto Rico, the lack of a paternal function is the effect of a colonial situation that leads to the fantasy of paternal suicide. What are the consequences for the law, language, society, and culture of Puerto Rico of this lack of a paternal function, and of the presence instead of the colonial fantasy represented by the phrase "a father beats himself to death"? *Mujer con sombrero Panamá* gives an answer to this question. It begins with a reference both to a melancholy and to a vexed place that Manolo cannot escape. The place is a labyrinth that is also a trap for all the male characters of the novels, and that is the main consequence of the colonial fantasy represented by the phrase "a father beats himself to death": "And I, well I was under a dark cloud, as if prone to the sadness of remembering my youth, and that big mess that came right out of her mouth made me remember that all men have that place that they cannot forget, where we return with the illusion of tasting happiness, even if only once, of tasting that bitch absolute happiness" (*Mujer*, 7).

Manolo's investigations into the murder-suicides of Carlos, Jimmy, Toño, and Tite lead him to face and learn to navigate a permissive society without laws, a culture abandoned to its own worst instincts, a community in complete chaos and disarray that acts out a deadly eroticized rage and speaks in a language punctuated by its rhythms. Not surprisingly, at the center of what is (for the narrator) an excuse for a society, nothing but a web of intrigue, a labyrinth without exit, the Puerto Rican Noir detective, Manolo, finds the familiar figure of the Femme Fatale. In the novels, this figure is also marked by a curious difference. The sex-starved vixens are also soccer moms, maternal figures devoted to their families, and willing to go to any lengths to protect their "cubs." Migdalia is Carlos's lover, a woman who is also married with children. Her mother (an abject Dominican widow) is behind Carlos's assassination, and she kills to protect Migdalia's social status and that of her family. Similarly, Arelis is married with children, and wants to recover compromising love letters with Jimmy in order to save her marriage. She is described by the narrator as a two-sided monster and compared to a transvestite, a mixture of tenderness and coldness, a castrating and seductive woman, a being that "only yesterday was blowing her brains out with cocaine and today is a militant member of the PTA, frying fritters at the field day on Friday nights" (*Mujer*, 27). It is no coincidence that Arelis is also the woman with the Panama hat of the title. She is, in the words of Manolo, "Arelis, the big mother" (ibid., 123). She wears the outward signs of the master, and is indeed his replacement in a context where the appeal to the loving father is impossible, in a colonial context where the paternal function has been removed and replaced with a suicidal fantasy.

But none of these matricidal figures hold a candle to The Scorpion: the nickname Manolo gives to his mother Eva Cáceres, the wife of Tite Pérez. Eva (Spanish for Eve) is the complementary figure that boldly steps into the vacuum or void left by the fantasy of Tite's symbolic suicide. She is the daughter of the aspiring and frustrated patrician class of Creole masters displaced by the new rulers from the United States, and she appears to exact her revenge on everyone around her for the fall from grace of her social class. If Tite is a modern-day *Josco,* marked by an archaic inward depression and empty melancholy gaze, Eva is a "narcissistic gorgon," a complementary monstrous figure, whose eyes have a petrifying effect on the young Manolo (*Mujer*, 109, 187). Haunted by his feelings of shame that extend to his complicity in the death of his own brother, Manolo remembers a sadomasochistic scene from his infancy when his mother pretended to beat him with a plastic *machete* (the iconic weapon of the Puerto Rican peasant) in a fit of pretend rage. Eva appears to act out her incestuous desire for her son with eroticized cruelty. "What affected me most was to see that evil smile behind my mother's pretend madness, the cruelty with which she would look at my little dick and tell me that I was given a short shrift," Manolo remembers (ibid., 149). Eva's incestuous desire has a strong hold, or casts a shadow, over Manolo even after her death. He represents himself not only as the passive object of her desire, a petrified victim of fear and anxiety, and a possessed slave to her will, but also as her tool, her instrument, and the figure of her uncanny desire.[20] Defending himself against the accusation of fratricide, Manolo says that a strange voice speaking through him made him feel powerful enough to do anything: "The thick voice and mocking tones of an animal archaically bound by noisy chains spoke through my mouth: I felt powerful and luminous" (ibid., 105). Manolo denies responsibility for the murder of his brother by claiming to be the medium for his mother's voice, and the unwilling instrument of her resentment and anger against his father.

The Split Son

In this way, The Scorpion at the center of the fantasy represented by the phrase "a mother beats me to death" displaces the beast at the center of the fantasy represented by the phrase "a father beats himself to death," even as Manolo continues to gives an uncanny voice to the hermetic bellows of the sacrificed bull. Indeed, the investigations of the Noir detective of *Sol de medianoche* and *Mujer con sombrero Panamá* suggest that these complementary fantasies are shared by Puerto Rican males, and lead them to repeat similar scenes of incestuous permissiveness with the objects of their love, desire, and affection whether they are wives, lovers, same-sex partners, or close friends. Moreover, the investigations further suggest that these archaic fantasies of permissiveness in turn give rise to a lawless society, and to a culture that indulges in a rampant eroticized sadomasochistic social violence. Finally, these complementary fantasies produce the figure of a Split Son that is a pathological version of the undecidable identity produced by the paternal function, according to Kristeva. Instead, the Split Son is a borderline subject who denies responsibility for a crime that he nevertheless commits.

Manolo is the beneficiary and the effect of these fantasies insofar as he is the Noir detective who investigates his own crimes. In both novels, Manolo is responsible in one way or another for the murders and deaths that happen around him. He betrays Carlos's affair to Migdalia's mother and causes his death. He sets Toño's lover against him by suggesting that Toño is keeping the winning lottery ticket from him, leading to Toño's murder. He betrays Jimmy's wishes and Arelis's confidence by sending copies of the compromising letters to Yvette, Jimmy's wife, leading to the disarray of both families. And Manolo even betrays his own brother Frank, whom he appears to kill after a binge of alcohol and drugs. But Manolo is in pathological denial about all of these betrayals and murders, to the point that he is a split character in the novels, constantly looking for the murderer even as he hides clues from himself. He even goes so far as to figuratively kill this other Manolo (the fratricidal Manolo of *Sol de Medianoche*), as he begins the second novel, having moved away from his earlier haunts at the beach to the interior of the metropolitan area, having changed cars, and having sworn off alcohol and drugs. All done in vain, of course, as his repressed self resurrects and returns to haunt him with an irrepressible anger and resentment.

Parricide the Colonial Way

The task for the detective of these novels, then, becomes the investigation not so much of the person of the murderer, but of the Noir Eros and the colonial shame that lies behind the fantasies that lead to his split personality and his pathological denials of responsibility. Manolo calls this force "a profound shame, only comparable to the humiliations of infancy or adolescence," or "an essential guilt, barely concrete" (*Sol*, 51, 96). His investigations of this shame suggest that parricide is indeed the original murder that lies hidden behind the melodramatic fantasies of Puerto Rican passion after all. But parricide is again different from the archaic murder told by Freud in his story of the primal horde and developed by Kristeva in her account of the story of the Christian Passion. Like the Minotaur in Borges's story, who is saved by a redeemer who frees the beast at the end by killing him, delivering the Minotaur from the horror of his labyrinth, parricide is also a form of liberation in these novels. It is an act of compassion inspired by a sense of pity, mercy, and shame about the abject, castrated, and irredeemable figure of the Victim Father. It is an act that is similar to the execution in the title *They Shoot Horses, Don't They?*, a 1935 novel by Horace McCoy that serves as the epigraph to *Sol de medianoche*.

Indeed, the novels reveal a complicity in an archaic parricide whose form is the result of a shameful colonial history, the story of "El Josco," which makes the son feel so ashamed for the father, and feel the shame of the father to such a degree, that he must kill him as an act of love. Manolo's descriptions of his father are examples of this symbolic parricide insofar as those descriptions contain both an eroticized compassion and a murderous shame, and insofar as they also lead to a disturbing act of identification with the now-abject father:

> I inherited his timid, poor-devil, side, his good-for-nothing side, his sense of being impaired, disabled, that drove him to drink, the side that he never revealed to his buddies, even when he was drunk, of which only his women were aware, mother before anybody else, to her great credit. Now, in my forties, I always wonder whether the old man had a small dick. (*Mujer*, 184)

The effect of this colonial version of the archaic parricide is the internalization of an abject and abjecting Victim Father and his permissiveness. Paradoxically, the criminal community that Manolo investigates results from this incorporation: a community governed by lawlessness, chronic misogynous, racist, and homophobic reactions; by rituals of defilement all resulting from the fascination, the attraction, and the repulsion of the abject. It also leads to a feeling that the literary critic Mercedes López Baralt, quoting Fanon, describes as the misdirected rage of the colonized, an anger aimed at his brothers in suffering rather than at the so-called oppressor (López Baralt 2000, 371), a feeling that I prefer to describe as the raging and fiery sword of an avenging angel, the other Manolo, who is driven to put society out of its misery out of compassion, who, rather than band together with his brothers to create a society, is driven to fratricide out of colonial shame:

> I grew mad with tenderness, there in the shore. I loved him; but I would have wanted to kill him without much ceremony. I was drowning in such compassion!, assaulted by an urgent pity. I couldn't bear to see him like that. He was a warrior, fearless; *he wasn't made for captivity*. Perhaps I only wanted to set him free, to give wing to that beautiful hawk, a prisoner to the stupidity of the world. (*Sol*, 105; my emphasis)

Manolo is referring to his brother Frank, but he could just as easily be describing his male clients, his father, or even the mythical *Josco*.

The Cover-Up

Rodríguez Juliá's version of the archaic parricide is also the site of a cover-up. Compassion from shame is far from the compassion produced by the Christian elaboration of the story of the primal horde, according to Kristeva: the identification with the Dead Father, and the embrace of the desire for the Noir Eros. Instead, Rodríguez Juliá's local, colonial account of the Noir Eros, his description of a dark, profound, and essential shame dramatizes the morbid repetition of an undigestible, unreedemable, and abject thing at the origins of the fantasies of the Victim Father, the Big Mother, and the Split Son. The shame, the colonial Noir Eros of his novels, produces a peculiar kind of rhythm a language, and a mode of writing that keeps the thing buried, hidden, and beyond sublimation, making it more difficult to confront and work through its Noir desire. In other words, the cover-up makes difficult the appeal to a loving father, and is another instance of the repeated perversion of Puerto Rican literature (see chapter 3 in this book).

The novels both dramatize and illustrate a mode of writing that is modeled after a noise that Manolo remembers from his days as the bass drum player in his school's military band, days that he remembers in two dreams that occur in the second half of the first novel. In the first dream, Manolo finds himself back in a private Catholic high school, subjected to a pep talk from the bandleader, an English-speaking North American priest or father whom Manolo calls Roberto, the madman. Roberto is a Teutonic good-looking liar who doesn't even know how to read music but boasts of being the star pupil of the famous drummer Gene Krupa. After demoting Manolo to bass drum player, the father tries to convince him of the importance of his new position as a player of what the North American exaggeratedly calls the very foundation of the band, its most lasting instrument. As he listens to this pep talk, Manolo stands naked in the center of a stage that he compares to a bull ring, covering his private parts. He also describes the priest as a bloodied Christ figure on the way to Golgotha, threatening to contaminate him with his diseased blood. As he gives him the pep talk, the North American priest first tries to catch a glimpse of Manolo's genitals, and then averts his eyes in a gesture of shame for Manolo's own shameful situation. Manolo is tempted to display his genitals, aware "that compassion, and not lasciviousness, was the weakness of that dreamer" (*Sol*, 80). But he is prevented from doing so by the screams of his fellow students who watch him from the bleachers.

The second dream finds Manolo attending a game of the 1958 Caribbean Baseball Series with Tite. He describes his father in ways that remind the reader of the North American father of the earlier dream. Tite is a liar who hides from his buddies his awkwardness with women. He is a dissimulator who dresses as a colonial master, "something he always wanted to be, but never was" (*Sol*, 183). And he hides his eyes behind large dark glasses. In this dream, Manolo is sitting on the bleachers as he watches the game and as a superstar of Cuban baseball, Minnie Miñoso, looks and smiles at him from the baseball diamond. The baseball player wears a remarkable baseball cap that is very attractive to Manolo (he calls it a precious object) and when the game ends, Miñoso throws the baseball cap up in the air in triumph. Manolo, his father, and the player, wait for the cap to come down, but it never does. They become very anxious, even desperate, and Manolo sees himself playing the bass drum, thinking that the baseball cap will come down if he plays with solemnity and enthusiasm (ibid., 186). They wait so long that Miñoso lies down on the grass and gradually wastes away. Everybody disappears, but the baseball cap never returns, and Manolo is left by himself, embarrassed and playing the bass drum.

Manolo's dreams dramatize a profound lack of self-knowledge, a lack of appreciation for the shameful nature of the colonial situation, an ignorance that affects all the father figures of the novels across the ideological spectrum (colonized or colonizers), and that is the cause of their downfall, according to the logic of the novels. The fathers are blind to their own abjection, best represented by the dream, a version of the Passion of Christ where the life-giving blood of his suffering body is instead the sign of a contagious disease. This lack of self-knowledge then leads to an ignominious and shameful display. And with this display comes a complex sentimental education that perpetuates a similar lack of modesty and self-deception that culminates in the degradation of the other. In short, the loss of self-respect results in a spectacular display of nakedness, of vulnerability, a desire to disrobe, to take the hat off, to throw the baseball cap up in the air, to make a show of a naked head. Or conversely, shame results in the desire for eroticized articles of clothing that become compensatory fetishes for lack, fantasies that cover over the naked head, empty signs of self-respect, such as the Panama hat that is a fixture of both novels. Either way, the shame-full dreams reveal the desire of the father, the lasciviousness of the priest that Manolo does not dare to face. Arelis asks Manolo, "Listen, so what does the 'M' on your baseball cap stand for . . . ?" "It stands for mama's boy or for faggot," Manolo retorts with characteristic self-hatred (*Mujer*, 182).

Indeed, Manolo the bass drum player is the object of this sentimental education. He appears fundamentally ignorant about his own abjection. He repeats willful disavowals of his contamination with the symbolic father's diseased blood. He repeatedly denies his complicity and responsibility in the eroticized murder of the Victim Father with exaggerated protestations that nevertheless reveal an intimate knowledge of the disturbing paternal desires: "How am I to blame for Toño's friends! I don't know anything about that. . . . Or about his weaknesses" (*Mujer*, 172). And he turns this feigned ignorance, the disavowals and denials, into a perverse desire to degrade himself and others, into a phantasmatic noise similar to the empty sounding words of the pep talk of the American father, into a noise full of compensatory false vacuous uplifting words, and into a shameful display of pity for the shame of the other. This hollow sound is also the noise of the bass drum at the center of these dream sequences. In Spanish, the word for bass drum (*bombo*) is used in an idiomatic expression that is similar to the English "bells and whistles." *Con bombos y platillos* is an expression that means an ostentatious display. It is the sound of a triumphant celebration, a pretentious display of bells and whistles, that screens, hides, covers over, even as it reveals both a self-deception and a profound lack of self-respect. Manolo, the bass drum player, survives, but only as a lasting and shameful caricature, making a pathetic display of his ignorance about his self. His lasting shame hangs over the first novel in the form of a howling dying cat.

It hangs over the second novel as the raging echo of the roar of a V-8 1971 Malibú that Manolo drives during his midlife crisis. And it remains as the angry and self-punishing tone that hovers over the perverse, pornographic scenes that he goes on to describe in his so-called confession: "I write this confession to give some order to my shame," he tells us, expressing both guilt and pleasure at exposing himself (*Sol*, 51).

Noir Grammar and Punctuation

And yet, ironically, these verbalizations of the Noir Eros that continues to haunt the Puerto Rican colonial subject also return a measure of order to culture and language. The ambiguous narrative voice that Rodríguez Juliá gradually develops in his detective novels is perhaps the most representative figure of this order that is open insofar as it is sensitive to the uncanny language of the Noir Eros. In developing this voice, Rodríguez Juliá's detective novels represent a partially successful appeal to a symbolic loving father who responds with a Noir grammar (or a dark punctuation) from the grave where the colonial tradition of Puerto Rican storytelling tries to bury him. From this perspective, the narrative voice of the last chapter of *Mujer con sombrero Panamá* is a surviving sign of sublimation in the midst of a wasteland of colonial self-violence.

Sol de medianoche ends with a characteristic gesture of self-deception and denial. Manolo disavows his murderous side in a first person singular voice that nevertheless also discloses the guilt of the character, and displays an internal split in his voice that is typical of the hardboiled genre of the police novel. These are examples of the cracks in the voice that denies its actual fragility: "But I didn't pay any attention [to the person or the thing that was hiding from me]; I didn't pay attention to any of it" (*Sol*, 194). The novel is thirteen chapters long, and the first eight don't show any signs of wavering from a firmly entrenched first person singular narrative voice. But beginning with chapter 8, we see a first crack in this voice, after Manolo, feeling possessed by an evil presence that makes his voice strange, takes drugs and refers to himself with the second person singular pronoun. He listens as an inner voice that he does not recognize as his own warns him of a coming horror that he cannot face and will soon overcome him: "some voice . . . that you do not recognize as perfectly yours," says Manolo (ibid., 107). This inner voice appears sparingly in the first novel and develops into the voice of another Manolo: the voice of a Manolo who looks at himself in the mirror; a voice that speaks the truths that Manolo cannot face directly; a voice that appears to know him better than he knows himself; and a voice that he suggests belongs to the Minotaur who knows the way out of his labyrinth. "One must listen to the other, guess at the sound of his footsteps in the wasteland. He knows how to exit," the voice says (ibid., 190). This disturbing voice counterbalances the empty-sounding and often-repeated quirk that is Manolo's verbal signature in the novel, a rhetorical "no sir" or "yes sir" that punctuate his declarations of intent, and gives these declaration a fake obsequiousness. The disturbing voice is the voice of the thing, the person, or (better yet) the corpse that hides from Manolo's last phrase of the novel. It bears witness to Manolo's shame and self-deception.

Mujer con sombrero Panamá ends with a gesture of disavowal that bears witness to a self-deception. The narrator says, "It would take a while for [the receipt] to sink; now nobody ever again would ask about the identity of that man" (*Mujer*, 222). The narrator refers to a receipt marked "Prime Printing, Carlos Matos" that is the missing clue to Manolo's guilt. The narrative voice describes the piece of paper as it sinks into the murky waters of a lagoon, forever lost, while Manolo races away in his vintage car. The voice is in the first person and it is singular, but it is very different from the voice that begins the novel. Significantly, Manolo begins the second novel by describing a haunting voice that pursues him, a voice that reminds the reader of the thing that so disturbed the narrator at the end of the first novel, a voice that appeals to him for help. "That morning, as I crossed the Moscoso Bridge, her voice haunted me; it was, above all, the insistent tone that I help her, that only I could help her, that exploded one time and another against my earlobe," the detective says (ibid., 7). Arguably, the voice that ends the second novel has been overtaken by that haunting insistent appeal. It is a voice marked by grammatical fluidity, by the temporal and spatial indeterminacy of pronouns that make it difficult (if not impossible) to fix its location and source. Perhaps the most vivid example of this eerie quality of the voice of the end of the novel occurs three-quarters into the novel when Manolo dreams that he has photocopied the love letters he is expected to return unread and untouched. At that moment, he produces the paradoxical phrase, "Something within you insisted that I, and not Arelis, was the keeper of that treasure" (ibid., 176). The phrase is riddled with the splits in the detective's personality. The voice refers to a thing inside the self. This thing is an other "I" that splits from the self (and that is also an undecideable voice that has no fixed place, time, nor person). This thing is also the voice of the keeper of the letters. This strange voice gains more autonomy as the novel progresses and in the last chapter it has separated completely from Manolo, and even becomes a separate character in the novel. It drives a different car from Manolo (a Dodge Challenger). It follows Manolo as he looks for his lost friend (Carabine Commander). And finally, it bears witness to Manolo's guilt and self-deception.

We cannot know the identity of this voice because it moves awkwardly between voices; between the voice of the other Manolo, the voice of his reflection in the mirror, the voice of his drugged self, the voice of an omniscient narrator and the voice of a mysterious character. All we know is that it is a pronoun as indeterminate and flexible as the second person singular that sometimes appears to call out to Manolo, and at other times addresses the reader of the novel. It is the flexible pronoun of phrases that sometimes order Manolo around and that sometimes stand in critical judgment of him: the voice says, "Wake up already, and feel how difficult it is. . . . Think yourself already dead, only to find out that your eyelids are heavy from so much alcohol and drugs" (*Mujer*, 214–15). The voice makes phrases like the ones that end both novels, which also suspend judgment and allow Manolo to escape from responsibility, but only by a very narrow margin. The phrases of this voice are a negative mode of writing that affirms by denying. They suggest Manolo's shame by declaring lost the incriminating evidence of his guilt. They contain the uncanny temporality of the conditional mode, the future of the past. They remain, like the lost receipt of something purchased, like soiled, buried, and abject proof of Manolo's shame. From this perspective, the voice that ends the second novel is an example of a form of writing that brings the deluded self back to reality. It is similar to the look of the other that Rodríguez Juliá describes in another context. It is a self-critical look back at the self from its abjection. It describes the memory, the antecedents, of a subject that is overcome by suffering. This is a subject that is racked with pain, and that is struck by history, as Rodríguez Juliá puts it (2003, 278). It is also the barely audible voice of a Dead Father. The testimony of a loving father that is barely alive.

The Survival of a Noir Eros

"El Josco" is a Puerto Rican form of the fantasy represented by the phrase "a father-son is beaten to death." It is a colonial elaboration of the story of the Christian fantasy as Kristeva understands it. Rodríguez Juliá's two police novels are efforts to work through the obstacles that such colonial storytelling puts in the way of the language of the Noir Eros. The novels work through these obstacles first by repeating the displacements and disavowals of Puerto Rican storytelling. In other words, the novels repeat and make visible again the familiar figures of the Puerto Rican symbolic family: the Victim Father, the Big Mother, and the Split Son. But the novels also add a revelation to this repetition. These detective novels also contain an interrogation of the perplexing Noir Eros that continues to haunt the subject, despite of, and because of, its repeated disavowals. As a result, *Sol de medianoche* focuses on the figure of the Big Mother and the fantasy represented by the phrase "a mother beats me to death" that emerges from the Puerto Rican tradition of storytelling. Similarly, *Mujer con sombrero Panamá* focuses on the obsessive displacement of responsibility that is at the center of the guilt-ridden Puerto Rican subject. They are both vexed appeals to the uncanny language of the Noir Eros. On the one hand, they attempt to return meaning by verbalizing its negative language. On the other, the uncanny language of the Noir Eros inevitably speaks through these novels, and they give it a means of expression.

The Noir Eros is an old and insistent component of subjectivity, older even than "El Josco." The literary critic Rubén Ríos Ávila has traced this component back not only to *El velorio*, the 1895 painting by the Puerto Rican painter Francisco Oller, but even to an archaic form of colonialism to which we all subject ourselves, whether we like it or not. For Ríos Ávila, this is the traumatic desire for (and desire of) the symbolic father of the law (2002, 20).[21] In this chapter, I suggest instead that the works of Díaz Alfaro and Rodríguez Juliá work through a Noir Eros (an incestuous sadomasochistic desire, a dread, and a joy) that is anterior to the Lacanian father of the law, and that is disavowed by their colonial contexts (see chapter 2 of this book). From this archaic perspective, "El Josco," *Sol de medianoche*, and *Mujer con sombrero Panamá* are examples in literature of the colonial version of a Noir Eros. They are literary events that represent the perversion of Puerto Rican culture, society, and laws. They are, in the untranslatable words of Ramos Otero, examples of the *culonización* of Puerto Rican humanity: the vexed erotization of abjection that results from colonialism. But they are also examples of colonial discourses that work through this Noir Eros. As such, these texts are also examples of sublimation. Vexed as they might be, they give form to the otherwise haunting fantasies of the colonial Noir Eros. In this sense, the works of Rodríguez Juliá are part of the same tradition of sublimation and perversion of the abject to which belong the other works of literature represented in this book.

6

Shame, Repetition, and Forgiveness in Queer Latino *Testimonio*

IMPOSSIBLE MOTHERHOOD AND *DIARIO DE UNA PUTA HUMILDE*

> I had twelve abortions in eleven years and they were the happiest years of my life.
>
> —Irene Vilar

> I knew I was addicted to blushing, which only happened when they said things to me that I would consider offensive at any other time. —Come on Bitch! Shake your ass you dirty faggot! Goddamned queer!
>
> —Caleb Acevedo

Both Vilar's *Impossible Motherhood, Testimony of an Abortion Addict* (2009) and Caleb Acevedo's *Diario de una puta humilde* (2012) are confessional and testimonial accounts characterized by the repeated representation of a bodily act of ejection or penetration that separates the speaking subject from the community. Whether it is male homosexual intercourse (safe or not) or whether it is abortion (legal or not), both works are constituted by the repeated representation of a bodily act that is shameful to their respective communities (Puerto Rican, American, or both). Both works are also constituted by the authors' ambivalent representation of that act, by their contradictory meditations on the meaning of that act, and by the voicing, performance, and overcoming of the ambiguous shame attached to that act. In what follows, I will argue that both works are representative examples of what Arnaldo Cruz-Malavé has called "queer Latino *testimonio*," an antidote to what Kelly Oliver has called the social melancholy of colonization. And I will argue that the curative effect of these *testimonios* is based on their ambiguous representation of colonial shame, on the one hand, and on their attempt to reconnect the abject body with language, on the other. Three ingredients characterize these testimonial antidotes to social melancholy: shame, repetition, and forgiveness.

Either the scandalous nature of both books, or perhaps their literary quality, has made them the object of notoriety and recognition: *Impossible Motherhood* was the winner of the 2010 Independent Publisher's Book Award for best memoir, and of the Latino Book Award for women's issues, while *Diario* received an honorable mention by the Pen Club of Puerto Rico for best memoir of 2013. Either way, they have certainly been the object of much commentary in the popular press and Internet blogs. However, they have also been the object of little serious study, at least so far. And it is remarkable that the little critical attention that they have received is disapproving, or ambivalent at best (see Ríos Ávila "Pornoliteratura" and Thompson). This essay is a contribution to this scarce bibliography in an attempt to elaborate on the ambiguous character and reception of queer Latino *testimonios* that are increasingly popular but that continue to generate little serious discussion—consider, for example, the works by Angel Lozada, *La patografía* (1998) and *No quiero quedarme sola y vacía* (2006), but also the parallel genre of dirty realism (see Birkenmeier). Arguably, the scant attention is a sign that such works are proving increasingly difficult to understand, perhaps because of the intensity with which our culture reduces them to mere scandalous and unspeakable (if also sometimes profitable) examples of shameful and meaningless colonized subjectivities. This chapter is an attempt to begin reversing that trend.

Colonial Shame

Ten years ago, Frances Negrón-Muntaner started a debate about colonial shame in the fields of Puerto Rican literary and cultural studies with the publication of *Boricua Pop: Puerto Ricans and the Latinization of American Culture* (2004). In that book, Negrón-Muntaner gives a social account of shame in the context of colonial transculturation. Drawing from both the work of José Luis González on colonial transculturation and from the work of Eve Kosofsky Sedgwick on gay shame, Negrón-Muntaner argues that colonial shame is not a private pathology. She argues instead that it is an affect generated in conflict "within asymmetrical power relations" (2004, xiii).[1] She describes colonial shame as both a symptom of colonial transculturation and as inseparable from Puerto Rican identity: "In fact, if it were not for the 'shame' of being Puerto Rican, [she writes] there would be no boricua identity, at least not as we know it" (ibid., xiii).

Negrón-Muntaner suggests that colonial shame is the effect of what she calls the Puerto Rican "entanglement" with the United States, which is in turn the effect of colonial transculturation: the blending of two cultures that results from colonialism and its cultural crossovers. Drawing from González's "El país de cuatro pisos" (1980), Negrón-Muntaner compares this "blending" process to a "freakish," violent, and sometimes deadly dream that is perceived as dangerous, that is unsuccessfully policed, that can be (and sometimes is) eroticized, and that allows subaltern cultures to flourish inadvertently. Drawing from Sedgwick's work, she also concludes that colonial transculturation is a process from which Puerto Ricans always awaken shaken, disturbed, changed or in a state of shame: "Yet from the grave, what is freakishly alive and cannot help but comfort us in these uncharted trips is the obstinate fact that even from the deadliest of dreams others, however shaken, always awaken" (Negrón-Muntaner 2004, 278).

In fact, according to Negrón-Muntaner, colonial shame is the central affect that haunts the identities that emerge from the process of colonial transculturation. And *Boricua Pop* is an account of the forms that colonial shame takes in so-called Boricuas, but also in Latinos, AmeRícans, or simply Americans. According to Negrón-Muntaner, colonial transculturation is accompanied by a long-standing contempt for Puerto Ricans, as well as by disciplinary and punitive measures that include shaming discourses that represent Puerto Ricans as inferior, as unmanly, cowardly, effeminate, meek, and as docile members of an inferior race. And Negrón-Muntaner argues that the effect of this process on Puerto Ricans is the production of a subject that is always in a state of shame and is also always trying to attenuate or to offset it: "[W]hat contemporary boricuas often share [she writes] are common sites of 'colonial' shame and resources to counter them" (Negrón-Muntaner 2004, 6).[2]

Negrón-Muntaner distinguishes between two main class-inflected ways of attenuating or offsetting this constitutive colonial shame: either disavowal or insolence, as Cruz-Malavé succinctly puts it (2007a, 111). She argues that if Puerto Rican elites disavow colonial shame by means of a nationalistic literary tradition, Puerto Ricans from the middle and working classes insolently redeploy and resignify colonial shame as shameless public spectacle. Of the two responses, Negrón-Muntaner clearly considers insolence more subversive. She insists on the transformational value of the "purposefully disrespectful . . . spectacles to upper-class decorum and masculinity" of the working class (Negrón-Muntaner 2004, 14), and of the attention that successful Puerto Rican entertainers such as Jennifer López and Ricky Martin pay to their eroticized, racialized, and shamed bodies in their performances.

Negrón-Muntaner also warns that even these efforts to attenuate colonial shame by redeploying it as a racially and sexually ambiguous commodity do not resolve the problem of colonial transculturation, and so the symptom of colonial shame remains and repeats. Ricky Martin is a case in point. She argues that he uses the global market to his advantage, and combines a strategy to overcome the shame of being Puerto Rican with a strategy to overcome the shame of being gay. In other words, he dances a straight rumba that whitens African traditions and keeps homosexuality at bay. But in the end, Negrón-Muntaner argues, colonial shame comes back to haunt even Ricky Martin, keeping him in the closet or turning him into a sellout.[3]

Sinverguencería, pudor, and *sentimiento*

Within five years of Negrón-Muntaner's effective combination of the theory of colonial transculturation with the theory of gay shame to produce the concept of colonial shame, a series of influential papers, essays, and books are delivered and published extending but also changing some of her conclusions. Critics of Puerto Rican studies such as Lawrence La Fountain-Stokes, Ríos Ávila, and Cruz-Malavé emphasize what Negrón-Muntaner merely suggests in her book.[4] They explicitly criticize the deployment of gay shame as a universal concept by queer theory, and emphasize its limited use in the Puerto Rican context, where it does not apply given the colonial inflection of shame. Second, they criticize the problematic reduction by mainstream queer theory of queer Latinos to the role of passive victim.[5] And third, they develop three concepts that not only take gay shame in a different direction from mainstream queer theory but also add different meanings to Negrón-Muntaner's colonial shame: La Fountain-Stokes's *sinverguencería* (shamelessness), Ríos Ávila's *pudor* (modesty), and Cruz-Malavé's *sentimiento* (discretion-shame).

Of the three concepts, La Fountain-Stokes's *sinverguencería* is perhaps the closest in spirit to Negrón-Muntaner's colonial shame. In a series of popular conferences (and in a followup essay), La Fountain-Stokes extends Negrón-Muntaner's insights about colonial shame and subversive shamelessness to the diasporic Puerto Rican homosexual subject, and he uses both colonial shame and subversive shamelessness to develop the somewhat different concept of Puerto Rican or Latino/a *sinverguencería*.[6] With this concept, La Fountain-Stokes describes a provocative, iconoclastic, guilt-free, and parodic reaction to shaming practices, a reaction that takes pride in transgression, and that originates in anger rather than in shame. He associates *sinverguencería* with its meaning in Spanish: a quick-witted reaction that does not do great harm (La Fountain-Stokes 2011, 72). And he ends his essay with an example of it.

La Fountain-Stokes describes his own ironic and bilingual use of the word *diarrhea* in a short story titled "Shit/La Mierda," a word that he reminds us is dramatized by the Puerto Rican actor Mario Montez in a film by Andy Warhol.[7] La Fountain-Stokes's bilingual example contrasts with the monolingual use of the same word by an attendee of a Gay Shame conference in 2003, who (according to Judith Halberstam) used the same word to demean the people of color presenting work at the conference by mocking the Puerto Rican accent of Montez.[8] La Fountain-Stokes suggests that the difference between the two shameless uses of the offensive word is twofold. On the one hand, he does not use the word to insult others, but aims the word squarely at himself: "I am pleased that my verbal shit preceded Warner's, and that on both occasions of its public display it has been for Spanish-speaking Latina and Latino audiences in New York, for people who know what I mean when I say *que cagarse encima es algo desagradable, pero total, así es la vida*" (La Fountain-Stokes 2011, 75). On the other, rather than use the word to do harm to himself, he uses it to establish a link with a community of interlocutors that is familiar not only with code switching, but also with the irony of a colonial situation that reaches even the language in which you try to protest. From this perspective, La Fountain-Stokes's concept of Latina/o *sinverguencería* both repeats Negrón-Muntaner's account of colonial shame and subversive shamelessness, but also goes beyond it. The self-inflicted nature of *sinverguencería*, and its emphasis on the presence of a receptive audience that understands this gesture of self-undoing and still offers community support, transcends the entanglement of colonial shame that is "impossible to undo" according to Negrón-Muntaner (2004, 8).[9]

Perhaps critic Ríos Ávila presents the strongest challenge to Negrón-Muntaner's account of colonial shame. More sympathetic than Negrón-Muntaner (and La Fountain-Stokes) to psychoanalytic theory, and drawing from the account of shame by film critic Joan Copjec, Ríos Ávila develops a theory of what he calls the *pudor* (modesty, shyness, or even remorse) of radical shame. He bases his theory on the principle that "we live in a world without an Other" (Ríos Ávila 2013, 6), which he draws from Copjec's book *Imagine There's No Woman* ("Queer Latino Shame," 18).[10] The theory rests on the distinction between psychoanalytic shame and guilt. Briefly put, psychoanalytic guilt is the result of not measuring up to the scrutiny of an other who desires us, whether this desire is direct or indirect. In psychoanalysis, this desire is usually paternal, and it is usually incorporated into the psychic structure called the superego. In other words, we feel psychoanalytic guilt because we owe an enormous debt to a superego that we cannot pay back. Psychoanalytic shame, on the other hand, is the feeling that we get from realizing that the superego is nothing but a fantasy that covers over a lack that nevertheless constitutes us. The fantasy of the superego is the effect of a constantly changing chain of names for that lack, which series together appears to give the lack the consistent appearance of a presence. When we realize that the superego and its other are in fact lacking, we realize that we have also laid bare or exposed our radical nakedness. In other words, we come to realize that the psychic mechanism that appears to cover our exposed nakedness with the trappings of civilization is all made up. It is but a mirage. When we realize that we stand figuratively naked in the world, or that we stand only with the fiction of an other giving us civilized form, at that moment we feel a radical shame accompanied by *pudor,* according to Ríos Ávila.

Radical shamelessness is what we feel when we react to this radical shame without *pudor*. Ríos Ávila argues that radical shamelessness is what we feel in the time of late capitalism, a moment in the development of Western liberal democracies when we have not only done away with the superego—and with all of the names that we used to give to it including the Paterfamilias, God, or the State—but we have even done away with the function that we had assigned to the superego, that is, the function to judge, to forbid, and to punish. Instead of living in a society that disavows colonial shame, Ríos Ávila argues we live in one that disavows the loss of the superego and the radical shame such a loss produces. And instead of deploying shamelessness as a strategy to attenuate or even transcend colonial shame, he argues that by ignoring our *pudor* to the point of forbidding prohibition itself, we succumb to radical shamelessness, and we make everything available to our senses. He suggests that lacking both a superego and the radical sense of shame from our exposed nakedness, we also feel no *pudor,* and we are not shy about exposing ourselves to every kind of experience no matter how morally objectionable or physically repulsive and abject.[11]

Ríos Ávila's argument suggests that analyses of colonial shame that indict consensual colonialism are in fact attempts to reinstate a superego that we have discovered does not exist.[12] It also suggests that such accounts are attempts to buttress or reinforce a phantasmatic structure that we know is not really there. For Ríos Ávila, critics such as Negrón-Muntaner disavow the lack of a superego that is apparent to our contemporary culture, and this disavowal leads to an unproductive resentment. In fact, our real problem, according to Ríos Ávila, is not the lack of a superego, but the lack of *pudor* with which we live that lack, or the disavowal of the radical shame that this lack makes us feel. If we don't get a grip on this problem, if we don't work, for example, on an ethics based on the understanding of our figurative nakedness, an ethics perhaps based on *pudor,* we will continue to be in the grip of radical shame, and as a result will continue to act shamelessly, or only according to our unconscious self-interest and pleasure, whether it be in the context of colonialism or liberal democracy. For Ríos Ávila, such an ethics might instead produce the knowledge that when we act we are only accountable to ourselves, and if this does not give us pause, it should give us enough sense to admit that we will probably be selfishly wrong in the end. At the very least, it should give us enough presence of mind to take responsibility for mistakes that are radically our own. But given his insistence on the fiction of the superego, and the so-called radical and constitutive lack at the center of the subject, Ríos Ávila fails to explain why his account of radical shame would necessarily lead to an ethics of *pudor,* and not simply take us back to nihilistic *sinverguencería.*

Almost simultaneously with Ríos Ávila's theory of *pudor,* and drawing from the work on shame by Silvan Tomkins and Carl D. Schneider instead of Lacan, Cruz-Malavé develops and deploys the more helpful concept of *sentimiento* in a series of introductory essays to what he calls a "queer Latino *testimonio*" by the Puerto Rican Juan Rivera (also called Juanito of the house of Xtravaganza).[13] Cruz-Malavé writes that he was paralyzed by shame when Rivera asked him to transcribe and to publish his *testimonio,* but that his feeling was different from the colonial shame of Negrón-Muntaner, as well as from the *sinverguencería* of La Fountain-Stokes: "[M]y particular sense of paralyzing shame . . . had neither to do with insolence nor the disavowal of personal disgrace," he writes (2007a, 111). Instead, Cruz-Malavé describes his shame as a form of *sentimiento*: "'He was struck by *sentimiento,*' they say when a child is confronted with an act that does not hurt her but damages her community instead—an act whose consequences might jeopardize the familial bond, betray the loyalty of those whom she loves the most" (ibid., 110).

In his description of the origins of *sentimiento,* Cruz-Malavé hints at a definition of transculturation that goes beyond González's and Negrón-Muntaner's definitions. He also points to the concept of discretion-shame, which similarly goes beyond colonial shame, *sinverguencería,* or *pudor*. For Cruz-Malavé, transculturation contains a strange and ambivalent identification between an individual self and the community that is left behind.[14] He writes, "My sense of shame had to do with wanting to live up to that impossibly simultaneous command at the heart of . . . *testimonio* both to shelter and expose, to divulge and protect" (2007a, 111). If we take this ambivalent identification to its logical conclusion, then transculturation also must be a paradoxical injunction to the migrant by the community that is newly joined. The injunction must be both to enter and to remain outside of the community. Either from the perspective of the community left behind, or from the perspective of the community newly joined, the individual self always experiences this ambivalent rupture and connection with the other, a strange link that simultaneously puts limits on the mutual relation of the self and the other, but also sets the conditions of possibility for their mutual existence, according to Cruz-Malavé.

He also argues that transculturation provokes not only the paradoxical feeling of loyalty and betrayal that is *sentimiento,* but it is also the origin of the similarly contradictory affect that Schneider calls discretion-shame: "that sense of shame that comes as a result of transgressing or breaching a community or personally sanctioned secret, mystery, or veil that proscribes indiscriminate access and sets limits to one's and others' invasive gaze," Cruz-Malavé writes (2007a, 111). According to Cruz-Malavé, discretion-shame is a form of tentativeness that results from the paradoxical injunction to the individual by the community of origin both to keep, but also to reveal its secrets. Like Ríos Ávila's *pudor,* Cruz-Malavé's discretion-shame is a source of ambivalent action, and it is the source of Juan Rivera's all-important minimal gestures of hesitation, elision, detour, and deviation in his *testimonio.*[15] These ambivalent gestures are in turn the source of Cruz-Malavé's ethical paralysis, which prevents him from publishing the *testimonio* for ten years. Paradoxically, these minimal gestures of hesitation are also the source of the hope that eventually leads Cruz-Malavé to answer Rivera's call, and to publish the queer memoir (ibid., 119). Indeed, insofar as *sentimiento* is the effect of an ambivalent command to keep the secrets of the community but also to betray them, and insofar as *sentimiento* also literally means "feeling" in Spanish, we can conclude that *sentimiento* is a radically ambivalent form of discretion-shame, which leads to a similarly ambivalent form of action.

From this perspective, Cruz-Malavé's *sentimiento* is a more paradoxical link between the self and the other than the connection to the bilingual community that La Fountain-Stokes describes in his account of *sinverguencería*. For La Fountain-Stokes, the link is a connection that gives him the feeling of being understood by that community, which allows him to act, speak, and write. For Cruz-Malavé, the link is a shifting and preexisting ground of engagement; it is both a command to stay and an invitation to leave; and it contains both shame and love. He writes, "For shame makes one pause . . . it also makes one . . . hyperconscious . . . of the irreducibility of one's engagement with the extra-communal other . . . even of one's love" (2007a, 99). The unstable ground of the *sentimiento* of discretion-shame allows Cruz-Malavé to accept Rivera's invitation ten years after receiving it. Similarly, the shifting ground of *sentimiento* allows Cruz-Malavé to publish Rivera's disturbing and hopeful queer Latino *testimonio* but only after an ambivalent gesture, after he loses the recording of his interview with Rivera (ibid., 9).

Social Melancholy

In *Colonization of Psychic Space* (2004), Oliver makes a compelling case against the ideal sovereign other or superego (which, arguably, critics such as Negrón-Muntaner would like to reinstate), but also against the notion of a constitutive lack at the center of the subject (which critics such as Ríos Ávila would like to face with *pudor*).[16] Drawing mainly from Kristeva's complementary notions of "intimate revolt" and "forgiveness," and also from Fanon's psychoanalytic study of the paradoxical effects of colonialism on the psyche of the colonized, Oliver gives an account of the complex affect that Cruz-Malavé calls *sentimiento*, but emphasizes its embodied nature. She also offers the sustained connection with this bodily affect as an antidote to the social melancholy of colonization.

Oliver describes in her book a circuit of affect where shame and forgiveness are as inseparable as the self is from the other. According to Oliver, shame is an archaic affect that is different from guilt in that it is the effect of a break in the primary contact or communication with an other or with others. But an equally fundamental insight is that subjectivity requires both this break and also the connection that must give rise to it. She writes, "In so far as shame signals the longing to belong, it can engender alternative forms of community" (Oliver 2004, 120). Shame, then, is simultaneously a feeling that confirms and even asserts individuality but that also gives rise to the hope and to the wish to reconnect with others. From this perspective, shame is the obverse of an equally primary already always existing ambiguous connection that makes possible both the return of the individual to the community and its original act of transgression against the community. In other words, Oliver's account of shame is similar to Cruz-Malavé's *sentimiento* of discretion-shame insofar as both are feelings associated with breaking with an other and also with the longing to belong.

Oliver also describes an equally important circuit of shame and language in her book. If shame is an archaic feeling, it is not necessarily experienced at the level of conscious thought. In fact, it is a feeling associated with the unconscious bodily affects, or the affects associated with bodily functions such as secretion, excretion, ejection, penetration, or incorporation. These bodily functions and their affects are the means through which the first boundaries of the subject are generated according to Oliver. But shame is also a feeling of a body that is already always in connection with (or in communication with) another body, even as that connection is continually broken and reestablished. That is, shame is also meaningful because it is social at its very origins. In fact, shame is at the origins of language insofar as shame is a form of address and a form of representation from its very archaic beginnings. Shame is a feeling subtended by a material connection to the other that is also an invocation, an interpellation, an ambivalent "yes," a hesitant "no," that generates meaningful difference and similarity between bodies that continuously come together and separate. In this, Oliver's account of shame is also similar to Cruz-Malavé's *sentimiento* of discretion-shame insofar as both are intimately related to the body and both are also ambivalent forms of embodied signification.

According to Oliver, shame and support, transgression and forgiveness, are circulating affects that generate the fluid connection and the difference between the self and the other, between body and language. And forms of oppression like colonialism, racism, and sexism threaten to interrupt this circuit of affect in a particular way. These forms of oppression produce the shame of the colonized, which Oliver calls social melancholy, a condition that is characterized by a doubling of shame, and that fixes the colonized other in a depressed position, separating the colonized self from the community forever, but also separating it from language. According to her, social melancholy is the symptom of the disavowal and of the displacement of shame by the community. In other words, the social melancholy of the depressed originates in the refusal of the privileged subject to carry the burden of their own shame, dumping it instead onto the colonized other. As bearers of their own constitutive shame plus the shame of the community, the colonized even feel ashamed of feeling shame, and they are radically othered. As carriers of the sum of the unwanted bodily affects of their community they become the irreducible and also unintelligible examples of what remains almost radically outside of the measure of the social. In other words, they are put shamelessly (without remorse or *pudor*) outside language, they are made both mute and unspeakable. Oliver's account of social melancholy is like Cruz-Malavé's paralyzing shame, insofar as both interrupt the necessary connection between body and language, and leave the subject almost immobile and speechless.

Hyperbolic Forgiveness

How do we listen to, read, let alone find meaning in unspeakable shame? How do we return meaning to a language and to a bodily affect that is not only silenced by a community, but that is constitutively distorted by that community at the most basic level: to the point that a speaking community disavows and displaces its bodily affect on to subjects that by their very definition will sound garbled and will write nonsense to us? Oliver suggests a process of idealization based on what I will call hyperbolic forgiveness as a solution to the problem of the colonized other and its unspeakable shame. "This process of idealization [she writes] does not punish but rather forgives (or fore-gives meaning)" (2004, 140). In other words, she calls for an attitude of radical responsibility that is both social and individual. This is an attitude that presupposes meaning from the very get-go, before we hear the first word or read the first line that will be nothing but nonsense to us. It is an attitude that we take even before the first sound or mark is made by those who do not have a voice, by those without a sanctioned language, by those without a means to express themselves in writing, and/or whose expression is certain to revolt us. This attitude is the key ingredient to Cruz-Malavé's definition of queer Latino *testimonio* insofar as it is what allows meaning to return to the otherwise unspeakable body at its center.

Hyperbolic forgiveness requires being in tune with a vibration, with a rhythm, that is originally a bodily affect that we abject, that we have grown accustomed to minimize and even to reject, an affect that has become all but impossible for us to feel in ourselves, let alone accept in the other: the reversible and transmissible affect of our own and the other's shame. And in the face of the close-to-impregnable nature of this archaic affect, hyperbolic forgiveness requires acting as if we nevertheless felt it, performing the whisper of discretion-shame as if we really heard it, interpreting the signs of *sentimiento* as if we in fact read them, and trusting that this ethical prolepsis is just enough to jumpstart the forgiveness or the responsibility that is necessary for meaning and that is the prior guarantee of sense. We must practice a hyperbolic forgiveness that requires anticipating the repetition of what will be nonsense to us, that offers an invitation to the recalcitrant nonsense that pushes against meaning: an attitude that always already represents *sentimiento* and that gives value to its discretion-shame.[17] Briefly put, hyperbolic forgiveness is the attitude of the speaking subject of the queer Latino *testimonio*.

Cruz-Malavé writes with this attitude when he titles his two introductions to Rivera's *testimonio* with the oxymoron "Listening Speaks." In fact, the oxymoron can even stand as a figure for the whole book in so far as *Queer Latino Testimonio* contains a form of reading with an eye for distorted signs, and a form of writing with an ear for jarring sounds. In it, Cruz-Malavé interprets signs and sounds by Rivera and Montez that appear to be nothing but nonsense. In it, Cruz-Malavé focuses on the very resistance, the ambiguity, and the density of a form of nonsense that is actually the sign of the *sentimiento* of discretion-shame. Such an example of reading and writing requires the attitude of hyperbolic forgiveness that does two related things for Cruz-Malavé. Hyperbolic forgiveness first allows him to transvaluate the nonsense that is loaded with discretion-shame into an invitation to engage: the invitation of minimal gestures of hesitation, elision, detour, and deviation that make up the queer Latino *testimonio* of Rivera and Mario Montez. Second, hyperbolic forgiveness also allows Cruz-Malavé to feel the vibration, to hear the rhythm, and to see the meaningful gesture of a body still alive inside this minimal morpheme, a body that is always a part of the language of *sentimiento,* and a body that is always a part of the work of queer Latino *testimonio.*[18]

In *Queer Latino Testimonio*, Cruz-Malavé promises to transcribe Rivera's *testimonio* according to the inner logic of Rivera's disturbing storytelling. With this promise he suggests that the driving inner logic of queer Latino *testimonio* is the feeling of discretion-shame. And Cruz-Malavé also promises to read the signs of a living body in Rivera's *testimonio*. With this promise he suggests that the expression of the feeling of discretion-shame at the center of Rivera's *testimonio* is the embodied language of *sentimiento*. Indeed, I would argue that transvaluating discretion-shame and learning to speak the body language of *sentimiento* are the two lessons of Cruz-Malavé's book. Both lessons are contained in the repeating epigraph: "Listening, your heart is in your throat." The quote is from a book on opera by Wayne Koestenbaum, and it suggests a paradoxical (some might say nonsensical) definition of listening first as a feeling, and second as the feeling when our heart is in our throat. When is listening a feeling? Is it when it goes beyond the conscious and mental act of hearing? And when is our heart in our throat? Is it when we are gripped by a feeling that makes our voice tremble with the rhythm of our heart? In the context of repeating forms of oppression such as colonization, racism, and sexism, the quote suggests that to listen ethically is to proleptically feel the *sentimiento* of discretion-shame. The quote also suggests that to reverse the social melancholy of colonization we must proleptically hear the voice of *sentimiento* in queer Latino *testimonio*. In short, we must anticipate the objection to the forgiveness inherent to *sentimiento* with a hyperbolic forgiveness. In what follows, I will draw from these two works by Oliver and Cruz-Malavé in order to describe the three ingredients that characterize two contemporary Puerto Rican queer Latino *testimonios*: shame, repetition, and forgiveness. By doing so, I hope to return a measure of meaning to two contemporary examples of the repeating scene of self-undoing that I study in this book.

Reading and Writing Nonsense

Irene Vilar (1969–) and Caleb Acevedo (1980–) are two writers from Puerto Rico who have spent a considerable part of their lives in the United States.[19] Vilar is the author of *The Ladies's Gallery: A Memoir of Family Secrets* (1996), a work written in Spanish but published only in an English translation by Gregory Rabassa. Caleb Acevedo is a poet, a writer of fiction, and a translator.[20] Their two latest *testimonios* have been both notorious and popular, and for the most part they have been ignored by the academic community with the exception of two sophisticated studies that appeared in 2014: one by a specialist on queer theory (Ríos Ávila) and the other by a specialist on feminist theory and motherhood studies (Thompson). The articles are written from two very different perspectives (one psychoanalytic, the other sociological), but they both focus on the central issue of shame or its obverse shamelessness, and they arrive at similar conclusions. Although they express their appreciation for aspects of the works, they also end by expressing a profound concern over what the works represent.

Thompson praises Vilar's *testimonio* for bringing the difficult subject of repeat abortion into the mainstream. She also praises Vilar's ability to make her readers see (and feel) the effect on women of our culture's negative attitude toward abortion with the metaphor of addiction, a sign of Vilar's symptomatic and representative ambivalence about her experience, according to Thompson. But she also finds much to criticize in Vilar's *testimonio*. On the one hand, she suggests that colonial shame drives Vilar away from identifying with the negative stereotype of out-of-control Latina reproduction. On the other, she suggests that a rhetoric of neoliberal personal accountability drives Vilar toward an idealized stereotype of antiabortion motherhood. And (Thompson continues) this rhetoric of personal shame and redemption is in turn based on the values and the privilege of the white middle class that Vilar aspires to join. For Thompson, *Impossible Motherhood* represents a concession and even a capitulation to an oppressive economic system organized according to patriarchal and neoliberal values.

Ríos Ávila praises *Diario* for its sharp and brilliant language. But he also suggests that its brilliance is in fact the result of the unmitigated *jouissance* that drives the writing. He argues that the *testimonio* belongs to a world dominated by an unrelenting Freudian death drive, which also gives the work its archaic, repetitive, even compulsory form. Ríos Ávila argues that the *Diario* begins by representing itself as a confession of guilt with the promise of redemption, but that in the end its form betrays its true nature as a work of literary pornography driven by radical shamelessness. In other words, Ríos Ávila reduces the *testimonio* to a work that stimulates all manner of erotic and aesthetic pleasures without remorse. And Ríos Ávila further argues that the attention that the book has received is but a symptom of a culture that is similarly abandoned to the shameless pursuit of aesthetic and erotic pleasure: a society that has lost its sense of judgment and prohibition, and that experiences a loss of *pudor*. For Ríos Ávila, the wide circulation of the book marks the entrance of Puerto Rican culture into a period of radical shamelessness that is overdetermined by neoliberalism and consumer capitalism.

The faint praise by these critics compounds the fact that both of them make these *testimonios* radically unspeakable. They make them unspeakable in the sense that they silence their disturbing singular voice. But they also make them unspeakable in the sense that they describe them as constitutively without a language, as shameful or shameless to the point of nonsense. In other words, these readings double down on the shame that the authors of the *testimonios* admit to, and are at pains to put into words. Instead, Thompson and Ríos Ávila load these works with the added shame of being either agents for a neoliberal economic system with patriarchal values, or with the ventriloquism of an unmoored and relentless death drive. Either way, Thompson and Ríos Ávila leave the two *testimonios* profoundly speechless, and firmly fixed on the other side of language: both on the other side of an ideological or analytical divide, and also on silence, the other side of language itself. Thompson, for example, does not elaborate on the damning statement "Many commentators pronounced Vilar to be mentally ill and dismissed her work for that reason" (2014, 134). And Ríos Ávila emphasizes that the narrator of Caleb Acevedo's queer memoir is trapped by a compulsive movement of serial repetition that lacks meaning: "[T]here is a conscious honesty in this content . . . but there is even more honesty in the form, in the way that the unconscious traps the story in a compulsive serial repetition," he writes (2014). In a profound sense, these *testimonios* always were and forever remain nonsense for these critics.

Constitutive Shame

Impossible Motherhood and *Diario* are *testimonios* that suggest that shame is constitutive of the subject. The subject of each book finds its origins in the struggle and embrace with an other (or with a community). Their shameful acts turn them into singular outlaws and rebels for an other. But the acts also reconnect them to a larger body. This connection can be negative, as underground pariahs. Or it can be positive, as agents that affirm the value and the need of individual survival despite the odds against them. And the subjects repeat acts that their communities also disavow or shame into hiding. The communities at the center of these two *testimonios* are very different. In the case of Vilar, the communities that she leaves and enters are the communities of her family in Puerto Rico and various communities in the United States. They are also the communities of women that engage in the ambivalent act of repeated abortion. The communities at the center of Caleb Acevedo's work are the Puerto Rican homophobic community and the underground homosexual community at the fringes of Puerto Rican society.

They are also the communities of hustlers that serve the needs of customers, many in denial about their own sexual ambiguity. Both *testimonios* bring out the presence of populations that engage in acts that the community at large wants to minimize, outlaw, or altogether deny. They also stand as evidence to the fact that the communities that outlaw these acts are also involved in their repetition. In other words, the *testimonios* put into practice what the theories about colonial shame suggest: namely, that shame is an ambivalent feeling that is produced by both a transgression but also by the obedience to a complex process of belonging. Shame is the effect of the separation from a community and of the longing to reconnect with that community, of the rejection by a community and of the invitation by that same community to repeat. Shame is an effect of an act that is simultaneously sanctioned and outlawed by the community.

Both *testimonios* draw from the victim-to-survivor narrative that is common to the trauma recovery services industry. But unlike this popular discourse based on what sometimes feels like a compulsory hopefulness and optimism, the survivor narrative articulated by Vilar and Caleb Acevedo confirms the ambivalence that comes from realizing the profound nature of their shame, its constitutive place in their subjectivity, instead of the disavowal that aims to erase shame. They are *testimonios* that suggest that shame can be lived, that it is possible to experience the paralysis and depression of a profound shame and simultaneously survive, or live together and side by side with it. Both *testimonios* describe the experience of hitting bottom in order to start again, but they also acknowledge the permanence of that bottom in the form of a pleasure that is simultaneously described and revealed, an attraction to the opposite force to the tendency to overcome the shameful pleasure, which both writers experience together with their respective communities. This other force is represented as equal to the drive to live. The *testimonios* are also attempts at describing the pleasure that the narrators derive not only from acts that are made shameful by their communities, but also from acts that are in a profound ambiguous relation to the affirmation of community and singularity. The *testimonios* describe the pleasure in an act of undoing that is experienced when coming close to the most abject forms, to the cadaverous form of material that also constitutes us, material which we embody and eject, material that we ingest, incorporate, and also expel and abort. This is the material of life; food that is turned into excrement, semen and ova that are turned into the organs of an other, a fetus. Kristeva calls the feeling that we experience when coming into contact with this material abjection. But even within Kristevan psychoanalysis abjection remains very much a work in progress. In these *testimonios,* we are witnesses to the effort to understand the paradoxical and ambiguous role that this shame-inducing abjection also plays in the desire to survive.

The *testimonios* also acknowledge the inherent limitation in understanding the will as an agency that is both separate and distinct from the body. Both Vilar and Caleb Acevedo reflect on the force of the body, but not as a thing that is always in opposition to the subject and its conscious, deliberative, and linguistic agency. Rather, the body has a constitutive role to play in the development of language and in the development of the subject, according to Vilar and Caleb Acevedo. Both *testimonios* reflect this role of the body when they describe its signifying effect: the role that desires and phobias play in the motivation of fantasy, action, and representation. Both *testimonios* consider the role that the body plays in the construction of the subject that signs itself Vilar or Caleb Acevedo. They both are a witness to the fact that the compulsively repeated act of penetration or ejection and their bodily affect (i.e., shame) are in fact the motors behind the act of language that is the *testimonio,* whether it is a confession or a description of that act. The acts of penetration, pregnancy, and abortion, begin and end sections of each of these *testimonios* and together these sections give form to the whole. These always disturbing acts are both responsible for the linear narrative that the *testimonios* tell, their stories of guilt and redemption, but also for the uncanny sense that these stories never quite move away from their starting point. They are at the origin of a linear temporality. This temporality is suggested by the daily recording of events, a recording that makes up these *testimonios.* This recording gives both works (and the subjects they represent) a sense of order, the sense of development of the self. But the abject acts are also at the origin of a different temporality. They are also at the origins of a different mode of signification that is perhaps closer to repetitive poetry than to linear prose. A form of signification that interrupts the very sense of development and stability of the subject that it too creates. This form of signification is closer to an accident, or a traumatic event that returns. It gives a necessary instability or motility to the subject without for that reason depleting it of sense or reason.

Both *testimonios* have their origin in the accidental temporality, and also in the rhythmic scansion, of the bodily acts of penetration and ejection. They also have their origins in acts of writing, more specifically in previous examples of similarly ambiguous *testimonios.* This double origin makes it difficult to decide whether they are based on the archaic signification of the body or on the linguistic signification that is simultaneous with the body. For example, both *testimonios* comment on earlier examples of their genre. And they criticize, reject, but also incorporate and repeat the earlier work. Vilar refers to her earlier memoir, *The Ladies' Gallery*, as a form of self-revelation and self-delusion, as telling the truth but not telling it fully. She describes the earlier memoir as both her doing and not her doing, as the result of the influence of her so-called master on her (her professor and ex-husband), but also as a result of a master that she discovers that she has created for herself. *The Ladies' Gallery* is also a memoir about the women in Vilar's life, about her famous grandmother (Lolita Lebrón) and perhaps more importantly about her mother (Gladys Méndez). It is a memoir that contains Vilar's troubled relation with both, and that acknowledges the ambiguous debt she owes to their influence on her. Not surprisingly, Vilar's *Impossible Motherhood* ends with a letter to her newborn daughter in the form of a diary, a letter that morbidly and lovingly anticipates for her daughter her own necessary death and their imminent separation.

Caleb Acevedo similarly refers back to the memoir *Paula* (1995) by Isabel Allende and suggests that his own *Diario* is but a repetition of it, or more specifically, a repetition of what he calls its *mala leche*. The phrase is a reference to the body, to the bad "milk" of the body (*leche* is also the word for semen in colloquial Spanish), to infected semen (the narrator of the *Diario* is HIV positive), and also to the "milk" from the mother's breast, a bad breast to be sure, but also belonging to a devoted, nourishing, and loving mother in the case of Allende. *Mala leche* refers to the resentment that hides behind the sentimental words of Allende's nonfiction, according to Caleb Acevedo. The work is presumably written for her daughter, but is simultaneously an act of betrayal and abandonment of her daughter, insofar as the writing allows Allende to move on. Both love and hatred, maternal feeling and maternal resentment are the emotions that give form to the nonfiction that is *Paula*, and also to the *Diario* by Caleb Acevedo. The *Diario* is also a "letter" to a man he both resents and loves. It is both a love letter and a "Dear John" letter addressed to Poe, a character that abandons the narrator.

In short, the *testimonio* is a cathartic form of writing that makes visible a negative affect that we try to hide with our pronouncements of love. This affect is what Caleb Acevedo calls *puro teatro*, a sham that resonates deep within us.[21] The *testimonio* is also an incorporative form of writing that takes in what is abject in the other, turning it into what Vilar calls an "internal theatrics," calculated to temporarily fool ourselves, always for the benefit of our relationship to the other.

Repetition and Reversal

If Vilar's and Caleb Acevedo's *testimonios* bear witness to the constitutive nature of shame, they also bear witness to the different ways in which oppression (ranging from colonialism to sexism, from homophobia to savage capitalism) doubles down on shame. In gambling, to double down is to stay put. It means to double your bet and not to withdraw. Consciously or unconsciously, Vilar's and Caleb Acevedo's *testimonios* show how shame can be doubled by the conditions of oppression experienced in the society and culture of Puerto Rico and the United States. They are examples of the projection of a shame felt by the majority cultures onto stigmatized individuals and groups that suffer the extra burden of carrying the shame of the privileged as well. One example of this extra burden is the consensual colonialism of Puerto Rican society, which is projected onto Vilar and her mother, both destitute subjects who then become willing servants in an effort to survive. Like the Puerto Rican writer Ramos Otero before him, Caleb Acevedo similarly remarks on the allegorical meaning of his sadomasochistic sexual practices and phantasies, which he hints might be an internalized form of the enduring colonial struggle.

Such forms of oppression in turn lead to a form of paralysis or social melancholia also described in these *testimonios* as a compulsive tendency to repeat shamed acts that the society has abjected, and to which these subjects are in turn reduced. The paralysis of repetition is accompanied by a reduction in language, which gradually is depleted of meaning, and which becomes empty of signification for these narrators. This depletion is illustrated by a repeating sound bite from Caleb Acevedo's *testimonio*: the word *Dale* or "hit me." The paralysis is also simultaneous with what could be described as an existentialist circular logic that begins with the attempt to avoid the fear of the nothingness to which these narrators have been reduced, only to find themselves back at the original void in the end. The logic goes from what Vilar describes as "hyperarousal excitement to disgust and shame" (2009, 203). It similarly traces what Caleb Acevedo describes as the "cycle of sex" when he writes, "You start with a psychological connection, you fuck, you exchange fluids, the connection is broken, and all that remains is the morgue" (2012, 39).

The *testimonios* are loaded with a pathologizing discourse that is perhaps the most visible sign of the internalization that results from doubled-down shame. The repeated and widespread abjection of homosexual practices and abortion shames both narrators into a discourse of addiction that both Thompson and Ríos Ávila have noted, and that both also have reduced (problematically) to either a self-help or to a New Age discourse. But Vilar's and Caleb Acevedo's narratives of addiction can also be interpreted as a sign that the abjection by their respective social environments has had its intended effect. Both narrators describe themselves as addicts, sex addicts or abortion addicts. They both demonize themselves, finding an unspeakable evil inside, an inscrutable evil object that becomes a social habit, and that is described and pathologized as an addiction. This discourse of addiction turns them into unwilling victims of their impulsive bodies, of their bodies' unquenchable sexual hunger, of their perverse desire to penetrate and be penetrated, to incorporate and to abort. The narrators also offer repeated examples of the depressive effect on them of this addiction. They describe their actions as involuntary forms of self-mutilation, self-humiliation, and self-undoing due to their addiction. Notably, the discourse of addiction also liberates these narrators from responsibility for their acts of self-violence.

But it is also clear that the discourse of addiction in these *testimonios* is not limited to its self-debasing aspect, or to a problematic form of freedom from responsibility. The discourse of addiction also reverses itself in these *testimonios*. Specifically, there is a discourse of cure that is simultaneous with the discourse of addiction in these narratives. And this discourse does not refer to the cure of the addiction, but instead refers to the notion that claiming responsibility for the addiction might also be a form of cure, a form of reversal of the lack of agency usually implied by addiction, and by its imposition of repetition. In other words, these *testimonios* reconsider and resignify addiction beyond the concept of a symptom of the social melancholia that comes from oppression, and suggest its simultaneous role as a cure for that very condition, and as a way out of melancholy.[22]

Both *testimonios* also contain reflections and meditations on the nature of addiction, explaining its logic, challenging our preconceptions about the condition. They suggest that addiction might in fact be a negative way out of an internalized death, as in the popular saying "one nail drives out another." At one point, Vilar tells the traumatic story of the death of her beloved dog Oliveira (due in part to her neglect of the animal). She tells the story to a Canadian publisher who is originally from Haiti and who does not respond to her sad tale. Vilar is shocked by his lack of response to her story until she learns that he has no sympathy for dogs because his family was killed by dogs trained by the Tonton Macoutes, the secret police of the Haitian dictator Papa Doc. The shocking revelation has nevertheless a calming effect on Vilar and reveals the internal and simple logic of her addiction. Greater pleasure like greater suffering minimizes or overwhelms. It makes us temporarily forget the earlier pleasure and suffering. In this case, the Haitian publisher provides the cure, but in the *testimonio,* the cure is mostly self-administered. It takes the form of a growing tally of repeated abortions, or of a gradual increase of risky behavior during penetration in the case of Caleb Acevedo. The growing risk temporarily shocks the narrators themselves out of the circular logic of their internalized and paralyzing shame. It brings them back to a more manageable reality. Momentarily shocked out of themselves, they can begin anew. The interrupting logic of the cure also returns meaning to an act that appears to make no sense.

Arguably, addiction understood in this way (as a cure) is a form of what Kristeva has called intimate revolt (another name for abjection) or the "possession of our intimacy, including the most demonic and most tragic, [which] remain our refuge and our resistance in the face of a so-called virtual world where judgments are blurred or assume an archaic and barbarous form" (2002a, 12). The *testimonios* considered in this way are forms of abjection in two specific senses. On the one hand, they have the power to shock and scandalize, to unsettle, disturb, the oppressive context that is responsible for the exclusion of homosexuals and of women in general, and of homosexuals and women that engage in unsafe or illegal sexual practices in particular. From this perspective, the scandalous *testimonios* have social repercussions. On the other, they also have more intimate effects. The *testimonios* also practice what Caleb Acevedo calls "small acts of terrorism," a series of otherwise invisible acts that return a measure of agency to the subject that occupies the shamed position. More to the point, they practice a reversal in style. They shift constantly from scandal to idealization, from objectivity to sentimentality. These reversals are signs of the survival of the imaginary even in subjects that have been reduced to their abjected bodies by their communities. They return a measure of resilience, visibility, and agency to the shamed subject. At the center of this reversal there is a hyperbolic forgiveness.

The *testimonios* are characterized by a form of temporality that is based on the experience of scandal and shock. This temporality is not the linear and teleological temporality of historicism; rather, it is a temporality based on the disturbing and interruptive, arbitrary and sudden, rhythms of the body, of repeated penetration and ejection. This is an accidental form of temporality that reverses the experience of the end, or the experience of finally hitting bottom. In other words, it is an interruption of the sense of an ending, and the necessary condition for a capacity to begin again. It is a form of temporality based on repetition and reversal, the kind of back-and-forthing required to get a wheel unstuck from the mud. It is a form of temporality that is required to overwhelm the paralyzing past and set it into motion again. It is a way to reverse the feeling that we are stuck in time, a timelessness. It is a temporality that instead allows the narrator to start again and to move on. From this new beginning, out of timelessness, these narrators imagine a hyperbolic agency that has forgiveness at its core, what Vilar calls "the renewable resources of life" (2009, 179), what Caleb Acevedo calls "the suffering of the planets" (2012, 201).

Forgiveness in these *testimonios* is not a gesture of condescension or mercy toward a guilty other from an unassailable superior position. Forgiveness is instead a gesture of support given in advance of any guilt or any shame, an attitude of watchfulness, inflected with anger and admiration in the case of Vilar. It is a form of nonjudgmental witnessing to the paradoxical forms that the subject must take in order to make a way in life for itself. A form of caring watchfulness or company that offers support without offering solutions or absolution. A form of support contained in the words of Vilar's paternal grandmother: "Nobody is dead until they are dead" (Vilar 2009, 125). And indeed, both *testimonios* place the maternal abject at the source of this uncanny and hyperbolic forgiveness. Both *testimonios,* ironically, grow out of the debt owed to the lessons of a maternal abject otherwise flushed down the toilet by Caleb Acevedo: "I taught you many things and you flushed them down the toilet," his mother tells him, and he replies: "Not all of them, I kept the best ones" (Acevedo 2012, 22). Both *testimonios* similarly grow out of what Vilar describes as the impossible motherhood of her grandmother and mother, out of what she calls "the burden of life interrupted," a burden that lives and dies with Vilar and is the prologue to her book (2009, 5). In short, *Impossible Motherhood* and *Diario* are queer Latino *testimonios* that contain the constitutive shame, the repetition reversals, and the hyperbolic forgiveness necessary to renew our social bonds. And they both do so at a time and in a place that has reduced shame and forgiveness to nonsense.

Conclusion

The Scene of Self-Sacrifice in Literary Discourse

BETWEEN PERVERSION AND SUBLIMATION

In a poignant essay about the reason why she writes, the poet, short story writer, and novelist Olga Nolla (1938–2001) asks herself why did the main character of her novel *El Castillo de la memoria*, Juan Ponce de León, have to die fighting against U.S. soldiers in the Spanish American War? After all, she had allowed the Spanish *Conquistador* to find the fountain of youth that Ponce de León died searching for in reality. So, why did she then make the first governor of Puerto Rico drink the antidote to eternal life in her novel? Why did she make Ponce de León kill himself in 1898? Nolla answers that something "visceral . . . something unnamable and incomprehensible" inside of her, "the very story I was telling made me do it, because it needed to end there so that I could find the meaning I was looking for" (Nolla 1998, 7).

In the essay, Nolla suggests that the American Century evacuates meaning not just from Puerto Rican history, but also from Puerto Ricans. "We were raised with the feeling that nothing had ever happened in Puerto Rico. . . . We were of no importance and of no value," she writes (Nolla 1998, 6). She also finds that this collective and unconscious process of self undoing begins to reverse itself in the late twentieth century, but that Puerto Ricans live the process of recovery still afraid of "finding a dragon in the basement of our own home" (ibid.). She suggests that the suicide in fiction of Ponce de León gives literary form to this fear. "Literature," Nolla writes, "helps us to process reality" (ibid., 7). More specifically, writing the scenes of *El Castillo* gives Nolla what she calls the particularity of somebody who knows where she came from. She writes, "I don't know why my hero had to die in the Spanish American War. . . . I only know that after writing *El Castillo de la memoria* I now have a national narrative . . . that holds me up" (ibid.). It is as if writing the suicide of Juan Ponce de León gave Nolla a meaningful (if also a precarious) form of psychological support.

In her essay, Nolla retells an earlier story that could stand for the origin of the suicide of her hero. In his famous chronicle of the Spanish American war, the Spanish soldier Ángel Rivero tells the tragic story of lieutenant colonel Puig, a soldier of unknown origin. Faced with the U.S. invading force in 1898, Rivero writes that the lieutenant colonel was ordered to retreat by the Spanish High Command. The morning after his retreat, Puig "dressed in uniform, went to the beach; when he got there he drew his sword, thrust it deeply into the sand, and holding the steel scabbard with his left hand, he shot himself in the right temple, falling down and bending the sheath as he fell" (Nolla 1998, 6–7). Nolla repeats and perhaps sublimates this earlier scene of self-undoing in her novel, a perverse scene that idealizes, decorates, and erotizes the suicide of a soldier even as it suggests the debasing effects of his fall.

In *Malady and Genius: Self-Sacrifice in Puerto Rican Literature*, I reveal the function of similar attempts to give form to the so-called dragon buried in the crypt of the Puerto Rican colonial psyche: a scene of self-sacrifice or self-undoing that repeats in the twentieth and twenty-first centuries. I return meaning to a literary obsession that both sublimates and perverts the fear of Puerto Rican meaninglessness: the abject at the origin of the Puerto Rican subject. The crux of my argument is that the Puerto Rican subject lives under the duress of colonialism and its effects, but still manages to claim its place in the world. I conclude that the colonial subject is alive and well and living in Puerto Rico and in the United States. That its powers of imagination are clearly altered by the experience of colonialism, but that they continue to perform their necessary and paradoxical work of sublimation and perversion.

In *Malady and Genius*, I also build on a long-standing tradition that represents self-undoing in writing as a defense against the violence of colonialism. This old tradition can be traced back to the works of Fray Bartolomé de las Casas, who deployed the scene of collective suicide by the indigenous peoples of the Caribbean as a rhetorical defense for the Amerindians.[1] This defensive use of the scene of self-undoing is elaborated centuries later by the Martinican psychoanalyst Frantz Fanon, who studies similar scenes as paradoxical examples of the effect of decolonization on the psyche of the colonized. It is further developed in the twenty-first century by philosopher Kelly Oliver, who interprets them as symptoms of a social melancholy in need of collective attention. In this book, I take further the efforts of these writers. I argue that the scene of self-undoing is valuable in and of itself. Indeed, that its representation in literature and writing is evidence of the dynamic and supple nature of the colonial psyche, and of its hyperbolic forgiveness, predating the humanist or humanitarian arguments that are developed in its defense.

As Fanon convincingly argues (and as Oliver elaborates), the experience of colonialism is pathological. Its gravest symptom is the result of its sustained attack on the psyche. Following Kristeva, I think of the imagination as a defense of the psyche that is similar to a breakwater. Like a porous seawall, the imagination is a boundary for the energy of a fluid environment that both gives in to its effects and transforms them into something more manageable over a lifetime. As Fanon and Oliver argue, colonialism is a sustained attack on this very defense of the psyche. Colonialism, in other words, leaves the psyche almost without a necessary form of support by producing the fantasy that the colonial subject is a dense and impermeable abject body incapable of making meaning. Given the island's five-hundred-year-old colonial experience, it is perhaps not surprising that some Puerto Ricans repeat to themselves the familiar litany that they are "lazy. Filthy. Thieves. Kept. Wanting everything to be handed to them. Without initiative. Nor talent. Stupid. Indolent. Disorderly. Unable to take responsibility. Just wanting to have a good time. Hateful of their fellow citizens. That the island is sinking. Falling into pieces. That it simply stinks." This according to journalist Torres Gotay (2014, 14).[2]

However, if one is sensitive to the radical ambiguity revealed by psychoanalytic postcolonialism (i.e., by critics such as bhabha, Shepherdson, Oliver, or Ríos Ávila), one can see that the chokehold of the colonial environment is also always imperfect, much like the prohibitions of all discourses and rituals, or like the laws of economic, political, and social practices. Its destructive force is always temporary. It is never foreclosed to alternatives. And it always produces an ambiguous remainder that contains the antidote to its own poisonous effects: the abject. This is particularly the case as colonialism develops and elaborates crucibles for its causes and effects, crucibles such as literature. In essence, literature is a social ritual turned into radically ambiguous language and paradoxical practices. From this perspective, literary practices in Puerto Rico represent both the perverse practices of colonialism and their sublimation. Like the environment that generates them, literary practices defile and purify the substance of Puerto Rican subjects, turning them into dense and impermeable objects, or more precisely turning them into the Kristevan abject. But because of its precarious nature as a copy, as a representation, or as a ritual at a second remove, literature (understood to include the broad spectrum of expression in writing) also sublimates the substance of the subject and its social order. In doing so, literature remains a royal road to the process that colonialism systematically breaks down but also imperfectly holds. Following Kristeva, I call this process abjection, and it has its most representative feature in the repeating scene of self-undoing in the literary practice of the Puerto Rican imagination.

The repeating scene of self-undoing can be studied from many perspectives, including historical, sociological, psychological, legal, anthropological, economic, political, or from the combination of some of these specialized forms of knowledge represented by what has come to be known as cultural studies. But my preference in this book has been to insist on the tradition of knowledge that I believe is most familiar with the double-meaning negativity of words. By this, I mean my preference for literary analysis and for its attention to language and to form, even as I also go beyond figurative and rhetorical limits. The scene of self-undoing and the literary practices that produce it are profoundly ambiguous, ambivalent, paradoxical, and even ironic. And they interpellate an interlocutor that is similarly possessed of instruments that are sensitive to these forms of expression, which otherwise would go without commentary or simply would go unnoticed. From this perspective, my book is a call to literary study, and an argument to continue paying attention to what makes literature singular and necessary, namely, its representation of our social rituals in a flexible set of signs that allows us to survive. This is not to say that other art forms, like the visual arts, for example, are not modes of representation in a language of their own—indeed, in this book I dabble in some of the pleasures of the art critic. It is, however, to say that there is a rich tradition in literary studies that I repeatedly turn to in this book, confident as I am in its sensitivity to the ambiguity that matters the most to me.

There is also in my approach in this book a concern with what sometimes I call an ethical or better yet a herethical dimension (to borrow a term from Kristeva). By this concern, I mean the attention to a dimension of literary practice and of literary analysis that shies away from the position of a judge who can discern with clarity the worth or worthlessness of the object of study, its authenticity or its deceitfulness, the justice or the egregious violence of its claims. Rather, my study of the works in this book leads me to try to be as aware as I possibly can of my blind spots and their disturbing effects on others, just as the practice of literature is to a large degree an attempt to bring us closer to the forces in our environment that remain outside our line of sight but that nevertheless constitute the condition of possibility of our selves. Similarly, I conclude that any form of analysis worth its salt must tend in some way or another to the unsurmountable debt that we owe to the invisible forces in our environment that are most responsible for our lives. Those forces are both material and figurative, and they are the substance of all our laws, rituals, and discourses including colonialism and its ritualized scenes.

Literature and literary analysis have the potential to face these forces squarely, "without sham innocence or modest self-effacement" (Kristeva 1982, 88). But the potential depends on our willingness to entertain the possibility that we are made and unmade by these forces, by the porous boundary between the sacred and the abject, between desire and knowledge, and between death and society, as Kristeva puts it (ibid.). The repeating scenes of self-undoing in the literature of Puerto Rico are a testament to the ability of the writers from that unincorporated territory to maintain the seawall that allows the waters of the unconscious to pass through, even if the waves of colonialism also threaten to level the breakwater of the Puerto Rican psyche. The literary elaboration of the scene of self-undoing is one example of the necessary boundary that forgives perversion and leads the subject to sublimation.

Notes

Introduction

1. Translations are mine unless otherwise noted. Whenever possible, I have used published translations of the works.

2. In 2013, the famous American philosopher and activist Professor Cornel West was invited to speak at the University of Puerto Rico (see West 2013). During the visit, West answered a question about religion and social change with a reference to the Puerto Rican nationalist Lolita Lebrón, who spent twenty-seven years in a federal prison for shooting at members of the U.S. Congress in 1954, in protest against the change in the colonial status of Puerto Rico to a U.S. commonwealth. Lebrón became famous as much for her act of rebellion as for her suicidal words. Two things interest me most about the visit by West. The first is West's reference to Lebrón's attack as an act of witnessing to colonial violence. The second is the laugh that West and his audience share when he says: "Lolita said the Lord's Prayer before she made a move on the U.S. Congress." I believe this laughter betrays an uncanny affect that accompanies the repetition of a scene of self undoing, and I believe that irony is what allowed the Puerto Rican audience both to release this strange affect, but also to bond with West. I believe that the irony behind this laughter is one of the essential components of the scene of self-undoing that repeats in the acts of the Puerto Rican imagination. I elaborate on this point in chapter 1 of this book.

3. By testimony here I mean a genre of Latin American writing called *Testimonio* in Spanish. The genre has been popular in Latin America and in U.S. academia, where it has been studied since the early eighties. Some argue that the genre became institutionalized by a literary prize first awarded in the category of *testimonio* by the Cuban publishing house Casa de las Americas in 1970.

4. By the metaphor of the soul I mean the mind, the ego, or the psyche, a byproduct and a secretion of material bodies that interact under historical conditions such as colonialism. Quoting Frantz Fanon, Kelly Oliver argues that the "soul" is a byproduct "secreted from . . . interacting bodies" (2004, 67). Following the psychoanalyst Julia Kristeva, Oliver suggests that the colonial interaction of bodies "hollows them out," infecting them in such a way as to produce colonial maladies of the "soul," or infecting the mind or the ego with colonial pathologies (ibid.).

According to Fanon, future humans will be beyond this infection. According to Kristeva and Oliver the so-called pathology or malady is a permanent feature of the relationship between self and other, but it is also accompanied by a simultaneous process of sublimation and resignification, a form of genius that must be recovered and emphasized at all costs. In this book, I follow Oliver's and Kristeva's definition of the soul, of its malady and of its genius, as it applies to the Puerto Rican subject.

5. I am referring here to a wide gamut of critical works including *Literatura y paternalismo en Puerto Rico* (1993) by Juan Gelpí, *La raza cómica* (2002) by Rubén Ríos Ávila, *Boricua Pop* (2004) by Frances Negrón-Muntaner, *¿Encanto o espanto?* (2008) by Van Haesendonck, and to the essays "Community at Its Limits: Orality, Law, Silence and the Homosexual Body in Sánchez's 'Jum' " (1995) and "Sobre el tráfico simbólico de mujeres: homosocialidad, identidad nacional y modernidad literaria en Puerto Rico" (1997) by Agnes Lugo-Ortiz, as well as to " 'What a Tangled Web': Masculinity, Abjection and the Foundations of Puerto Rican Literature in the United States" (1996) and "The Oxymoron of Sexual Sovereignty: Some Puerto Rican Literary Inflections" (2007) by Arnaldo Cruz-Malavé, among others. These works are in turn part of a wider tradition of postcolonial psychoanalysis, or psychoanalytic postcolonialism that includes works such as homi bhabha's *The Location of Culture* (1994), Gayatiri Spivak's "Can the Subaltern Speak" (1988), and Anne McClintock's *Imperial Leather* (1995), among others.

6. Kristeva associates this malady with the dark side of belief that is similar to the nihilism that accompanies the convictions of the adolescent. She writes, "In light of the adolescent malaise and the psychosexual development model in *Three Essays* which I've just summarized, I would like to posit the following binary schema in which my reasoning will play out today: Let us oppose the polymorphous perverse child dependent on partial pleasures, who 'wants to know' and whose thought develops thanks to his sexual theorization with the adolescent who idealizes the object relation to the point of succumbing to what I call 'the malady of Ideality' which pushes him to relish both the fantasy of an absolute Object as well as of the fantasy of its vengeful destruction. The polymorphous perverse theoretician versus The adolescent believer" (Kristeva 2007, 716).

7. The word *dormidos* in the title of this novel literally means "sleepers," but in the novel the word is also a euphemism for the corpses of people who have committed suicide, and it is also a symbol for larger community of Puerto Ricans. The title is translated as *Captain of the Sleepers*, a better translation of the title might have been *Captain of the Suicides*.

Chapter 1. Psyche, History, Language, and Body in *Antígona Pérez* by Luis Rafael Sánchez

1. Sánchez is the author of *La pasión* (1968) and twelve other plays. They include *Cuento de la Cucarachita Viudita* (1959), *Los ángeles se han fatigado* (1960),

Farsa del amor compradito (1960), *La espera* (1960), *La hiel nuestra de cada día* (1962), *O casi el alma* (1965), *La balada de las hogueras* (1965), *Mil sueños tiene la calle* (1965), *Tablado puertorriqueño* (1966), *Parábola del andarín* (1979), *Quíntuples* (1985), and *Necesitamos a Marlon Brando* (n.d.). He is also the author of one book of short stories: *En cuerpo de camisa* (1966); several important essays and collections: *La guagua aérea* (1994), *No llores por nosotros Puerto Rico* (1998), *El himno de la vida* (2003), *Devórame otra vez* (2005), *Abecé indócil* (2013); and three novels: *La guaracha del Macho Camacho* (1976), *La importancia de llamarse Daniel Santos* (1988), and *Indiscreciones de un perro gringo* (2007).

2. The Spanish title is a reference to the idiomatic expression *en mangas de camisa,* which is in turn the Spanish version of the English expression "in shirtsleeves." In the title, Sánchez plays with the notion of the naked body in language. A translation of the title that preserves this word play might be *In Bodysleeves.*

3. The bibliography about *La pasión* is extensive. For a partial account of the bibliography about the play, please see Hernández Vargas and Caraballo Abréu 1985, 257–60. For an account of the bibliography about the various plays of Sánchez, please see Colón Zayas 1985, 111–16. For an account of the bibliography about the various works of Sánchez, please see Perivolaris 2000, 192–203. For a description of the Theater of Protest in Puerto Rico, see Colón Zayas 1985, 26–27.

4. For a comprehensive history of the transition of contemporary Puerto Rican theater from a period of social realism (1938–1947), to a period of poetic realism (1948–1959), to a period of intensification of the elements of poetic realism (1960–68), please see *Contemporary Puerto Rican Drama* by Jordan Phillips (1972).

5. *La pasión* was first performed at the Tapia Theater in San Juan Puerto Rico in May–July of 1968 (Hernández Vargas and Caraballo Abréu 1985, 284).

6. The brothers are two friends of Antígona who were killed in an assassination attempt against Creón, the dictator of the imaginary republic of Molina.

7. In her work on autobiography in Latin America, Sylvia Molloy focuses on this histrionic difference as the characteristic that distinguishes European autobiographies from their colonial counterparts in Latin America.

8. Less convincingly, self-sacrifice is also for Žižek a radical political and democratic act, a display of revolutionary autonomy and sovereignty that interrupts the temporal progress and the so-called global circuit of slave morality.

9. Cruz-Malavé finds a similar promising distance from a repeating fantasy of self-abjection in Sánchez's novel *La guaracha del Macho Camacho* (1996, 154).

10. When Monsignor Escudero warns Antígona that her imminent death requires her confession, she replies that death is the least serious question facing mankind (*La pasión,* 81). The words affirm Antígona's secularism in front of the church official, and they suggest that the question of death is less serious for her than life. Later in the play, however, Antígona suggests the opposite to Pilar when she claims that to die is to love absolutely (ibid., 119).

11. *Fascinerosa* and *fascinar,* the word in Spanish meaning "to enchant" or "to cast a spell," have the same root": *facere* ("to do," in Latin). *Fascinerosa* is one

who can only do evil acts, one who enchants and casts a spell by her very nature, one whose action and evil are one and the same: a witch.

12. This book by Ferré is not translated. The adjective *desangrada* has been variously translated into English as wounded, bloodless, bleeding etc. However, in Spanish, *desangrada* also connotes a reflexive meaning as in something that the body does to itself: it depletes itself of blood. This reflexivity in turn carries the meaning of a forgiving self-violence that is characteristic of the works of the collection.

Chapter 2. The Gift of Abjection

1. For some critics this character is also a figure for the Puerto Rican subject (Cruz-Malavé 1995, 142).

2. In her essay "The Look of Love," Oliver develops what I would call an environmental ethics based in part on the work of Luce Irigaray. Oliver argues for an ethical approach to subjectivity based on the debt that the subject owes to what she does not see. The subject does not see but feels the effect nonetheless of an uncanny hold and release that defines her own limits or boundaries negatively. Oliver fleshes out this hold as the air and the light that surrounds us, as a circulating substance that puts us in constant relation with others, that gives us our contours, and that we dismiss at our peril. In fact, she argues that the account of the alienated subject by the psychoanalyst Jacques Lacan and the philosopher Jean-Paul Sartre is but a symptom of this untimely dismissal. Instead, she argues for a form of recognition that is based on taking stock of this uncanny substance that circulates around us, connecting and separating us from others. Oliver asks us to consider the political ramifications of defining the subject not as radically alienated, but as one fundamentally loved, and indebted to her environment.

3. Historians Ayala and Bernabe describe the crisis as a consequence of the end of the postwar expansion of the Puerto Rican economy: "Real yearly gross national product fell from 7 per cent in the 1960´s to 3.3 percent in the 1970s to 2.1 percent in the 1980s. The official unemployment rate had never dipped below 10 percent, but by 1980 it had risen to 17 percent. . . . Between 1970 and 1990, federal transfers to individuals in Puerto Rico—through food stamps and other programs—rose from $500 million to $6 billion. Their share of personal income went from 15 to 30 percent" (267).

4. Charles Pilditch concludes the first book-length study of Marqués's works stating that "for his sometimes comic, sometimes tragic, and more often than not pessimistic but sympathetic acceptance of the absurdities which he finds in man, the world and life in general, Marqués ranks not only as Puerto Rico's best author but as one of the leading literary figures writing anywhere in Spanish today" (243). Josefina Rivera de Álvarez writes that Marqués was not only a leading short story

writer of his generation, but that he remains one of the greatest contemporary Puerto Rican writers (495, 604).

5. One year after the publication of *La mirada,* literary critic Efraín Barradas wrote a devastating review of the novel, concluding that it was a failure due primarily to Marqués's investment in the values of a displaced landed bourgeoisie, and also due to his ideological confusion. According to Barradas, this confusion led to a crisis in Marqués's writing that extended from his baffling treatment of the theme of homosexuality to defects in the novel's structure and form (Barradas 1977, 80). One year after Barradas's piece, María Solá repeated Barradas's and Quintero Rivera's claim that Marqués represented the values of a social class in crisis, which included sexism, or the view that female sexuality limited human capacity. She also argued that Marqués was not misogynistic and that his representation of the psychology of his female characters was complex, even as he repeated the sexist stereotype of women as either mothers or whores. She pointed out that Marqués criticized the patriarchal and traditional values that reduced women to objects and drove them into psychological conflicts that destroyed them, in short stories such as "Purificación en la Calle del Cristo" (Solá 1979, 93). Ten years later, Arcadio Díaz Quiñones echoed Barradas's assessment of *La mirada* as a failure. He repeated the argument that Marqués represented the outdated and outmoded values of a defeated social class. But he also described his work as a criticism of the values of modern capitalist society with the latest innovations of the art of storytelling (1982, 43).

6. Much of the criticism that has followed Barradas's and Solá's initial assessment, as well as Díaz Quiñones's reassessment, have largely repeated their claims about Marqués's conservative ideology, including Lugo-Ortiz (1991), Juan Gelpí (1993), Cruz-Malavé (1995), Alfredo Villanueva-Collado (2007), and more recently Ríos Ávila (2009, 2011). Some, such as Lugo-Ortiz, describe Marqués's violent stories of femicide and self-undoing as paranoid homosocial fantasies that act out against the modernization of Puerto Rico. Others, like Cruz-Malavé and Villanueva Collado, affirm that Marqués was a homosexual writer who considered his homosexuality abject and kept it a secret in the name of a future self-identical, autonomous, national identity. Others still, such as Ríos Ávila and Cruz-Malavé, have suggested that the violent exclusions and repressions of Marqués's so-called homo-fascistic narratives are in fact responsible for the "tics" and the phobic figures that also haunt his writing as forms of the return of the repressed.

7. My comments in this section are gleaned from the third chapter of that book, titled "From Filth to Defilement."

8. In *La mirada,* the main character also echoes the words of the man on the cross: "Father, my father! Why have you [forsaken] me?" (*The Look,* 63).

9. According to the Death Penalty Information Center, "Puerto Rico abolished the death penalty in 1929, two years after their last execution. In 1952, when

Puerto Rico drafted and ratified their own constitution, it included the decree 'the death penalty shall not exist'" (see "Puerto Rico" 2015).

10. The other three nationalists were Rafael Cancel Miranda, Andrés Figueroa Cordero, and Irving Flores Rodríguez.

11. Perhaps not coincidentally, Marqués had divorced his wife of fifteen years, and the mother of his three children in 1957, one year before writing these two works. My interpretation is indebted to a tradition of criticism that is sensitive to the role of sexual difference and objectification in the works of Marqués, but a tradition that also appears to be blind to the role of the abject in Marqués, that is to say blind to a figure that stands in between the binary opposition object/subject. This blindness threatens to reify the binary structures that some of these critics are trying to undermine. Three examples of this tradition are the groundbreaking essays by Concha Meléndez, María Solá, and Lugo-Ortiz. From the point of view of stylistics, Meléndez criticizes Marqués for privileging unimportant objects in his narratives. With references to the Spanish philosopher Ortega y Gasset, she suggests that the *infrarrealismo* of Marqués is an escape from the monumental forms of the soul, a regrettable escape that is characteristic of modern and secular narrative. From a feminist angle, Solá makes the argument that in some stories by Marqués women interiorize the patriarchal values that have turned them into purely decorative objects and that requires their destruction as these objects become polluted. This explains, for Solá, the group suicide of the sisters in the story "Purificación en la Calle del Cristo" (93). From a poststructuralist angle, Lugo-Ortiz also repeats the binary opposition that systematically pits a valuable subject against a devalued object in her account of the function that Marqués assigns to the figure of the writer. She argues that Marqués preserves the agency of the masculine subject by affixing the feminine to the status of object (Lugo-Ortiz 1997, 266).

12. For a different psychoanalytic interpretation of this shame in Marqués, please see Ríos Ávila's "Sobre la masculinidad." Where I see a feeling associated with the dread and the joy of the abject, Ríos Ávila sees the primary insufficiency or the lack at the origins of the subject.

13. Martin emphasizes the ambiguity of the works of Marqués even to the point of undermining his political intentions. She writes, "Marqués' drama evinces an evolution from melodrama and the presentation of black and white solutions of conflicts to dramas of more subtle denouement. As Marqués increases the subtlety of the problems and solutions, so also his characters become increasingly complex—showing human merits and shortcomings. The development in this direction is fairly constant, with only minor slips into melodrama (*Mariana, or the Dawn*) and biting political outbursts (*Carnival Outside, Carnival Inside*). As his artistry becomes more sophisticated, Marqués runs into a dilemma with thesis, for his message is not as sharply delineated. It forces the audience to muse upon the drama's subtlety and to reach its own conclusions. This may account for Marqués choosing thesis over art in a drama of his mature period—*Mariana, or the Dawn*—where the dramatist preferred

to unequivocally exhort his islanders on the centennial of the Lares insurrection, rather than cloud his purpose with artistry and subtlety" (Martin 1979, 143).

14. The theory is posited in the essay "El puertorriqueño dócil," where Marqués writes that the so-called *machista* Puerto Rican culture is under siege by the matriarchal North American Welfare State. Feminist, poststructuralist, and postfeminst critics such as Solá, Lugo-Ortiz, and Ríos Ávila, have criticized Marqués's description of this pattern as either a sign of his sexism or of his sexual paranoia. Their criticism is not unfounded, and yet I think it also misses the point of Marqués's work, and the reason why it is important to continue to read him. Arguably, Marqués's "matriarchal pattern" is an example of the perverse erotization of the abject (see my "Colonial Fetishism"). According to Kristeva, perversion and sublimation are the two paths that open up to the subject when abjection is "faced squarely": she writes, "Our eyes can remain open provided we recognize ourselves as always already altered by . . . language. Provided we hear in language . . . the basic incompleteness that conditions the indefinite quest of signifying concatenations . . . Here two paths open out: sublimation and perversion" (Kristeva 1982, 88–89). If this chapter follows the path of sublimation in some of the works by Marqués, the next chapter of this book elaborates on the path of perversion in others, as well as in some of the works of the writers that followed him.

15. Ríos Ávila has noticed this tendency in the writing by Marqués, and he suggests that it points to the writer's fantasy of plenitude, and to his desire to return to an undifferentiated state (Ríos Ávila 2011). The critic sees in this tendency a repetition of the romantic vision that dates the supposedly superannuated writing of Marqués. I would argue instead that his continued technical experimentation is a measure of the adolescent nature even of his last works, now open to the possibility of an ethical environmental law.

Chapter 3. Vicissitudes of Perversion

The verse quoted in the first epigraph comes from the song "Triángulo," composed and performed by the Puerto Rican crooner Bobby Capó (1922–1989) in an album from 1962. According to the gossip surrounding this song, the woman referred to in the verse was the late Jacqueline Kennedy (later Onassis) whom Rodríguez visited at the White House during the short-lived presidency of the late John F. Kennedy. Rodríguez dedicated another song on the same album to the former first lady, giving it the title "Jack, Jack, Jacqueline."

In the second epigraph, "Lita" was Ramón Emeterio Betances's (1830–1898) beloved niece (María del Carmen Henry). According to legend, the famous Puerto Rican doctor embalmed his niece for her final journey back to Puerto Rico from Le Havre, France, in 1859. Cayetano Coll y Toste preserved the legend in his short story "La novia de Betances."

1. Vieques is a part of the Commonwealth of Puerto Rico. It is a small island off the coast of Puerto Rico to the northeast.

2. By perverse desires I do not mean here the opposite of normative desires, or desires that stand opposed to those that correspond to a genital organization according to Freudian psychoanalysis (Laplanche and Pontalis 1973, 306–309). Following Kristeva, by perversion I do mean the erotization of abjection. In other words, perversion is the underside of the process of sublimation that I described in chapter 2, the erotic cult of abjection as a melancholy means to defend against the losses of colonialism. Kristeva writes, "This erotic cult of the abject makes one think of a perversion . . . our borderlander is . . . threatened with losing . . . his whole life. To preserve himself from severance, he is ready for more—flow discharge, hemorrhage. . . . The erotization of abjection . . . is an attempt at stopping the hemorrhage: a threshold before death, a halt or a respite?" (1982, 55). I believe that colonial relations overdetermine desires that are both perverse (sadism, masochism, and voyeurism) and erotically abject in this sense. If in this chapter I focus on the malady of perversion, in chapter 4, I focus instead on the genius of the turn to the abject in the journal *Zona. Carga y Descarga*. Following Kristeva, in that chapter, I refer to this turn as a mereversion.

3. In her book, Oliver suggests that the socially constructed maternal abject (a reduction of maternity to "repellent or asocial animality" [2004, 110]) is a foundational model for other forms of social abjection, denigration, devaluation of selves that turn the homosexual, the lesbian, the feminine, the colored into nonselves, or the negative of self. This social abjection, denigration, and devaluation produces a sense of loss of self and a concomitant shame in being that is so radical that the individual so defined finds it almost impossible to mourn this loss and to overcome this shame. Instead, she becomes radically depressed. Oliver also argues that sons and daughters identify with these depressed mothers, they eroticize "their sorrow and suffering as the secret, silent pain that binds mother and child" (ibid.). This identification turns sons into sadists and daughters into masochists (ibid., 112). Their interaction in turn sets the conditions of possibility for social abjection, or for what Oliver calls the colonization of psychic space, which follows the structure of the self-fulfilling prophesy. In this way, the erotization of maternal abjection is the key to what Oliver calls social melancholy (see chapter 6 of this book).

4. In an otherwise insightful analysis of the Vieques crisis, Pabón suggests that the good feelings that the crisis produced among all Puerto Ricans were the result of a highly suspect, consensus-driven discourse of "Puertorricanness" at the center of Puerto Rican neo-Nationalism, a discourse that covered over and hid a nostalgia for an epical account of history, an account of struggle of good forces against evil that erased more "messy" accounts of Puerto Rican history. In his essay, Pabón shows that the source of the so-called good-feelings of self-satisfaction in "Puertorricanness" produced in part by the struggle for Vieques hid a conservative, class-inflected project that served the normative and consumer-centered ideologies of

the postmodern and globalized state. To his credit, Pabón suggests that this agenda is not only suspect, but it is also precarious, and more than anything else, quickly and easily reversible (2002, 429).

5. See my essay "Colonial Fetishism" for a detailed development of this claim.

6. In his history of Puerto Rican literature, Manrique Cabrera famously coined the term "the trauma generation" to refer to the Puerto Rican writers psychologically affected by the military occupation of Puerto Rico after the Spanish American War of 1898. Marqués and Manrique Cabrera, as well as other members of their generation, were concerned with the effects of "shell-shock" or trauma on veterans of war, a concern that can be traced back to the military context in which the psychological sciences developed in Puerto Rico (see Rivera Ramos).

7. For a sustained analysis of Paz's book and its figures from this perspective, please see my book *Remembering Maternal Bodies* (and particularly the chapter on maternal *jouissance* in Elena Garro's *Recuerdos del Porvenir*) as well as Norma Alarcón's "Traddutora, Traditora: A Paradigmatic Figure of Chicana Feminism." For a comparisson of Paz's and Marqués's essays focusing on the construction of the figure of the intellectual facing the development of the modern state, please see Gelpí (2006).

8. For a study of the role of Marqués's emphasis on virile subjectivity, and its implicit deployment of the feminine in the construction of a homosocial social economy, please see Lugo-Ortiz (1997).

9. In his book, Stabb suggests that the state of crisis is actually made normative by a generation of positivist thinkers practicing a symbolic form of medicine on the Latin American continent.

10. Like bhabha's notion of ambivalence in colonial discourse, this kinship is a sign of the ambiguous (both recalcitrant and productive) nature of the forces that all of these writers try to shape into figures for the Puerto Rican national subject (bhabha 1994, 66). For a more systematic study of this shared ambivalence please see chapter 2.

11. Labrador-Rodríguez offers an accurate description of the meaning of the phrase *hacer una descarga*: "It is a Puerto Rican idiomatic expression of the popular classes that leads to a verbal agression, that is to say outloud what everybody knows but keeps silent" (2007, 250).

12. My essay could be described as an attempt to burrow deeper into the origins of this aesthetics.

13. For a more detailed analysis of the debt owed to Cortázar by Ferré for her own (more violent) use of collage, please see Labrador-Rodríguez.

14. I am referring here to a passionate form of support of an archaic not-yet-object that Kristeva calls abjection (1982, 1–2).

15. Ferré was familiar with police surveillance, as policemen were posted at her house during the government of her father, Luis A. Ferré, from 1968–1972.

While the intention of such measures certainly was to protect her (Ferré's government weathered an exceptionally turbulent moment of Puerto Rico's labor history), their effect was just as certainly intimidating for a daughter who spoke publicly against her father's political ideal, months before an election to a second term, an election, by the way, that her father lost.

16. For a compelling account of Montero's novels as a Caribbean narrative driven by the absence or lack at the center of desire please see Vera León's essay "Mayra Montero: Las islas del deseo."

17. The characters of Andrés's father (Frank), his mother (Estela), and his friend (J. T. Bunker) make up the initial triangle of the novel. This geometric figure then changes into another by the end of the novel, a love triangle that includes Andrés, Frank, and J. T., at the center of which the corpse of Estela lays buried.

18. In the novel, J. T. is the son of a United States Air Force fighter pilot who was an advisor to President Woodrow Wilson.

19. On March 13, 1950, Antonio Fernós Isern, the resident commissioner for Puerto Rico, presented a bill (H.R. 7674) to the U.S. House of Representatives. According to historian Morales Carrión, "the bill recognized the principle of government by consent, stating that the proposed act would be 'adopted in the nature of a compact so that the people of Puerto Rico may organize a government pursuant to a constitution of their own adoption'" (275). After clearing both houses, President Truman signed the bill into Public Law 600, setting the stage for a referendum that would begin a new constitutional process and for a Nationalist uprising. Four months later, armed troops of Nationalists occupied two small towns and attacked the governor's mansion in San Juan. The uprisings did not stop the consequences of Public Law 600, which led to a referendum and then to a new constitution in 1952, which in turn set the legal foundation for the unique political relationship between Puerto Rico and the United States that has ruled the island ever since.

20. The historical record shows that five Nationalists were killed and two policemen were wounded during the uprising. The government responded with equal if not greater force, sending in the National Guard. This action in turn resulted in the death of thirty-three persons throughout the island, and in the imprisonment of Pedro Albizu Campos, the leader of the Nationalist movement.

21. Montero suggests that these suicides are victims of colonialism. Their lands have been expropriated by the Navy, and they have to abandon their island to survive. In the novel, the corpses represent the return of the repressed colonial violence, and their coffins become the means to smuggle arms for the uprising.

22. The character of Urbano appears to have been modeled after a real-life Brazilian hunger artist who made the rounds of Caribbean vaudeville in the mid-fifties with the stage name of El Faquir Urbano. Hunger artists were very popular vaudeville acts in Europe during the nineteenth century, but were in decline by

the beginning of the twentieth century, as Kafka showed in his homonymous short story written in 1922. They survived well into the twentieth century both in Latin America and the Caribbean.

23. The *Qur'an* is made up of 114 *surat* (of varying length). Each *surat* is made up of verses. Yasin is the name for the thirty-sixth *surat.* One of its verses reads, "They shall say: O woe to us! who has raised us up from our sleeping-place. This is what the Beneficent God promised and the apostles told the truth" (*Qur'an* 36.52). I am grateful to Professor Alia Al-Saji for pointing out this reference to me.

24. "And if We please, We would certainly put out their eyes, then they would run about groping for the way, but how should they see?" (*Qur'an* 36.66).

25. Lupus is a disease of the autoimmune system, which loses its ability to tell the difference between foreign substances and the body's own cells and tissue, in essence pitting the body's defenses against itself.

26. The subject of the poem is Betances's incestuous necrophilia for his niece, Lita. Betances was one of the "founding fathers" of Puerto Rican nationalism. He organized uprisings against Spanish colonial rule during the nineteenth century as well as the Puerto Rican Revolutionary Committee. The latter was instrumental in the failed Nationalist revolt known as the *Grito de Lares* (1868). Ferré's scandalous poem has the effect of returning relevance to a figure that has become both obsolete and mythical (or obsolete because mythical) by suggesting the perverse nature of the ideals of Betances.

27. The English version of the novel ends with the expression "Sleep tight!" which is a good translation of *Que sueñes con los angelitos* (*Capitán,* 215). Perhaps, the nursery rhyme "Don't let the bed bugs bite" also conveys the meaningful music of the children's lullaby with which Montero ends her novel.

Chapter 4. *Zona. Carga y Descarga*

1. I am here referring to the so-called Boom of the Latin American novel, which ocurred in the early sixties in that region when a constellation of influential and popular works was published. This list changes but almost always includes *La ciudad y los perros* (1962) by Mario Vargas Llosa, *La muerte de Artemio Cruz* (1962) by Carlos Fuentes, *Rayuela* (1963) by Julio Cortazar, and *Cien años de soledad* (1963) by Gabriel García Márquez. With the reference to the "boom," I am also referring to a period of history in Latin America characterized by political unrest and explosive violence associated with the Cold War.

2. Referring to the notorious French novelist Sidonie-Gabrielle Colette, Kristeva writes, "In an ingenious intuition, Colette guesses that it is by appropriating her mother, by creating the mythical figure of Sido, that she will be able definitely to transmute perversion—*père-version,* turning toward the father—into *mère-version,*

turning toward the mother, to reconcile herself with her always somewhat humiliated femininity and to finally install herself in the oblatory sensuality of a henceforth fateful writing" (2002, 13).

3. Thomas Kuhn describes the black-body problem or the problem of black radiation in the following way. "If a cavity with perfectly absorbing (i.e., black) walls is maintained at a fixed temperature T, its interior will be filled with radiant energy of all wavelengths. If that radiation is in equilibrium, both within the cavity and with its walls, then the rate at which energy is radiated across any surface or unit area is independent of the position and orientation of that surface" (1979, 3).

4. Barbara Johnson traces the origins, consequences, and meaning of this turn or revolution to the materiality of writing in her essay on "Writing" (1990, 39–49). For an example of the consequences to the Western philosophical tradition of this modernist turn to the materials of signification, which he refers to as the trigger, the frame, the scission, the temporality, the tain, the column, and the graft, see Jacques Derrida's influential 1969 commentary on a novel by Phillipe Sollers (1981, 289–366). Aníbal González traces the long-standing ethical attention by Latin American literature to this linguistic turn, or to the violent effects of the Derridean definition of writing in his book *Killer Books.*

5. Bleys defines homotextuality as "a heuristic catch-all term, which is diachronic instead of being tied to all-too-reifying notions of 'homosexual' or 'gay' identity. It allows for cross-cultural comparison and avoids the pitfalls of Eurocentric conceptualization. It is inclusive at once of artistic expressions of homoeroticism, as of their perceptions by various audiences. It embraces an image's potential reception as a site of homotextual meaning, even when not intended so by the artist him/herself. It also includes 'documentary' images that, while neutral on a primary semantic level, reveal something of a hidden, codified homosexual content when properly contextualized and that appear as visualizations of an *ambiente,* clearly recognizable by an informed eye" (2000, 11).

6. There is a reference to Sánchez's departure in an editorial of *Zona* 4 where the editors explain that she is leaving the group after they decided to better define their political position. The editors emphasize that they understand and respect her decision, and underscore her generosity, her talent, and her enthusiasm in the defense of Puerto Rican culture (*Zona* 4: 3).

7. By 1971, Sánchez was an established artist. She had held her first individual exhibit nineteen years before, in 1953, and had participated in more than twenty five individual and group exhibits in Havana, Paris, Madrid, Mexico City, Sao Paulo, Barcelona, Washington, D.C., and San Juan.

8. See excerpts in *Zilia Sánchez: tres décadas* of comments by Stephen Spector (*Arts Magazine*), Leo Soretsky (*City East*), Gordon Brown (*Arts Magazine*), Dolores Prida (*La Nueva Sangre*), and Mario Peña (*El Tiempo*), all from New York;

and from Marta Traba (*Zona. Carga y Descarga*), Ernesto Ruiz de la Mata (*The San Juan Star*), and Antonio Molina (*El Mundo*), in Puerto Rico.

9. Sarduy published seven articles in the journal *Tel Quel* from 1965 to 1978. Phillipe Sollers, a member of the group, published an article on Sarduy's work in *Tel Quel* in 1970, and translated *Cobra* into French. In his work, Sarduy made references to articles from *Tel Quel* written by Hollier, Baudry, Kristeva, and Sollers. He reviewed a book by Marice Roche published in the *Tel Quel* series. Roberto González Echevarría writes that "*Tel Quel* allows Sarduy to recover Cuba, to give it meaning through writing" (1987, 47). González Echevarría also writes that Sarduy gleans a different way of asking the questions from the theoretical approach of *Tel Quel*, questions that the Cuban Revolution was also asking of culture and history (ibid., 45). For a helpful summary of the first period of Sarduy's work, including his participation in *Tel Quel*, see González Echevarría 1987, 133–35.

10. The debt of Sánchez's erotic (and, as we shall see, particularly feminine) manipulation of space to the *ambiente* (to use another of Bleys's terms) of New York during the heyday of the gay liberation movement is clearly beyond the scope of this essay, but such a study would doubtlessly offer new perspectives on the homotextuality of her work, including her work for *Zona*. For a discussion of Sarduy's own deconstruction of the telquelian ideology, and on his critique of its eurocentrism, please see González Echevarría 1987, 46.

11. As if to underscore this reflective quality of her work, several photographs of her canvases from her catalogues are set on the beach and under the bright sun. Not surprisingly, Sánchez chose a light-sensitive and similarly reflective silver paper for the remarkable cover of the 1970 catalogue of her exhibit (conversation with Sánchez, July 29, 2008).

12. The Spanish words *carga y descarga* can be translated into either "loading and unloading freight" or into "electric charge or discharge."

13. From September 1968 to November 1970 more than 137 explosive devices were placed in eighty-one different locations in Puerto Rico. Losses mounted to more than four million dollars (Baralt 1998, 112). Bonus was the first experimental nuclear reactor to produce electricity in Latin America. It was built in 1964 on the west coast of Puerto Rico and closed only four years later, in 1968. It was part of the government program Atoms for Peace. A radiation leak forced the hasty closing of the plant under false premises (ibid., 10–11).

14. In 1970, Báez studied the technique of collography with Clare Romano at the Pratt Institute (Fernández Zavala and Droz 2001, 68). For a more detailed description of the technique and its development by Báez, please see Fernández Zavala's essay (ibid., 66–68).

15. For an example of this self-undoing merversion in the literature of Puerto Rico from the sixties, see chapter 2 of this book, and my analysis of René Marqués's gift of abjection.

16. For a discussion of this aspect of Báez's work please see Fernández Zavala (2001, 46–53).

17. Labrador-Rodríguez points to another possible interpretation for the size of the journal when she reminds her readers that Ferré associated the dimensions of *Zona* to those of a tabloid newspaper, which stood in opposition to the format of the Puerto Rican newspaper *El Nuevo Día,* owned by her father and managed by her brother, Antonio Luis Ferré (Labrador-Rodríguez 2007, 248 n.388).

18. According to Sánchez, she met Sarduy in his neighborhood in Havana, which was close to the theatre *Las Máscaras* owned by Andrés Castro, where Sánchez was responsible for the marquee, and where she also exhibited some of the artwork she completed while still an art student at San Alejandro University (conversation with Sánchez, July 29, 2008).

19. For a list of Sarduy's contributions to *Ciclón* from 1955 to 1956, please see Guerrero's bibliography (Sarduy 1999, 1845).

20. For an essay that summarizes Sarduy's theory and represents his writerly practice please see "Cubos" (Sarduy 1989, 82–83). González Echevarría is correct in describing what is most characteristic and audacious in Sarduy's work from this period as "an economy of loss (wound) that produces an excessive surplus (proliferation)" (1987, 134).

21. This sadistic violence is best represented by the incarceration of the Marquis de Sade for Sarduy. Aníbal González has carefully studied the ethical imperative of Latin American writing, and the various modes that violence takes in the nineteenth and twentieth centuries (2001a, 18–23). This essay is indebted to his emphasis on this ethical question, at the same time that it tries to take it in a slightly different direction, more herethical than ethical. While I do not wish to deny the violence that appears to be inherent to the origin of writing producing what González calls a "graphophobia," here I also try to emphasize its local, regional, and even sexually specific manifestations, or modalities, and particularly its self-inflicted form in Puerto Rico (ibid., 2).

22. I am grateful to Gelpí for pointing out to me that *Zona* published only certain writers from the Boom.

23. Ibáñez has compiled a helpful list of the reviews and interviews as well.

24. The other two were Emilio Díaz Valcárcel and José Donoso.

25. For a discussion of this and other topics please see the editors's "conversation" with Díaz Valcárcel published in *Zona* 2. For a symptomatic and contemporary example of the exclusionary practices characteristic of the Boom, see Harss's famous 1966 book, where Lezama Lima's writing is summarily dismissed as made of the "green dreams and onanist prose of a tropical adolescent" (464).

26. Considerations of space do not allow me to develop the claim that the Boom of the Latin American novel was characterized by the erotization of the abject. However, in chapter 3 of this book I suggest the ambiguous legacy of this perversion in the works by Ferré and Montero, close readers of the Boom writers.

27. Michel Fossey was a journalist and poet working and living in Paris and Barcelona. He published his interview with Sarduy in *Imagen* in 1971 and again in *Insula* in 1972 (Sarduy 1999, 1874). By the time Nolla's review was published in *Zona*, *Cobra* already had been reviewed at least eight times in journals in Mexico, Paris, Caracas, Buenos Aires, and even Holland such as *Siempre*, *Libre*, *Le Nouvel Observateur*, *Prensa*, *Imagen*, *Nieuwe Gazet*, *Combat*, *La Opinión*, and *Promesse* (ibid., 1857–73). The fact that there is no reference to the poems, the interview, or the review in the bibliographies of Sarduy that I have consulted appears to confirm that *Zona* was and remains invisible to the critics in the world of academic writing. Why this remains so is at least in part the subject of this essay (González Echevarría 1987, 255–69; Sarduy 1999, 1844–76).

28. I borrow the term *herethics* from Kristeva's description of the effort to stop the petrifying, stultifying, and murderous effects of a paradoxically matricidal maternal imaginary on us all (Trigo 2006, 13; Kristeva 1987, 263).

29. Rama uses the expression in Spanish, *a pie juntillas*, which refers to a self-sacrificial posture common in children's games where the feet and the legs are firmly joined together, to signify a certain force in passivity, the power of standing upright and remaining immovable, supported by an unquestionable sense of duty and an unshakable belief in the face of overwhelming odds. Like a proud soldier in front of a firing squad.

30. In a letter published in *Zona*, Rama gave his "apostolic blessing to the newly born tropical girl, who will happily exchange blows with the literature, the arts, the knowledge, of the island of Puerto Rico and of any island that dares to cross its path. So be it" (*Zona* 3: 23).

Chapter 5. Colonial Sublimations of a Noir Eros in "El Josco" and Two Detective Novels

1. The Noir Eros is a form of abjection inflected by the genre of police detective fiction. For a definition of abjection, please see chapter 2 of this book.

2. Kristeva's analysis of the fantasy represented by the phrase "a father-son is beaten to death" is an elaboration of an earlier fantasy described by Freud with the phrase "a child is being beaten." In an essay with that title, Freud distinguishes between masculine and feminine forms of fantasies (both in visual and verbal form) that work through what he calls the wounds of the Oedipus complex, or that sublimate a sadistic and masochistic dynamic with the father figure (a dynamic that Freud suspects is primary to human subjectivity). His analysis also suggests (and he himself points out) that the fantasies are a part of a multiphase and multilayered process of inversions and transformations that doesn't have a fixed but rather a dramatically flexible order and organization, which changes from sadism to masochism, from passivity to activity, from unconscious to conscious images, and from Father

to Mother figures. In her development of Freud's essay, Kristeva argues that those fantasies and phrases are forms of the prohibitions, the laws, and the language that emerge out of the ritual murder of the Symbolic Father in the story of the primal horde, sublimations that are both disturbing but that also make culture possible. For Kristeva these are sublimations or perlaborations that have the virtue both of temporarily suspending the prohibitions, and of allowing the Noir Eros to express itself. They are processes, phases, and phrases that in their optimal form allow us to work through the Noir Eros by bringing it in and out of consciousness, by allowing it to acquire verbal and nonverbal form, by continuing to mutate its form from Father to Mother, from Father to Son, from Daughter to Mother, by sustaining what she calls the never-ending journey through the death drive. They are, in short, forms of abjection.

3. The figure of the *jíbaro* has a profound ideological and political meaning in Puerto Rico (to the point of being the symbol for one of the political parties on the island). The bibliography on this figure and its genealogy is extensive. Since the nineteen seventies, critics of cultural nationalism have argued that the *jíbaro* is a romantic chimaera deployed to whiten the race. Some of these writers argue that the *jíbaro* is an illusion meant to disavow the influence of the institution of slavery, and the trace of the African population on the Spanish-identified Creole man of letters during the nineteenth and twentieth centuries in Puerto Rico. Later critics of a resurgent neonationalism argue that such figures are constantly repeated and redeployed to generate a disturbing form of political consensus at the cost of a much needed self-examination.

4. The phrase is full of pity, identification, and compassion. It is followed by resentment and reproach. It displaces and disavows a Noir affect. This affect inhabits the gruesome description of the fight between the competing bulls. It also inflects the perverse description of the bull's sacrifice.

5. The phrase *se esnucó de rabia*, "he broke his neck in a rage," suggests that the deadly fall could be either a sacrifice or a suicide. On the one hand, the bull could have been so blinded by his rage that he did not see where he was going and fell, breaking his neck, a sacrifice to his rage. But on the other, the Melancholy Bull might have actually jumped to his death in a rage, possessed by the anger of being unjustly and unnecessarily replaced by the other bull. Killing himself as an act of rebellion, rather than submit to the humiliation of the yoke.

6. The story is different from the Christian Passion according to Kristeva's account, and from the fantasy she finds in it, represented by the phrase "a father-son is beaten to death." The story does not work through the sadomasochism at the origins of the primal story of the horde. Neither does it verbalize or sublimate into laws, culture, and language the Noir impulses or the death drive at the origins of subjectivity. Instead, "El Josco" is a fantasy that dramatizes and makes visible the incapacity to work through the death drive. It covers over, veils, but also screens those impulses with phrases that leave the deadly force of the impulse intact.

7. For examples of this repeating moment of Kenos in Marqués's works see chapter 2.

8. In "El Josco's" version of the Passion, the Father figure is not beaten to death. Indeed, the sons of the story (the collective voice of the Puerto Rican peasants) go to great lengths to deny responsibility for the death. They cheer their bull (or the Father) on, when the bull successfully asserts his claim over the herd (or the females of the clan) in an epic battle against an usurper. And when the bull is found dead, they displace the responsibility back to the Father figure. On the one hand, the peasant expresses his pity for the bull and interprets its supposed accidental death as the effect of a suicidal rage. He produces the phrase, "My dear Josco, he broke his neck in a rage." On the other hand, the peasant lays the blame squarely at the feet of the bull with the reproach: "I warned you, that bull was a native stud; he was not born to live under the yoke" (Díaz Alfaro 1984, 65).

9. Several historians have made the point that by virtue of its strategic military location, Puerto Rico in particular (and the Caribbean archipelago in general) has suffered from a pattern of endless attacks dating back to the expansion of the Spanish Empire in the fifteenth century, and to its violent institutions of government and control such as the infamous Encomienda system. Morales Carrión calls this pattern "a cycle of aggression," and it leads to what Gordon Lewis calls "a military society." More recently, Patricia Gherovici has suggested that this history or pattern of endless attacks precedes Spain's colonial rule. She includes in this history of relentless attacks a longer history of deadly impulses that include not only the invasions of the warring Caribe Indians in pre-Columbian times, but also the assaults of hurricanes and disease (2003, 127, 130). All of which is woven into a defensive mechanism, a psychic agency, that helps to protect from this long history of deadly impulses. Following Freud, she compares this agency to "a garrison in a conquered city" (ibid., 128).

10. With the phrase, the *jíbaro* also seems to say, "This was no accident, nor was it a suicide, you killed him, and you will be punished for this."

11. As Lugo-Ortiz notes, the story of "El Josco" contains foundational myths regarding Puerto Rican national identity internalized by many Puerto Ricans (1998, 79). She has convincingly argued that in the story "national identity is a matter of masculine identity, of patrilineal reproduction, and domination over 'the virgin soil'" of Puerto Rico (ibid., 81). Moreover, the national and masculine identity constructed by the text and internalized by its many readers is one where "masculine bodies become objects of incessant transfigurations on the basis of intense power struggles with and against female bodies and desires" (ibid., 83). For Lugo-Ortiz, the threat of castration is at the center of these transfigurations. The author of "El Josco" raises this threat to the level of a foundational narrative. In other words, according to Lugo-Ortiz, the survival of the gendered Puerto Rican national subject paradoxically needs and relies on the castration threat that that very subject purports to fight.

12. Kristeva has written three detective novels to date: *Murder in Byzantium* (2006), *Possessions* (1996), and *The Old Man and the Wolves* (1991).

13. Later in that conference, Kristeva suggests that the Holocaust did for Freud what the death of her biological father did for her, namely open an approach or a passage to a Noir Eros that she again describes as a sadomasochistic desire for a symbolic father and of the father of the law. "After the Holocaust, the Freudian approach was the only one which emphasized the sadomasochistic desire for the law of the father which feeds the moral order, as well as the dark eros which underpins the perversion and the sublimation of homo religiosis" (2015).

14. From this perspective, José Rosado is right to interpret the police or detective novel in Puerto Rico as a mode of the social critique of other Latin American detective novels, which interrogate the insufficiency of the state and accuses it of corruption, merging a literary style with yellow press journalism.

15. For an analysis of Kristeva's police novels, please see my *Kristeva's Fiction*.

16. In Borges's version, the Minotaur tries to kill himself, but without success. He only gets bloodied by throwing himself off the cliffs of the labyrinth.

17. In a lucid analysis of the debt of the novel *Sol de medianoche* to Sartrean existentialism, Van Haesendonck describes the space of the novel as the space of the abject, which is the space marked both by the desire for separation from the maternal body and by the inability to become autonomous from the maternal substance, according to Kristeva (Van Haesendonck 2008, 139). He argues that the detective is an abject subject who inhabits this space, whose identity is between object and subject, and because of this indeterminacy develops both a sense of his own contigency and errancy as well as an existential nausea (ibid., 140). He further argues that the detective tries to rid himself of this feeling, of this condition, through acts of purification such as murdering his twin brother, or by swimming across the bay, a metaphor for an impossible wish to return to the uterus, according to Van Haesendonck. For him, the space of the abject represents the indeterminacy of the colonial situation. The effect of this indeterminacy is depression and melancholy, the matricidal impulse now aimed at the self (ibid., 142). According to Van Haesendonck, the novel is an existentialist attempt to give a name and a form to what Kristeva calls the abject.

18. This look is the opposite of the look of love in Marqués's last novel, which I argue is a form of abjection in chapter 2 of this book.

19. In the essay "A Child is Being Beaten," Freud describes in some detail the different phases and phrases from the masculine and feminine mode of these fantasies, all of which work through and sublimate a primary sadomasochism that is shared by both. In his discussion of the masculine mode of the fantasy, Freud describes a process that displaces disturbing masochistic and unconscious feelings (verbalized by the phrase "I am beaten by my father") with the masochistic but conscious phrase "I am beaten by my mother." The masochistic phases and phrases

are then further developed into a sadistic similarly conscious fantasy and phrase "Some boys are beaten by a mother." Freud's analysis suggests that the figure of the Beating Mother is a convenient fantasy that screens disturbing incestuous feelings originally associated with the Father, ambivalent feelings of love and hate that the Father both expresses and provokes, and that the subject displaces and sublimates into fantasies and phrases.

20. Torres Caballero is essentially correct when he identifies an obsession with the maternal figure in Rodríguez Juliá's novels from this period (2007, 44). And he is right in his diagnosis of this obsession as the sign of the impossibility or the incapacity to balance the psyche's competing death and sex drives (ibid., 62). As he puts it, the maternal obsession reveals the need to be desired by the other/Mother (ibid., 68). I take this argument in a slightly different direction. I argue that this obsession is not so much the result of a traumatic event, or due to a confrontation with the maternal figure that gives origin to the detective's dark side, to his homicidal side. Instead, I argue that this obsession is the result of a matricidal fantasy that develops out of the colonial attempt to displace and disavow the shame for the love of the symbolic Father, and the shame from covering it up. Negrón-Muntaner will call this shame a consent to colonialism in her book *Boricua Pop* (see chapter 6 of this book).

21. In his book, Ríos Ávila redeploys the term coined by Ramos Otero to signify the universal and traumatic version of the process that results in the making of a subject. Ríos Ávila argues that there are two modes of approaching this traumatic process, and he believes that giving it the form of a story helps in the process of working through its trauma. He interprets Rodríguez Juliá's writing as an approach that is less helpful, as a punishing form of representation of the traumatic desire of the Father that draws no benefit or pleasure from its process of subject formation. Here I suggest instead that Rodríguez Juliá's writing, like all colonial writing, contains the promise of resignifying the original trauma into a loving symbolic response, a promise that turns on an act of interpretation.

Chapter 6. Shame, Repetition, and Forgiveness in Queer Latino *Testimonios*

1. Negrón-Muntaner makes a reference to Sedgwick's 1996 essay "Queer Performativity: Warhol's Shyness/Warhol's Whiteness," but Sedgwick's most well-known essay on the subject dates back to 1993 and is titled "Queer Performativity: Henry James's The Art of the Novel."

2. Drawing from the work of writers such as Marqués and Sánchez, Negrón-Muntaner provocatively argues that Puerto Rican shame is characterized by an implicit consent of colonialism. She argues that sometimes Puerto Ricans

interiorize this state to the point that they both represent themselves as docile, and they also punish themselves for this self-representation. She also argues that at other times they respond less violently by attenuating or offsetting the shame that consent brings. In fact, she suggests that Puerto Rican pride is an overcompensation for, or an attenuation of, the "shame" of colonial transculturation.

3. Negrón-Muntaner published her book before Ricky Martin announced that he was gay in 2010, suggesting the limits of her analysis.

4. I am referring to a series of presentations by La Fountain-Stokes delivered between 2005 and 2009 and published in 2011 with the title "Gay Shame, Latina- and Latino-Style: A Critique of White Queer Performativity." I am also referring to Cruz-Malavé's book *Queer Latino Testimonio, Keith Haring, and Juanito Xtravaganza: Hard Tails* (2007), and to another series of essays and papers, this time by Ríos Ávila, including "Queer Latino Shame" (2007), "Queer Nation" (2007), "La creencia y la verguenza" (2013), and "Pornoliteratura" (2014).

5. The offending essay was a paper by Douglas Crimp originally delivered at a conference in 2003 and published in 2009 with the title "Mario Montez, For Shame."

6. La Fountain-Stokes also draws his theory from a series of events where queer Latinos/as felt that they were excluded, objectified, or shamed by white gay scholars. These events include an undated Garden Party in New York City, the already mentioned paper and essay by Crimp, and a hostile exchange at a conference on Gay Shame at the University of Michigan in 2003.

7. Móntez first performed the word in a film by Warhol (*Screen Test #2*) made famous by Crimp in his essay "Mario Montez, For Shame." For a careful analysis of this controversy, see Cruz-Malavé (2007b, 114–18).

8. Halberstam says, "It was left to Hiram Pérez, one of the few people of color presenting work at the conference, to address an angry and impassioned critique at Hansen when Pérez finally had his turn to speak on the last panel of the conference. Hansen responded defensively to Pérez. . . . The painful session only ended when Michael Warner grabbed the mike and mimicked Móntez saying 'diarreah' " (quoted in La Fountain-Stokes 2011, 75).

9. While Negrón-Muntaner concludes that this "defining entanglement" seems "impossible to undo," she also suggests that there is one way to cut the Gordian knot at the center of Puerto Rican identity (2004, 8). But to do so, she continues, Puerto Ricans have to choose between two equally unpalatable options. Either they sacrifice their culture and become a state of the United States or they sacrifice their wealth and become a sovereign nation-state. Following the thrust of Marqués's argument in "El puertorriqueño débil," she writes that "boricuas will be differently constituted . . . only if they risk themselves in the pursuit of social desires that may entail death, a 'death' that in the context of contemporary politics in Puerto Rico has been defined as either loss of culture (statehood) or loss of access to metropolitan wealth (independence)" (ibid.). Negrón-Muntaner's suggestion that

Puerto Ricans must sacrifice either their culture or their wealth is an example of the scene of self-sacrifice that I describe in this book.

La Fountain-Stokes suggests that Negrón-Muntaner's account of colonial shame might be more relevant for first generation diasporic Puerto Ricans than for the second generation in *Queericans* (2009). In that book, he applies her account of colonial shame to the community who tries to escape a colonial environment that is made even more intolerable by homophobia. And he suggests that this homosexual exile community, and particularly its first generation, takes the shameful contradictions of the colonial entanglement to an extreme. In one of the chapters of his book, La Fountain-Stokes focuses on Ramos Otero, a representative member of this community's first generation. He suggests that Ramos Otero exhibits symptoms of colonial shame in his short story "Página en blanco y staccato." The narrator of that story, a first-generation white Puerto Rican migrant dying of AIDS, is killed by a second-generation black, racially mixed, also Puerto Rican character as an act of vengeance against a past act of colonial violence. Echoing Negrón-Muntaner, La Fountain-Stokes writes that the "unintended or willing sacrifice" of the narrator "serves as a form of redemption for the complicity of island elites" with colonialism (2009, 56). In other words, the narrator is a member of the Puerto Rican elite (he is white and Spanish speaking), but he sacrifices himself as an act of atonement for the shameful consensual colonialism of his social class. In this way, and through a suicidal gesture that exceeds (but is also in the spirit of) the heroic self-sacrifice called for by Negrón-Muntaner, first-generation Puerto Rican exiles cut the Gordian knot of colonial shame. But this sacrifice does not appear to be required of the second generation of queerricans, according to La Fountain-Stokes.

10. He also draws from Copjec's essay "May 68, The Emotional Month" (2006) for his analysis of the relationship between shame and late capitalism.

11. Ríos Ávila suggests that the expulsion without any feeling of remorse of millions of Puerto Ricans during the nineteen fifties for the benefit of a program of industrialization that benefited, and continues to benefit, a relative minority of Puerto Ricans is the most egregious example of the radical shamelessness that drives the late capitalist regime or liberal democracy in Puerto Rico.

12. Consensual colonialism is the notion that Puerto Ricans give their consent to being colonized. The concept is an elaboration of the notion of the related concept of colonial guilt, first introduced by Sánchez in 1979 (cf. "Cinco problemas").

13. Cruz-Malavé criticizes the way that Academia has studied, deployed, and obscured the subaltern voices of the oppressed in the controversial genre of testimony in Latin American literature. Drawing in part from the work of Doris Sommer, but also from queer theory, he proposes a different approach that listens to *testimonio* rather than trying to make it speak. *Queer Latino Testimonio* is both an example and a description of this approach, which has deviancy at its center, but deviancy understood as a necessary disturbing turn that is contained by *testimonio* and to which the reader should pay heed.

The house of Xtravaganza was the most famous collective group to emerge from the New York City underground LGBTQ ballroom culture. Rivera's queer Latino *testimonio* was about his life and his relationship with the famous artist Keith Haring.

14. Considerations of space do not allow me to develop the idea that the identification at the center of Cruz-Malavé's *sentimiento* has many points of contact with the concept of "disidentification" as developed by José Muñoz, particularly with the paradoxical notion that the identification with one's opposite is a form of subject formation more common than our culture is willing to admit.

15. Unlike Ríos Ávila's *pudor*, Cruz-Malavé's discretion-shame is not a reaction to the radical nakedness or to the radical separation that characterizes the Lacanian subject. Instead, Cruz-Malavé's discretion-shame confirms the preexisting, necessary, and surviving link between the self and the other, between the subject and the community. Cruz-Malavé calls this link *sentimiento*.

16. For reasons of space, I will focus on Oliver's description of this complex affect rather than on her respective arguments against both the idealization and the so-called lack of the other.

17. Like theoretical astrologists, we might draw some confidence from the fact that it is only because this presumed forgiveness and responsibility must exist that it is possible for us to imagine hyperbolic forgiveness to begin with.

18. Cruz-Malavé describes this signifying body as follows, "I myself would rather dwell on Mario Montez's own insistently minimal gestures: the brushing of his unruly hair, his distracted listening to Tavel, his staring at the camera as if it were his own private mirror in his own private boudoir, his sudden unexpected turn to the camera, through his tangle of hair, in a vampy, devouring gaze. I myself would rather listen to the language spoken by these gestures—resistant, ambiguous, dense, as all language must be that must traverse the silencing barrier of shame" (2007b, 119).

19. Vilar was born in Puerto Rico but left the island when she was nine years old. She has lived most of her life in the United States, and she currently resides in Boulder, Colorado. Caleb Acevedo was born on the island but lived in Hartford, Connecticut, for fourteen years. He now lives back in Puerto Rico.

20. He is the author of two books of poetry (*Bestiario en nomenclatura binomial*, 2009; *Empírea o la Saga de la Nueva Ciudad*, 2012) and a novel (*El oneronauta*, 2014). He is also the co-author of a book of poems in English with Charlie Vázquez titled *Hustler Rave XXX* (2013).

21. "Puro teatro" is a song by the Puerto Rican composer Tite Curet that was made famous in the late sixties and early seventies in Latin America and in Puerto Rico by the renowned Cuban singer Guadalupe Victoria Yoli (La Lupe).

22. Perhaps in the same melancholy way that Susan Bordo famously described the paradoxical agency of anorexia, for example.

Conclusion

1. In his famous attack against the cruelty of the conquering Spaniards, *Brevísima relación de la destrucción de las Indias* (1542), Fray Bartolomé de las Casas tells the story of a sick indian woman who kills herself and sacrifices her one-year-old son when faced with imminent death by the vicious dogs of the Spanish conquistadors (105). By contrast, El Inca, Garcilaso de la Vega, and Fernández de Oviedo retell the story of collective sacrifice to argue instead that the Indians from that region of the world were exotic but also slothful and full of vice; see *La Florida* (133), and *Historia general y natural de las Indias* (71). The different rhetorical uses of the scene of self-sacrifice suggests the ambiguous character of its material.

2. As this book goes to press in 2016, Puerto Rico is facing bankruptcy. Like the thirty-six cities, counties, and municipalities that have filed for bankruptcy in the United States since 2010, the Commonwealth of Puerto Rico has borrowed more money than it can pay back. The size of the debt is monumental relative to the size of the Puerto Rican economy. Its Gross National Product is in the order of 69 billion dollars, and it is in debt for 72.6 billion dollars. The Commonwealth of Puerto Rico is poorer than the poorest state of the Union and it faces daunting obstacles including a loss of population greater than the Great Migration after World War II, an unemployment rate higher than 12 percent, low productivity growth, government operating deficits for more than ten years, etc. The crisis is partly due to its colonial status, insofar as this status has made the unprotected triple-tax-exempt government debt appealing to a depressed municipal bond market—as an unincorporated territory Puerto Rico's bankruptcy cannot be ruled by Chapter 9 of the U.S. Bankruptcy Code.

Works Cited

Acevedo, David Caleb. 2012. *Diario de una puta humilde*. San Juan de Puerto Rico: Erizo Editorial.

Alarcón, Norma. 1989. "Traddutora, Traditora: A Paradigmatic Figure of Chicana Feminism." *Cultural Critique* 13: 57–87.

Allende, Isabel. 1994. *Paula*. New York: Harper Libros.

Associated Press. 2009. "Raid Targets Puerto Rico Drug Gang." *CBSNews*, Oct. 2. http://www.cbsnews.com/stories/2009/10/02/ap/latinamerica/main5359620.shtml. Accessed July 26, 2015.

Ayala, César, and Rafael Bernabe. 2007. *Puerto Rico in the American Century; A History Since 1898*. Chapel Hill: University of North Carolina Press.

Baralt, Guillermo A. 1998. *La Razón del equilibrio: La Vida de Luis A. Ferré*. II. San Juan: Fundación El Nuevo Día.

Barradas, Efraín. 1977. "El Machismo existencialista de René Marqués." *Sin nombre* 8, no. 3: 69–81.

———. 1981. *Para leer en puertorriqueño: acercamiento a la obra de Luis Rafael Sánchez*. Río Piedras: Editorial Cultural.

Bátiz, Martha. 2010. "El Estatuto de la verdad y las variaciones discursivas dentro del estado de excepción en La pasión según Antígona Pérez, de Luis Rafael Sánchez." *Corrientes* 2: 3–22.

Ben-Ur, Lorraine Elena. 1975. "Myth Montage in a Contemporary Puerto Rican Tragedy." *Latin American Literary Review* 4, no. 7: 15–21.

Benítez, Marimar, ed. 1983. *Francisco Oller (1833–1917)*. Ponce: Museo de Arte de Ponce.

Bettaglio, Marina. 2012. "Surveiller, et punir: The Body of Evidence in Luis Rafael Sánchez La pasión según Antígona Pérez." *Latin American Theater Review* 45, no. 2: 45–55.

bhabha, homi. 1994. *The Location of Culture*. London and New York: Routledge.

Birkenmeier, Anke. 2006. "Dirty Realism at the End of the Century: Latin American Apocalyptic Fictions." *Revista de Estudios Hispánicos* 40, no. 3: 489–512.

Bleys, Rudi C. 2000. *Images of Ambiente; Homotextuality and Latin American Art, 1810-Today*. London and New York: Continuum.

Bordo, Susan. 2003. *Unbearable Weight: Feminism, Western Culture, and the Body.* Berkeley: University of California Press.

Borges, Jorge Luis. 1981 (1947). *El Aleph.* Madrid: Alianza-Emecé.

Burgos, Julia de. 1997. *Song of the Simple Truth. Obra completa poética. The Complete Poems of Julia de Burgos.* Edited and translated by Jack Agüeros. Willimantic, Curbstone Press.

———. 2008. *Obra poética* I. Madrid: Ediciones de la Discreta.

Butler, Judith. 1990. *Gender Trouble: Feminism and the Subversion of Identity.* New York: Routledge.

Coll y Toste, Cayetano. 1928. *Leyendas y tradiciones puertorriqueñas.* Barcelona: Maucci.

Colón Zayas, Eliseo. 1985. *El Teatro de Luis Rafael Sánchez; códigos, ideología, lenguaje.* Madrid: Editorial Playor.

Contexto puertorriqueño: del rococó al arte global. Catálogo acompañante de la exhibición permanente del Museo de Arte de Puerto Rico, reestructurada en 2007. San Juan: Museo de Arte de Puerto Rico, 2007.

Copjec, Joan. 2003. *Imagine There's No Woman: Ethics and Sublimation.* Cambridge: MIT Press.

———. 2006. "May 68, The Emotional Month." In *Lacan, The Silent Partners,* edited by Slavoj Zizek, 90–114. London: Verso.

Cordero, Juan Giusti, et al. 2002. *Vieques ante el 2003: posibilidades y peligros.* San Juan: Editorial LEA.

Cortázar, Julio. 1974. *Octaedro.* Buenos Aires: Editorial Sudamericana.

Crimp, Douglas. 2002. "Mario Montez, For Shame." In *Regarding Sedgwick: Essays on Queer Culture and Critical Theory,* edited by Stephen M. Barber and David L. Clark, 63–75. New York and London: Routledge.

Cruz-Malavé, Arnaldo. 1995. "Toward an Art of Transvestism: Colonialism and Homosexuality in Puerto Rican Literature." In *¿Entiendes?: Queer Readings, Hispanic Writings,* edited by Emilie Bergmann and Paul Julian Smith, 137–67. Durham: Duke University Press.

———. 1996. " 'What a Tangled Web!': Masculinity, Abjection, and the Foundations of Puerto Rican Literature in the United States." *differences: A Journal of Feminist Cultural Studies* 8, no. 1 (Spring): 132–51.

———. 2007. "The Oxymoron of Sexual Sovereignty: Some Puerto Rican Literary Inflections." *Centro Journal* XIX, no.1: 50–73.

———. 2007a. *Queer Latino Testimonio, Keith Haring, and Juanito Xtravaganza: Hard Tails.* New York: Palgrave Macmillan.

De la Vega, Garcilaso. 1988. El Inca. *La Florida.* Introducción y notas de Carmen de Mora. Madrid: Alianza Editorial.

Deleuze, Gilles, and Félix Guattari. 1985 (1975). *Kafka: Toward a Minor Literature.* Minneapolis: University of Minnesota Press.

del Rosario, Rubén. 1980. *Vocabulario puertorriqueño.* Río Piedras: Editorial Edil.

De Oviedo, Fernández. 1959. *Historia general y natural de las Indias*. Edited by J. Pérez de Tudela Bueso. Bilioteca de Autores Españoles Vol. 1. Libro III. Madrid.

Derrida, Jacques. 1981 (1969). *Dissemination*. Translated and with an introduction by Barbara Johnson. Chicago: University of Chicago Press.

Díaz Alfaro, Abelardo. 1984 (1959). "El Josco." In *Cuentos Puertorriqueños de Hoy*, edited by René Marqués, 57–63. Río Piedras: Editorial Cultural.

Díaz Quiñones, Arcadio. 1982. "Los Desastres de la guerra: para leer a René Marqués." In *el almuerzo en la hierba; lloréns torres, palés matos, rené marqués*, 133–68. Río Piedras: Ediciones Huracán.

Díaz-Valcárcel, Emilio. 1972. *Figuraciones en el mes de marzo*. Río Piedras: Editorial de la Universidad de Puerto Rico.

Dolores Hernández, Carmen. 2000. "Nuestros escritores ¿Quiénes son? ¿Cómo son? Entrevista a Rosario Ferré." Revista Domingo. *El Nuevo Día*, 6 de agosto, 8–9.

Duchesne Winter, Juan. 1992. *Las Tribulaciones de Juliá*. San Juan: Instituto de Cultura Puertorriqueña.

Edwards, Jorge. 1974. *Persona Non Grata*. Barcelona: Barral Editores.

Fanon, Frantz. 1965 (1959). *A Dying Colonialism*. Translated by Haakon Chevalier. New York: Grove Weidenfeld.

———. 1967 (1952). *Black Skin, White Masks*. Translated by Charles Lam Markmann. New York: Grove.

———. 2004 (1961). *The Wretched of the Earth*. Translated by Richard Philcox. New York: Grove.

Faulkner, William. 1992 (1929). *The Sound and the Fury*. New York: The Modern Library.

Fernández Zavala, Margarita, and Vanessa Droz, eds. 2001. *Myrna Báez: una artista ante su espejo An Artist and Her Mirrors*. San Juan: Universidad del Sagrado Corazón.

Ferré, Luis A. 1972. *El Propósito humano*. México: Ediciones Nuevas de Puerto Rico.

Ferré, Rosario. 1975. "Comedia Non Grata." *Zona. Carga y Descarga* 3, no. 8: 27–28.

———. 1975a. "Ocho caras del miedo." *Zona. Carga y Descarga* 3, no. 8: 11, 31.

———. 1982. *Fábulas de la garza desangrada*. México: Joaquín Mortiz.

———. 1986. "The Writer's Kitchen." Translated by Diana L. Vélez. *Feminist Studies* 12, no. 2: 227–42.

———. 2005. "Apuntes sobre *Zona de Carga y Descarga*." Ensayo leído en congreso celebrado en torno a la obra de Rosario Ferré celebrado por Brown University y organizado por el Dr. Julio Ortega en la UPR en Mayagüez en junio de 2005. TS. Rosario Ferré Archive. Columbia University. New York, New York.

———. 2007. *Fisuras*. San Juan: Ediciones Callejón.

Flores, Juan. 2000. *From Bomba to Hip-Hop; Puerto Rican Culture and Latino Identity*. New York: Columbia University Press.

Freud, Sigmund. 1953–1974 (1905). *Three Essays on the Theory of Sexuality.* In *The Standard Edition of the Complete Psychological Works of Sigmund Freud.* 24 volumes. Edited and translated by James Strachey in collaboration with Anna Freud. London: The Hogarth Press and the Institute of Psycho-Analysis.

———. 1953–1974 (1919). "'A Child Is Being Beaten' A Contribution to the Study of the Origin of Sexual Perversions." In *The Standard Edition of the Complete Psychological Works of Sigmund Freud.* 24 volumes. Edited and translated by James Strachey in collaboration with Anna Freud, vol. 17, 179–204. London: The Hogarth Press and the Institute of Psycho-Analysis.

———. 1963 (1927). "Fetishism." In *Sexuality and the Psychology of Love*, edited and with an Introduction by Philip Rieff, 214–19. New York: Collier Macmillan.

———. 1981. "Beyond the Pleasure Principle; Group Psychology and Other Works." In *The Standard Edition of the Complete Psychological Works of Sigmund Freud*, translated by James Strachey, vol XVIII. London: The Hogarth Press and the Institute of Psycho-Analysis.

———. 1989 (1912–13). "The Return of Totemism in Childhood." In *The Freud Reader*, edited by Peter Gay, 481–513. New York: W. W. Norton.

García Pinto, Magdalena. 1988. *Women Writers of Latin America; Intimate Histories.* Translated by Trudy Balch and Magdalena García Pinto. Austin: University of Texas Press.

Geirola, Gustavo. 2008. "Los Avatares de la sexualidad en los estudios literarios latinoamericanos en Estados Unidos." In *Treinta años de estudios literarios/culturales latinoamericanistas en Estados Unidos. Memorias, testimonios, reflexiones críticas*, edited by Hernán Vidal, 311–50. Pittsburgh: Instituto Internacional de Literatura Iberoamericana.

Gelpí, Juan. 1984. "Apuntes al margen de un texto de Rosario Ferré." In *La sartén por el mango: encuentro de escritoras latinoamericanas*, edited by Patricia Elena González y Eliana Ortega, 133–35. Río Piedras: Huracán.

———. 1993. *Literatura y paternalismo en Puerto Rico.* Río Piedras: Editorial de la Universidad de Puerto Rico.

———. 2006. "Retórica, subjetividad y procesos de modernización en la ensayística de Octavio Paz y René Marqués." In *Para romper con el Insularismo; Letras puertorriqueñas en comparación*, edited by Efraín Barradas and Rita de Maeseneer, 91–104. Amsterdam: Rodopi.

Gherovici, Patricia. 2003. *The Puerto Rican Syndrome.* New York: Other Press.

González, Aníbal. 2001. *Abusos y admoniciones: ética y escritura en la narrativa hispanoamericana moderna.* México: Siglo XXI.

———. 2001a. *Killer Books; Writers, Writing, and Ethics in Spanish America.* Austin: University of Texas Press.

González, José Emilio. 1983. "Puerto Rican National Culture in the Nineteenth Century and Francisco Oller." In *Francisco Oller (1833–1917)*, edited by Marimar Benítez, 75–87. Ponce: Museo de Arte de Ponce.

González, José Luis. 1950. "En el fondo del caño hay un negrito." *Asomante* VI, no. 3 (julio-septiembre): 88–91.

———. 1980. *El País de cuatro pisos y otros ensayos*. San Juan de Puerto Rico: Ediciones Huracán.

González, Rita. 2009. "Boricua Gazing; An Interview with Frances Negrón-Muntaner." In *Gay Shame*, edited by David M. Halperin and Valerie Traub, 88–100. Chicago: University of Chicago Press.

González Echevarría, Roberto. 1987. *La Ruta de Severo Sarduy*. Hanover: Ediciones del Norte.

Harss, Luis. 1966. *Los Nuestros*. Buenos Aires: Editorial Sudamericana.

Hernández Vargas, Nélida, and Daisy Caraballo Abréu, eds. 1985. *Luis Rafael Sánchez: crítica y bibliografía*. Río Piedras: Editorial de la Universidad de Puerto Rico.

Hintz, Suzanne S. 1995. "*Zona. Carga y Descarga*; Nascent Postmodernism in Puerto Rican Letters." Paper Presented at XIX LASA Congress in Washington, DC. http://lanic.utexas.edu/project/lasa95/hintz.pdf. Accessed November 15, 2015.

Ibáñez, Jorge. 1992. "Índice de autores publicados en *Zona de Carga y Descarga*." *La Torre* 6, Issue 155.23: 333–47.

Irizarry, Guillermo. 1993. "Dramatic Structure in Two Plays by Luis Rafael Sánchez." MA thesis. The University of Texas, Austin.

Jiménez, Félix. 2001. *Vieques y la prensa: el idilio fragmentado*. Carolina: Editorial Plaza Mayor.

Johnson, Barbara. 1990. "Writing." In *Critical Terms for Literary Study*, edited by Frank Lentricchia and Thomas McLaughlin, 39–49. Chicago and London: University of Chicago Press.

Kafka, Franz. 1928. "A Hunger Artist." In *The Penal Colony*. Translated by Willa and Edwin Muir. Prague: Schocken Books.

Kangro, Hans. 1976. *Early History of Planck's Radiation Law*. London: Taylor & Francis.

Kazin, Alfred. 1960. "In Puerto Rico." *Commentary* 29, no.2, 108–14.

Kristeva, Julia. 1982. *Powers of Horror: An Essay on Abjection*. New York: Columbia University Press.

———. 1987 (1983). *Tales of Love*. Translated by Leon Roudiez. New York: Columbia University Press.

———. 1995 (1993). *New Maladies of the Soul*. Translated by Ross Guberman. New York: Columbia University Press.

———. 2002. *Colette*. Translated by Jane Marie Todd. New York: Columbia University Press.

———. 2002a. *Intimate Revolt: The Powers and Limits of Psychoanalysis*, vol. 2. Translated by Jeanine Herman. New York: Columbia University Press.

———. 2002b. "'Forgiveness,' interview with Kristeva." *PMLA* 117, no. 2: 278–323.

———. 2002c. *The Portable Kristeva*. Edited by Kelly Oliver. New York: Columbia University Press.

———. 2007. "Adolescence, a Syndrome of Ideality." *Psychoanalytic Review* 95, no. 5 (October): 715–25.

———. 2009. *This Incredible Need to Believe*. Translated by Beverley Bie Brahic. New York: Columbia University Press.

———. 2010 (2005). *Hatred and Forgiveness*. Translated by Jeanine Herman. New York: Columbia University Press.

———. 2011. "La Reliance, ou l'erotisme maternelle." *Revue française de psychanalyse* 75, no. 5: 1559–70.

———. 2015. "A Father Is Beaten to Death." *Julia Kristeva Site Officiel*, July 26. http://www.kristeva.fr/father.html. Accessed November 15, 2015.

Kuhn, Thomas S. 1979. *Black-Body Theory and the Quantum Discontinuity. 1894–1912*. Oxford: Oxford University Press.

Labrador-Rodríguez, Sonia. 2007. "Un Capítulo de la 'estética de la furia': La revista *Zona. Carga y Descarga*." *Hispanismo; Discursos culturales, identidad y memoria. VII Congreso Nacional de Hispanistas*. Vol. II. Edited by Flawiá de Fernández, Nilda María, and Silvia Patricia Israilev, 247–57. Universidad Nacional de Tucumán.

La Fountain-Stokes, Lawrence. 2009. *Queer Ricans; Cultures and Sexualities in the Diaspora*. Cultural Studies in the Americas 23. Minneapolis: University of Minnesota Press.

———. 2011. "Gay Shame, Latina- and Latino-Style: A Critique of White Queer Performativity." In *Gay Latino Studies; A Critical Reader*, edited by Michael Hames-García and Ernesto Javier Martínez, 55–85. Durham: Duke University Press.

Laplanche, J., and J.-B. Pontalis. 1973. *The Language of Psychoanalysis*. Translated by Donald Nicholson-Smith. New York: W. W. Norton.

Las Casas, Bartolomé de. 1965. *Tratados. Brevísima relación de la destrucción de las Indias*. México: FCE.

Lewis, Gordon. 1963. *Puerto Rico: Freedom and Power in the Caribbean*. New York: M. R. Press.

Lewis, Jim. 2007. "Havana Nights." *The New York Times Book Review*, February 19, 1, 8.

López-Baralt, Mercedes. 2000. "'I hate to see that evening sun go down;' Los múltiples rostros del *Sol de medianoche* de Edgardo Rodríguez Juliá." *Revista de estudios hispánicos* 27, no. 2: 363–74.

Lozada, Ángel. 2013. *El Libro de la letra A/The Book of the Letter A*. New York: Sangría.

Lugo-Ortiz, Agnes. 1995. "Community at Its Limits: Orality, Law, Silence, and the Homosexual Body in Luis Rafael Sánchez's 'Jum.'" In *Entiendes? Queer Readings, Hispanic Writings*, edited by Emilie L. Bergman and Paul Julian Smith, 115–36. Durham, London: Duke University Press.

———. 1997. "Sobre el tráfico simbólico de mujeres: homosocialidad, identidad nacional y modernidad literaria en Puerto Rico (apuntes para una relectura de El puertorriqueño dócil de René Marqués)." *Revista de Crítica Literaria Latinoamericana* 23, no. 45: 261–78.

———. 1998. "Nationalism, Male Anxiety, and the Lesbian Body in Puerto Rican Narrative." In *Hispanisms and Homosexualities*, edited by Sylvia Molloy and Robert McKee Irwin, 77–100. Durham, London: Duke University Press.

Manrique Cabrera, Francisco. 1986. *Historia de la literatura puertorriqueña*. Río Piedras: Editorial Cultural.

Manzotti, Vilma. 1996. "Mayra Montero y su ritual del deseo desterritorializado." *Alba de América: Revista Literaria* 14, no. 26–27: 363–71.

Marqués, René. 1944. *Peregrinación: poemas*. Arecibo: Imprenta Venezuela.

———. 1971. "Purification on Cristo Street." In *Cuentos: An Anthology of Puerto Rican Short Stories*, translated by Charles Pilditch, 49–61. San Juan de Puerto Rico: Instituto de Cultura Puertorriqueña.

———. 1972 (1966). *Ensayos (1953–1971)*. Río Piedras: Editorial Antillana.

———. 1975. "Carta a Rosarito Ferré." *Zona. Carga y Descarga* 3, no. 8: 26.

———. 1976 (1960). *The Docile Puerto Rican*. Translated by Barbara Bockus Aponte. Philadelphia: Temple University Press.

———. 1976a. *La mirada*. Río Piedras: Antillana.

———. 1976b. *Los Soles truncos*. In *Teatro*. Vol. 1, 6–66. Río Piedras: Cultural.

———. 1977 (1960). *El Puertorriqueño dócil y otros ensayos. 1953–1971*. Río Piedras: Editorial Antillana.

———. 1981 (1959). *Cuentos puertorriqueños de hoy*. Edited by René Marqués. Río Piedras: Editorial Cultural.

———. 1981a (1959). "En la popa del barco hay un cuerpo reclinado." In *Cuentos puertorriqueños de hoy*, edited by René Marqués. Río Piedras: Editorial Cultural.

———. 1983. *The Look (La Mirada)*. Translated by Charles Pilditch. New York: Senda Nueva.

Martin, Eleanor J. 1979. *René Marqués*. Boston: Twayne.

McClintock, Anne. 1995. *Imperial Leather*. New York: Routledge.

Meléndez, Concha. 1955. "Cuentos de René Marqués." In *Otro día nuestro (cuentos)*, 7–18. San Juan de Puerto Rico: Imprenta Venezuela.

Mirabal, B. et al. 2010. "Homicides among Children and Young Adults—Puerto Rico, 1999–2003." *MMWR* 55: 361–64. Reprint: *JAMA* 295, no.18 (2006): 2133–34. http://jama.ama-assn.org/cgi/content/full/295/18/2133. Accessed November 15, 2015.

Molloy, Sylvia. 1981. *At Face Value: Autobiographical Writing in Spanish America*. Cambridge: Cambridge University Press.

Montalvo-Barbot, Alfredo. 1997. "Crime in Puerto Rico: Drug Trafficking, Money Laundering, and the Poor." *Crime and Delinquency* 43, no. 4 (October): 533–48.

Montero, Mayra. 2003. *El Capitán de los dormidos*. Barcelona: Tusquets Editores.

———. 2005. *Captain of the Sleepers*. Translated by Edith Grossman. New York: Farrar, Straus and Giroux.

Morales Carrión, Arturo. 1983. *Puerto Rico; A Political and Cultural History*. New York: W. W. Norton.

Morely, Jefferson. 2006. "What is Hamas?" *Washington Post*, July 17. http://www.washingtonpost.com/wpdyn/content/article/2006/07/17/AR2006071700898.html. Accessed July 26, 2015.

Muñoz, José Esteban. 1999. *Disidentifications: Queers of Color and the Performance of Politics*. Minneapolis: University of Minnesota Press, 1999.

Negrón-Muntaner, Frances. 2004. *Boricua Pop: Puerto Ricans and the Latinization of American Culture*, New York: New York University Press.

Nolla, Olga. 1998. "La Guerra hispanoamericana y el inconsciente colectivo puertorriqueño." *Revista Domingo, El Nuevo Día*, July 19, 5–7.

Oliver, Kelly. 2001. "The Look of Love." *Hypatia* 16, no. 3: 56–78.

———. 2004. *Colonization of Psychic Space: A Psychoanalytic Social Theory of Oppression*. Minneapolis: University of Minnesota Press.

Ortega y Gasset, José. 1966. "La Deshumanización del arte." In *Obras completas*, Vol. 3 (1917–1928). Madrid: Revista de Occidente.

Pabón, Carlos. 2002. *Nación postmortem; ensayos sobre los tiempos de insoportable ambigüedad*. San Juan: Ediciones Callejón.

Pedreira, Antonio S. 1934. *Insularismo: Ensayos de interpretación puertorriqueña*. San Juan de Puerto Rico: Biblioteca de Autores Puertorriqueños.

Perivolaris, John Dimitri. 2000. *Puerto Rican Cultural Identity and the Work of Luis Rafael Sánchez*. Chapel Hill: North Carolina Studies in the Romance Languages and Literatures.

Perry, Donna. 1993. *Backtalk: Women Writers Speak Out*. New Brunswick: Rutgers University Press.

Phillips, Jordan B. 1972. *Contemporary Puerto Rican Drama*. New York: Plaza Mayor Ediciones.

Pilditch, Charles. 1976. *A Study of his Fiction*. New York: Plus Ultra Educational Publishers.

Planck, Max. 1959. *The Theory of Heat Radiation*. New York: Dover.

"Puerto Rico." 2015. *Death Penalty Information Center*. www.deathpenaltyinfo.org/puerto-rico-0. Accessed July 13, 2015.

Quintero Rivera, Ángel. 1976. *Conflictos de clase y política en Puerto Rico*. Río Piedras: Ediciones Huracán.

The Qur'an. 2008. Translated by Tarif Khalidi. New York: Viking.

Ramos Otero, Manuel. 1991. "De la colonización a la culonización." *Cupey* 8: 63–78.

Ríos Ávila, Rubén. 2002. *La Raza cómica del sujeto en Puerto Rico*. San Juan: Ediciones Callejón.

———. 2007. "Queer Nation." In *Los otros cuerpos: antología de temática gay, lésbica, y queer desde Puerto Rico y su diáspora*, edited by Luis Negrón, Moisés

Agosto Rosario, and David Caleb Acevedo, 293–307. San Juan de Puerto Rico. Editorial Tiempo Nuevo.

———. 2007a. "A Bite of Visibility: On Queer Latino Shame." Online video clip. *Writers House Homepage. University of Pennsylvania*, November 5. http://writing.upenn.edu/wh/calendar/1107.html#5. Accessed July 26, 2015.

———. 2009. "La Nación más transparente: René Marqués y la dama de occidente." *La torre* 14, no. 51/52: 179–95.

———. 2011. "Sobre la masculinidad." *80grados*, April 21. http://www.80grados.net/sobre-la-masculinidad/. Accessed July 26. 2015.

———. 2013. "La Creencia y la vergüenza." *80grados*, November 22. 2013. http://www.80grados.net/la-verguenza/. Accessed July 26, 2015.

———. 2014. "Pornoliteratura." *80grados*, January 17, 2014. http://www.80grados.net/pornoliteratura/. Accessed July 26, 2015.

Rivera de Álvarez, Josefina. 1983. *Literatura puertorriqueña: su proceso en el tiempo.* La Habana, Madrid: Ediciones Partenón.

Rivera Ramos, Alba Nydia. 1991. *Hacia una psicoterapia para el puertorriqueño. Enfoque psico-social.* Río Piedras: EDIL.

Rodríguez Juliá, Edgardo. 1981. *Las tribulaciones de Jonás*. Río Piedras: ediciones huracán.

———. 1999 (1995). *Sol de medianoche*. Barcelona: Mondadori.

———. 1999a. " 'Incursiona Rodríguez Juliá en novela policíaca,' entrevista con el autor," Cynthia Palacios-Goya. In *El Universal, suplemento "Cultura,"* November 28. http://www2.eluniversal.com.mx/pls/impreso/noticia.html?id_nota=2168&tabla=cultura. Accessed April 13, 2001.

———. 2003. *Mapa de una pasión literaria.* Río Piedras, Universidad de Puerto Rico.

———. 2004. *Mujer con sombrero panamá*. Barcelona: Mondadori.

Rosado Rodríguez, José A. 2000. "El Género policial en Puerto Rico; el periodismo investigativo, el encubrimiento, y el enigma histórico." *Revista de Estudios Hispánicos* 27, no. 2: 351–62.

Sánchez, Luis Rafael. 1979. "Cinco problemas al escritor puertorriqueño." *Vortice* II, no. 2–3: 117–21.

———. 1989. *La pasión según Antígona Pérez.* Río Piedras: Editorial Cultural.

Santos Silva, Loreina. 1981. "*La Pasión según Antigona Pérez*: la mujer como reafirmadora de la dignidad política." *Revista/review Interamericana* 11, no. 3: 438–43.

Sarduy, Severo. 1969. *Escrito sobre un cuerpo; ensayos de crítica.* Buenos Aires: Editorial Sudamericana.

———. 1970. "Las *Topologías eróticas* de Zilia Sánchez." In *Estructuras en secuencias. Catalogue of exhibit of work by Zilia Sánchez at Museo Universidad de Puerto Rico*. [San Juan, Puerto Rico]: n.p., N.pag.

———. 1989. *Written on a Body.* Translated by Carol Maier. New York: Lumen Books.

———. 1999. *Obra completa*. Edited by Gustavo Guerrero and Francois Wahl. Vols. 1,2. Colección Archivos. Madrid: ALLCA XX, Universite Paris X.

———. 2000. "Las *Topologías eróticas* de Zilia Sánchez." Reprint. In *Zilia Sánchez; Heróicas Eróticas*. Catalogue of exhibit of works by Zilia Sánchez at Museo de las Américas, San Juan, Puerto Rico. 3 pages. No page numbers. San Juan: Impresión Elmendorf Colors.

Schneider, Carl D. 1977. *Shame, Exposure, and Privacy*. Boston: Beacon Press.

Sedgwick, Eve Kosofsky. 1993. "Queer Performativity: Henry James's *The Art of the Novel*." *GLQ: A Journal of Lesbian and Gay Studies* 1: 1–16.

———. 1996. "Queer Performativity: Warhol's Shyness/Warhol's Whiteness." In *Pop Out: Queer Warhol*, edited by Jennifer Doyle, Jonathan Flatley, and José Muñoz, 134–43. Durham: Duke University Press.

Shaw, D. L. 1968. "René Marqués' *La Muerte no entrará en palacio*: an analysis." *Latin American Theater Review* (Fall): 31–38.

Shepherdson, Charles. 2009. "Antigone; The Work of Literature and the History of Subjectivity." In *Bound by the City; Greek Tragedy, Sexual Difference, and the Formation of the Polis*, edited by: Denise Eileen McCoskey and Emily Zakin, 47–80. Albany: State University of New York Press.

Silva, Loreina. 1994. "El Josco: A Political Fable." *Atenea* 14, no. 1-2: 35–42.

Solá, María. 1979. "René Marqués: ¿escritor misógino?" *Sin nombre* 10, no. 3: 83–97.

Sommer, Doris. 1999. *Proceed With Caution, When Engaged by Minority Writing in the Americas*. Cambridge: Harvard University Press.

Spector, Stephen. 1970. "Cecilia [*sic*] Sánchez at Sarduy." *Arts Magazine* 44, no. 8: 60.

Spivak, Gayatiri. 1988. "Can the Subaltern Speak." In *Marxism and the Interpretation of Culture*, edited by Cary Nelson and Lawrence Grossberg, 271–316. Urbana: University of Illinois Press.

Stabb, Martin. 1967. *Quest of Identity; Patterns in the Spanish American Essay of Ideas 1890–1960*. Chapel Hill: University of North Carolina Press.

Thompson, Mary. 2014. "Misconceived Metaphors; Irene Vilar's *Impossible Motherhood: Testimony of an Abortion Addict*." *Frontiers* 35, no. 1: 132–59.

Tomkins, Silvan. 1995. *Shame and Its Sisters: A Silvan Tomkins Reader*. Edited by Eve Kosofsky Sedgwick and Adam Frank. Durham and London: Duke University Press.

Toral Alemañ, Begona. 2001. "Reescribiendo el Caribe: Entrevista a Mayra Montero." *Caribe: Revista de Cultura y Literatura* 4, no. 1: 58–66.

Torres Caballero, Benjamín. 2007. *Para llegar a Isla Verde de Edgardo Rodríguez Juliá*. Río Piedras: La Editorial Universidad de Puerto Rico.

Torres Gotay, Benjamín. 2014. "La Campaña contra Puerto Rico." *El Nuevo Día*, September 7, 14.

Traba, Marta. 1971. *Propuesta polémica sobre arte puertorriqueño.* Río Piedras: Ediciones Librería Nacional.

Trigo, Benigno. 2000. *Subjects of Crisis; Race and Gender as Disease in Latin America.* Hanover: Wesleyan University Press.

———. 2006. *Remembering Maternal Bodies; Melancholy in Latina and Latin American Women's Writing.* New York: Palgrave-Macmillan.

———. 2009. "Colonial Fetishism in René Marqués." *Revista Canadiense de Estudios Hispánicos* 33, no. 3: 507–24.

———. 2014. *Kristeva's Fiction.* Albany: State University of New York Press.

Van Haesendonck, Kristian. 2008. *¿Encanto o espanto? Identidad y nación en la novela puertorriqueña actual.* Madrid: Iberoamericana-Vervuert.

———. 2011. "'Light' Colonialism in the Caribbean in the Context of Global Empire Building." In *Perennial Empires: Postcolonial, Transnational, and Literary Perspectives,* edited by Silvia Nagy-Zemkin and Chantal Zabus, 173–98. Amherst, NY: Cambria Press.

Vera León, Antonio. 1996. "Mayra Montero: las islas del deseo." *La Torre (NE)* 10, no. 38: 183–201.

Vilar, Irene. 1996. *The Ladies' Gallery: A Memoir of Family Secrets.* New York: Random House.

———. 2009. *Impossible Motherhood: Testimony of an Abortion Addict.* New York: The Other Press.

Villanueva-Collado, Alfredo. 2007. "René Marqués, Angel Lozada, and the Constitution of the (Queer) Puerto Rican National Subject." *Centro Journal* XIX, no. 1: 179–91.

Waldman, Gloria. 1988. *Luis Rafael Sánchez: pasión teatral.* San Juan: Instituto de Cultura Puertorriqueña.

West, Cornel. 2013. "Dialogue between Excluded Communities: Challenges and Hope for Social Transformation." Cornel West at the University of Puerto Rico Theatre." USTREAM, September 26. http://www.ustream.tv/recorded/39268250. Accessed July 26, 2015.

Zeno Gandía, Manuel. 1978. *La Charca (crónicas de un mundo enfermo).* Río Piedras, Puerto Rico: Editorial Edil.

Zilia Sánchez: tres décadas. 1991. Humacao: Museo Casa Roig. Puerto Nuevo, Puerto Rico: Elmendorf Colors.

Zilia Sánchez: heróicas, eróticas. 2000. San Juan: Museo de las Américas. Puerto Nuevo, Puerto Rico: Elmendorf Colors.

Žižek, Slavoj. 2004. "From Politics to Biopolitics . . . and Back." *Southern Atlantic Quarterly* 103 no. 2/3: 501–21.

Index